DESCARTES
SELECTIONS

The Modern Student's Library

PHILOSOPHY SERIES

THE Modern Student's Library has been enlarged to include a series of volumes containing writings of the great philosophers. These volumes are edited by the most competent authorities at home and abroad. The selections are comprehensive and suited to the special needs of students and the general reading public. Each volume contains an introduction giving a brief outline of the system of the author and indicating his place in the history of thought.

The Philosophy Series is under the general editorship of Ralph Barton Perry, Professor of Philosophy, Harvard University.

[*For a complete list of* THE MODERN STUDENT'S LIBRARY *see the pages following the text*]

CHARLES SCRIBNER'S SONS

DESCARTES, René
SELECTIONS.

Edited by

RALPH M. EATON

ASSISTANT PROFESSOR OF PHILOSOPHY
HARVARD UNIVERSITY

CHARLES SCRIBNER'S SONS

NEW YORK   CHICAGO   BOSTON   ATLANTA
SAN FRANCISCO   DALLAS

B
1835
.E3
(2)

INTRODUCTION

I - background

René Descartes, more than any other figure in the seventeenth century, marks the intellectual transition from the Middle Ages to the modern world. He stands where the streams of European thought meet. The current of mediævalism flows into his philosophy and runs strongly through his metaphysics and theology, but the stream of modernism, the current of mechanical science that has borne along the European mind into the twentieth century, flows from his philosophy. In his attitude toward the Church and the mysteries of the Christian religion, Descartes might have been a good Catholic of the twelfth century. Here the spirit of Duns Scotus, St. Anselm, and St. Augustine is still alive. In his views of the physical world and the scientific method, he breaks sharply with the Middle Ages; he brings together in a complete system the leading ideas of the century of scientific discovery which produced Galileo, Bacon, Hobbes, Leibniz, Spinoza, Huygens, Harvey, Locke, Boyle, Newton.

Not that Descartes was a scientist to be ranked beside Galileo or Newton. Only one of his achievements in exact science remains of value to-day, his geometrical method, now known as analytical geometry. He lacked the patience in observation, the love of fact for its own sake, which enables the scientist to build carefully, brick on brick, a solid structure of detailed knowledge. Like Aristotle, he was enamored of the *a priori*. He sought brilliant generalizations which, in a flash, set everything in order—an order that was often reckless of details. And again like Aristotle, he had the genius to seize on the generalities which were fruitful for future thought. Descartes did not lay many solid particular bricks in the structure of modern science, but he did foresee, and sketch with a vigorous hand, the entire plan of that structure. His intuition of the general nature of things leaped far beyond the seventeenth century. In this respect, Descartes stands to modern science in much the same relation as Aristotle to mediæval theology and metaphysics: both of these thinkers provided the theoretical framework for an epoch.

"Give me matter and motion and I will make a world." This is the formula in which Descartes is said to have summed up his physical principles. The universe of material things is a machine which is governed by no other laws than those of matter in motion; the heavens are a machine, vast swirling vortices of particles separated out from an original undifferentiated matter; the human brain and body are machines, delicately adjusted to the flow of the blood and animal spirits, like the fountains of a French formal garden. Here is mechanism, however crude in detail, proclaimed and generalized, and waiting only for the labors of succeeding generations of observers to fill in the relevant facts.

The mechanical picture of the physical universe has repeated itself again and again since Descartes. It has taken its place in the background of the scientific mind; its lines have been drawn more and more clearly in each age. Whether or not it is the true picture, it has guided scientific observation since the seventeenth century; and Descartes' was the mind that first framed it with something approaching completeness.

The greatness—and weakness—of Descartes in the field of science appear in the judgment he passed on his illustrious contemporary, Galileo. He writes to Father Mersenne in 1638: "I shall commence this letter by my observations on the work of Galileo. I find in general that he philosophizes much better than the average, in that he abandons as completely as he can the errors of the Schools, and attempts to examine physical matters by the methods of mathematics. In this I am in entire agreement with him, and I believe that there is absolutely no other way of discovering the truth. But it seems to me that he suffers greatly from continual digressions, and that he does not stop to explain all that is relevant to each point; which shows that he has not examined them in order, and that he has merely sought reasons for certain particular effects, without having considered the first causes of nature; and thus that he has built without a foundation. Indeed, because his fashion of philosophizing is so near to the truth, one can the more readily recognize his faults."

Descartes is searching for the first causes of nature; Galileo is content to inquire into the reasons for certain particular effects; both are seeking to examine physical matters by the methods of mathematics. Descartes' imagination springs at once to the whole. He wishes to see nature as a complete scheme, whose principles are linked together as are the axioms and theorems of a mathematical system. "There is no phenomenon in nature," he declares in his *Principles of Philosophy,* "which has not been dealt with in this treatise." Galileo is content to experiment with bodies rolling down inclined planes, carefully timed by a water-clock, until he can state with mathematical exactitude the law of their descent. The age needed both Galileo and Descartes, the one to build and invent, the other to speculate; and far more important than their difference of temperament, is their agreement on the method of science,—that scientific truth is to be obtained only by the use of mathematics in the examination of nature.

This is the discovery, or rediscovery, of the seventeenth century, which brought modern science to birth. Pythagoras and Plato were aware of the power of mathematics as a key to nature; but Aristotle had underrated mathematics, and the Middle Ages were the offspring of Aristotle. The Pythagorean and Platonic insight, that the order of nature can be expressed in exact mathematical form, had been blurred; the dominating trend of mediæval thought was away from quantitative statement. Things were understood through specific qualities or forms. To explain the descent of heavy bodies and the ascent of light bodies—as in liquids—it was assumed that everything sought its proper place. The place of heavy bodies was below, the place of light bodies, above; thus heaviness and lightness were absolute qualities of things. It was only fitting, therefore, that a stone should lie on the earth, because this was its final end, to seek its resting place; and it was only proper that a flame should rise, for, being light, its very nature was to mount upwards, just as the very nature of a plant was to take nourishment and grow, and of a man to think.

But all the while mathematics was at work beneath the surface of mediæval culture, and in the age of Galileo and Descartes mathematics bursts again upon the world, not merely as a discipline for its own sake, but as a light that clarifies the nature of physical relationships. Kepler states the laws of the motions of the planets about the sun, in exact mathematical terms; Galileo describes the descent of falling bodies, the motion of the pendulum, the flight of projectiles, in exact mathematical terms. On hearing of the invention of the telescope in 1608 by Johannes Lippersberg, an obscure Dutch optician, Galileo, "after one night's profound meditation on the principles of refraction," which were mathematical principles, succeeded in producing a telescope of threefold magnifying power. Christian Huygens, whose achievement belongs to the second half of the century, carries forward triumphantly the mathematical standard in physical inquiry; he examines the principles of centrifugal force, constructs the first pendulum clock, generalizes the idea of the center of gravity,—always in exact mathematical terms. The whole century is conspiring toward the "victorious synthesis" of Newton. Mechanical science, once it sets its foot on the straight mathematical path, rushes forward in the space of three generations to its culmination in Newton's *Principia*. By 1687, the date of the publication of that work, the vision of Pythagoras had been realized; mathematics had struck the foundations, or at least very close to the foundations, of nature.

No wonder that in such a century Descartes believed he could finish off the whole of knowledge by a universal mathematics. In the *Discourse*—that extraordinary intellectual biography which served as preface to his scientific essays—he declares, in speaking of his early studies: "Most of all was I delighted with Mathematics because of the certainty of its demonstrations and the evidence of its reasoning, . . . but I was astonished that, seeing how firm and solid was its basis, no loftier edifice had been reared thereupon." His own philosophy was to be that loftier edifice, reared according to the rules of a universal science, whose essence was order and measurement. "As I considered the matter carefully," says rule IV of the *Regulae*, "it gradually came to light

that all those matters only were referred to Mathematics
in which order and measurement are investigated, and
that it makes no difference whether it be in numbers,
figures, stars, sounds or any other object that the question of measurement arises. I saw consequently that
there must be some general science to explain that
element as a whole which gives rise to problems about
order and measurement, restricted as they are to no
special subject matter. This, I perceived, was called
'Universal Mathematics.' "

Order and measurement are to replace the specific
qualities of the mediævals. Order and measurement—
these are foundations of science. Here indeed is the
true general insight of the new-born physics.

But mathematics, with all its power as an instrument
of physical inquiry, could not have brought forth modern
science, had it not been joined, in the closest possible
union, with observation. Kepler and Galileo, Huygens
and Newton, were observers of infinite patience; the
great physiologists, Vesalius and Harvey, were tireless
observers. "Nature to be commanded must be obeyed,"
wrote Francis Bacon in the Novum Organum (1620);
and the obedience nature exacts is unremitting attention
to her details.

The two dominant motives of the new science, pains-
taking observation and exact mathematical formulation,
worked separately in the two seventeenth century proph-
ets of science, Bacon and Descartes. The English
philosopher assigns to mathematics only a modest rôle
as a useful tool in collecting instances and performing
curious experiments. He has no vision, as does Descartes, of a system of physical laws rationally connected
and deduced from a few first principles. Bacon's science, beside Descartes', is like the work of the ant of
his own simile: "The men of experiment are like the

ant; they only collect and use; the reasoners resemble
spiders, who make cobwebs of their own substance."
What the Englishman and the Frenchman have in common is their hatred of the barren learning of the
Schools; both of them plead for a clean intellectual
slate, a new beginning of knowledge with a mind unencumbered by the sophistries of a previous age. Bacon
would have classed Descartes among those thinkers who
"fly from the senses and particulars to the most general
axioms, and from these principles, the truth of which
it takes for settled and immoveable, proceeds to judgment and to the discovery of middle axioms;" while
Descartes was of the opinion that Bacon's instances
and experiments, though valuable, played a subordinate
part in science, whose true aim was "to arrive at a
knowledge of things *a priori* from the knowledge of the
order of nature which controls them."

Bacon's skill as a scientific observer was scarcely
equal to his eloquence in pleading the cause of scientific
observation. The wearisome tables of instances on the
cause of heat which fill the *Novum Organum* are more
barren than any page of Aristotle's scientific works.
Bacon's force is in the eloquence of his pleading; he is
always the lawyer, rarely the scientist. But Descartes
—at least in that aspect of the new science which attracted his mind, its aspect of order, measurement, and
mathematical generality—is more than proficient; he is
a creative genius.

Descartes knows that observation and experiment
are necessary, but he cannot stop for them. Thus,
though he remarked to a visitor who wished to see his
library, "These are my books," pointing to the animals
he had dissected, his anatomical researches brought to
light no single new fact. He wrote at length on the
circulation of the blood, but his experiments never en-

abled him to go beyond the ancient theory of Galen, that the heart expands by an innate and mysterious heat. "He was acquainted with Harvey's work, but he had not been convinced by Harvey's arguments; he was not familiar enough with the details of physiological inquiry to feel the full force of Harvey's reasonings. He admitted Harvey's great and new conclusion, the greater circulation, the passage of the blood from the arteries to the veins, but he would not admit what Harvey insisted, and truly insisted upon as the keystone of his whole argument, the propulsion of the blood by the systole, the contraction of the heart. He clung in the main to the old doctrines."[1]

In physiology as in mechanics, what seemed important to Descartes was the general outline of the theory. Man was a machine, inhabited and ruled by a rational soul, which touched the body only at one small point, the pineal gland in the center of the brain. The actions of the human organism were for the most part automatic, while animals, having no rational souls, were nothing but automata. The solar system, a living body, the fountains playing in the garden of the royal château —all were mechanisms, at bottom to be explained on the same principles. This was the idea in physiology that fascinated Descartes, and if we put aside the question of the rational soul, it was the same idea that the physiologists of the next three centuries worked out, with more and more careful descriptions of the mechanisms within mechanisms which make up a living organism.

II - Life

Descartes' life and personality partake of the drama of his age. It is a life of passionate devotion to re-

[1] M. Foster, "History of Physiology," 1901.

search, of discoveries, of sudden illuminations, of wandering and unrest, of bitter controversy. He becomes early in his career "the celebrated M. Descartes," and remains so till long after his untimely end in Sweden; the celebrated M. Descartes, who is looked upon, in some quarters, as an atheist and suspected as a member of the Rosicrucians, but who, in his own mind and in the minds of his friends, never wanders from the faith of the beloved teachers of his youth, the Jesuits of the college of La Flèche.

"He had," says his biographer, Baillet, "a special talent for dividing scholars amongst themselves, and for prolonging the disputes which he had aroused." Thus we hear Henry More, the English Platonist, referring to him as "that pleasant wit, Renatus des Cartes;" we find Gassendi addressing him jocularly as a disembodied mind; we see the Dutch authorities taking steps, as a result of the dissension he stirred up in the universities of Utrecht and Leyden, to have his writings publicly destroyed by the hangman.

Descartes is a storm-center of his time, and this is probably the reason why he preferred to remain in retirement in Holland during the most productive period of his life. He declared that the air of Paris stifled him, he could not breathe or think there; and when he left for Holland in 1629 he vowed never to return. But Descartes was not out of touch with the learned world in Paris. His old school companion, Father Mersenne, kept the post-roads between Paris and Holland warm with communications. Through the agency of the good father, Cartesianism acts at a distance, but with unabated vigor, on Arnauld, Pascal, Gassendi, Hobbes,—on most of the brilliant intellects of the day.

It is difficult to know what manner of man M. Descartes was. There is a portrait by Frans Hals which says more than any of his biographers can: it shows him proud, self-contained, cool, even cold, shrewd, inscrutable, subtle. There is nothing of the ascetic and much of the man of the world in the face; the eyes are distant with much thinking, the mouth firm. There can be no doubt that this is a great man, but much doubt that it is "une âme simple, 'naïve,' au sens vrai de ce terme si français, une âme sincèrement religieuse, mystique même," as a recent French writer describes Descartes.[1] One sees in the portrait an ego, which might have torn down the world to build it again upon itself. In all, there is a mask-like quality in the features, hiding—what? Descartes as a person is a riddle.

Born the last day of March, 1596, at La Haye, in Touraine, Descartes was a gentleman of good provincial French stock. As a child his health was delicate; he writes that he had inherited from his mother, who died a year after his birth, "a dry cough and a pallid complexion" which remained with him until he was twenty. This may have been in part the cause of his meditative habits in youth, which led his father to speak of him, even before he was at school, as "my philosopher." The years he spent at the Jesuit college of La Flèche, from the age of eight to sixteen, sufficed for a grand tour of the world of learning, a journey which ended in disillusionment. But La Flèche had fixed upon him his habits of meditation. The Jesuit fathers had perceived his genius, and, partly on this account partly because he was a young man of station, they had granted him special privileges. He was allowed to rise as late as he chose and to meditate in bed in the mornings, a custom which he pursued throughout life. "It was thus," says one of his biographers, "that he discovered his so-called algebra, the key to all the liberal sciences and

[1] J. Chevalier, "Descartes," Paris, 1921.

rts, and the best method of distinguishing the true
from the false." Before he had turned seventeen, he
put aside his books, having squeezed them dry, and,
gentleman that he was, after a few lessons in fencing
and horsemanship, went up to the great world of Paris.

At that time Paris had its charms for the young René.
But Baillet remarks that the boy of seventeen, who had
no other guardian than a valet de chambre, and no over-
seers but lackeys, showed sufficient strength of character
"to keep himself free of debauched ways of living and
not to fall into the disorders of intemperance; but that
he was not proof against the companions who involved
him in excursions, in gaming, and other amusements
which passed for indifferent in the world. One thing
that caused him to be particularly fond of gaming was
his good luck, especially in those games which depended
on calculation rather than chance."

Descartes' thoughtful temper soon reasserted itself
under the influence of Father Mersenne, and he retired
to an obscure lodging in the Faubourg Saint-Germain
to meditate. It soon became apparent, Baillet continues, "that he had changed in his taste for pleasures.
Games and excursions no longer had the same attraction
for him as before; and the delights of 'les voluptés'
worked only very feebly within him against the charms
of Philosophy and Mathematics, in which his worldly
companions could have no share."

But the lesson in the great book of the world was
not yet complete. The restless mind of the philosopher
displayed a taste for adventure mixed with his mathematics. "Resolving to seek no other science than that
which could be found in myself," says the *Discourse*,
"I employed the rest of my youth in travel, in seeing
courts and armies, in intercourse with men of diverse
temperaments and conditions, in proving myself in the

various predicaments in which I was placed by fortune." The period between 1618 and 1628, from his twenty-second to his thirty-second year, was spent in wandering; first as a volunteer in the army of Prince Maurice of Orange in the Netherlands, then in the Bavarian army, at Neuberg on the Danube and in southern Bohemia, again, in the military service in Hungary. It was a life that gave him much time for thought during the long months of idleness in winter quarters. But after a few years, in 1621, "he carried into execution a resolve which he had taken a long time before, no longer to carry a musket." He did, however, continue his travels in Switzerland and Italy, after a brief sojourn in his father's house at Rennes, and in Paris. But he had no fixed plan of life until he finally went into seclusion in Holland in 1629. From then onward, at the advice of his friends, he began setting down for publication the philosophical ideas which had been in gestation during the decade of his wanderings. At thirty-two he was already recognized by the circle of Father Mersenne in Paris as a mathematician and philosopher of the first magnitude.

Descartes displays in his writings, especially in the *Discourse* and the *Meditations,* the true Gallic love of the histrionic. He has a genius for setting the stage, creating a situation, and dramatizing himself; and beyond a doubt there was a situation to be dramatized. Descartes' inner life during this period was intense and troubled. After years of despair, irresolution, doubt, after the world of knowledge had fallen about him and left him with nothing but his native wit, a sudden flood of light burst upon him, in the year 1619, and he solemnly resolved to devote the remainder of his days to the pursuit of truth, and to that alone. He recounts in a lost work, the *Olympica,* of which his biographer gives a summary, how, "having gone to bed (on a certain memorable day) all full of his inspiration and wholly occupied with the thought of having discovered that very day the foundations of a wonderful science, he is visited by three consecutive dreams in a single night, which he believes to have come from above." In one of these dreams he hears a clap of thunder, which he interprets as "the Spirit of Truth descending to take possession of him;" and the following morning he prays God to give him light and to lead him in the search for truth, vowing at the same time to make a sacred pilgrimage to the shrine of Loretto to seek the aid of the Blessed Virgin. It is recorded that the pilgrimage was accomplished. The incident explains the fervour of Descartes' appeal to the "natural light" of reason, and his faith that the eternal truths of mathematics, physics, and metaphysics are guaranteed by the goodness of God.

The important years between 1629 and 1649, spent for the most part in Holland, brought Cartesianism to a full expression. The *Discourse*, the *Geometry*, the *Dioptrics*, the *Meditations*, the *Principles of Philosophy*, make their appearance during the first fifteen years; Descartes answers objections, engages in disputes, conciliates the clergy; but all the while remains in seclusion from the world, with his servants, and, for a short time, in the company of his natural daughter, Francine, who died at the age of six. Baillet records that "he wept for the child with a tenderness which gave him proof that the true philosophy never extinguishes the natural."

Shortly after he came to Holland, the philosopher prepared the manuscript of a work on physics, which was to be complete and revolutionary. But "M. Descartes," remarks Bossuet, "was always afraid of coming under the notice of the Church, and we see him taking precautions in this matter which go to excess." He had before him the fate of the philosophers of the preceding century who had ventured to question the accepted physical doctrines. Ramus, Bruno, Campanella, Vanini, had suffered for their opinions, and Descartes did not propose to join their company. A French historian of philosophy gives the following picture of these men of the sixteenth century: "True knight-errants of philosophy, they wandered from university to university, breaking their lances against Aristotle. Followed from city to city by the terrible accusation of impiety and atheism, they found no fixed dwelling-place on the earth. To slake the burning thirst for truth that consumed them, they dipped into every spring, into antiquity, into cabalism, into magic and alchemy, into the dreams of their own imagination. Carried away by their blind rashness, they surrendered themselves, so to speak, into the hands of judges and inquisitors; they languished in horrible dungeons, they were condemned to do public penance, tortured, dragged to execution. Such is the spectacle they presented to the people! This is how Ramus, Giordano Bruno, Campanella, Vanini, lived and how they died. We can say of the whole century what Campanella, in a play of words on his name, said of himself: 'I am merely the bell that proclaims a new dawn.'"

Descartes, too, raised his lance against Aristotle, but not to shatter it. He was ready to soften the blow for the sake of the Church. Toward the end of the year 1633, he wrote to Father Mersenne that he had intended sending him his new physical treatise, *Le Monde,* as a New Year's gift, but that he had just been at Leyden and Amsterdam to ask after Galileo's cosmological system, only to be told that it had been printed but that every copy had been burned at Rome, and that Galileo had been himself condemned to do some penalty. Descartes thereupon dispatched his revolutionary treatise to a distant part of the country so that the temptation to publish it might be put out of his way. Only a fragment of it appeared after his death. The vicious doctrine of the treatise, that the earth was in motion, was later included in his *Principles of Philosophy* in a mitigated form. Motion, says M. Descartes in this later statement, consists in a change of the relations of a body to its immediate surroundings. Thus the earth, carried round the sun in a stream of subtle matter which immediately envelops it, is no more in motion than a man asleep in a ship that is passing from Calais to Dover.

Toward the end of his life, Descartes formed a friendship with the Princess Elizabeth, the eldest daughter of the exiled elector palatine, who was then living with her mother, the Queen of Bohemia, at the Hague. The princess is the first of "les femmes savantes", later satirized by Molière. She is a true savant, enamoured of mathematics and physics, and worthy of the honor Descartes did her in dedicating to her his *Principles of Philosophy*.

His second royal pupil, Queen Christina of Sweden, the daughter of Gustavus Adolphus, was less of a scholar. Through the French ambassador at the Swedish court, the young queen, not yet twenty, conducted a learned correspondence with the celebrated philosopher, beginning with a philosophical analysis of love and ending with a complete essay from Descartes on *The Passions of the Soul*, the most important of his later works. The queen begged Descartes to come to Stockholm. After much hesitation and against the advice of his friends, he set out in September, 1649, on the long journey. He reached Stockholm toward the end of October, but almost at the moment of his arrival, despite the gracious reception of the queen, he wished that he might depart. Anxious that he should have a part in the celebration of the peace of Westphalia in December, the queen set him to composing a ballet; but, "worse still, our philosopher, who had always been accustomed to remain in bed till a late hour, was obliged, at the pleasure of the queen, to arise before sun-up; it was at five o'clock in the morning that this exacting woman chose to make appointments with him, in her study, to learn from him 'how to live happily in the sight of God and man.'

"He suffered cruelly with the cold: the thoughts of the people of this country, he said, chilled him as did the water. He was unable to resist this fashion of living. He took cold as he was going from the embassy to the court and fell seriously ill. Christina sent a German doctor to attend him, whom he believed to be his enemy and received unwillingly. When the doctor desired to bleed him, he said, 'You shall not shed a drop of French blood'; and he would accept nothing but a homely remedy, which consisted of a weak infusion of tobacco in a warm drink. The fever became more intense; the lungs were affected; on the 11th of February, 1650, at four in the morning, after having dictated a letter to his brothers commending his old nurse to their care, and after having received the religious offices with fervour, he exclaimed, 'Now, my soul, it is time to depart.' He then breathed his last, 'passionately moved that he was about to discover and possess a truth that he had sought all his life.' He was not yet fifty-four years of age."[1]

The queen offered the principal church of Stockholm for the funeral services, but the French ambassador declined: "a gentleman who was Catholic and French could not lie in ground that was foreign and Lutheran."

[1] J. Chevalier, "Descartes," Paris, 1921.

Descartes' remains were deposited in the cemetery for children who had died before baptism; a few years later, in 1667, his body was brought to Paris and placed in the church of Sainte-Geneviève, and in 1819 it was transported to the church of Saint-Germain des Près, where it now reposes. Even at that time, in 1667, a royal order was issued to prevent the Chancellor of the University of Paris from pronouncing the eulogy he had prepared for the occasion of Descartes' burial in French soil. The storm of opposition to Cartesianism was beginning to burst, but it was too late.

III — Descartes' philosophy

The Cartesian philosophy is usually described as dualistic, which means that it divides the universe into two mutually exclusive realms, spirit and matter. The physical world with its motions, its geometry, its measurable relationships, constitutes one realm, and the soul with its free will, its thoughts, its sensations, constitutes the other. But this is not all. There is a third realm, or entity, which is not on the same level as the others and yet is essential to Descartes' universe. This is the Divine Being, who creates and sustains the realms of spirit and matter. Cartesianism is really "trialistic." Its basic realities, substances, Descartes calls them, are three—mind, matter, and God. The first two are the created substances; the third, the uncreated substance. Matter and mind need only the concurrence of God to exist, they do not depend on one another; while God requires nothing but Himself. The examination of these three realms of being and of their relations to one another constitutes the system.

Cartesianism thus harbors under a single roof the elements of at least three widely different philosophies, pantheism, materialism, and idealism. Make mind and matter coördinate aspects of God, who becomes the indwelling substance of all things, and you have the pantheism of Spinoza. Abolish the realm of thinking substance and explain thought as a function of the bodily machine, and you have the materialism of Hobbes or La Mettrie. Absorb matter into spirit, as a thought in the Divine Mind, and you have the idealism of Malebranche and Berkeley. Descartes stoutly resisted all these ways of thinking, which were later to grow out of his premises. Mind and matter are not for him mere aspects of God: they are God's creatures, brought into being by a free act of His will, and hence they are distinct from Him. Matter is much more than a thought in the Divine Mind or in the human mind: it is a substantial reality, issuing from God as its source. And, though the bodily machine can do many remarkable things, Descartes would never grant, with the materialists, that it could think.

Descartes' doctrines of the Divine Being are his link with the Middle Ages; his doctrines of mechanics and mathematics, his link with the modern world; while his theory of the soul, as a thing not to be embraced within mechanical categories, gives scope to physical science to develop, unembarrassed by questions of psychology, morality, and religion. But his views on the soul and the Divine Being would not have sufficed to write his name large at the beginning of modern philosophy; in these matters he is a conservative. His radicalism expresses itself in his theory of the physical world. From the point of view of the twentieth century, the realm of matter completely overshadows the other realms of the Cartesian universe.

The great French philosopher is always, first, a mathematician. The germ of his thought appears in his brilliant, and permanent, mathematical invention, the method of analytical geometry, which is a way of correlating algebraic equations with geometrical figures. No idea is ever without its roots, and Descartes had his predecessors as well as his successors in this field. The idea of the application of algebra to geometry is found in Appolonius, (Greek geometer of the third century B. C.), in Vieta, (French mathematician of the sixteenth century) and even among the Arabs; while Fermat, Descartes' contemporary, advanced notions similar to his own on this subject, and Leibniz (the great German philosopher of the seventeenth century) somewhat later introduced the term "coördinates," if not the idea. But Descartes was the first to formulate, in a generalized and effective way, the principles of analytical geometry. To him goes the credit for this important step forward in mathematics, as well as for numerous minor additions to the same science. He introduced numerical exponents to indicate the powers of numbers; he made use, for the first time, of the letters at the end of the alphabet for unknown quantities and those at the beginning for known quantities; he stated the rule of signs for determining the number of negative and positive roots of an equation.

These inventions were of slight importance, however, beside his geometrical method. The analytical power of that method fired his mind to generalization; hence, the Cartesian system. It is easy to understand how the philosopher, in the light of this discovery, might say, as he does in the *Principles*: "I do not accept or desire any other principle in Physics than in Geometry or abstract Mathematics, because all the phenomena of nature may be explained by their means, and a sure demonstration can be given of them."

Analytical geometry is a method by which a **numeri-**

cal, or algebraic, expression can be found to represent
any spatial figure. Numbers and spatial figures become like two languages which can be translated back
and forth; and Descartes has discovered the key to the
translation. This translation is effected by making use
of coördinates or axes, that is, lines drawn at right
angles to one another, on which various quantities can
be measured off from the point of intersection, called
the "origin." (Descartes employed oblique rather than
rectangular coördinates.) Thus it is possible to represent a function of two varying quantities by a figure.
For example, if the quantities measured off on the verti-
cal axis are years in a person's life, and those on the
horizontal axis are his height at the end of each year,
a curve can be drawn showing his rate of growth. The
method is familiar to everyone who has seen a statistical
chart. Now, if every property of space, including
motion, can be translated by this method into numerical
form, and if the essence of the material world is extension and motion in space, as Descartes believed it
to be, then this geometry is the key to the material
world. This is the vision of a "wonderful science",
which moved Descartes to make a pilgrimage to the
shrine of the Blessed Virgin.

The confidence with which the philosopher sets out
bare-handed to construct a mathematically water-tight
theory of all things, could come only at the dawn of an
era. Behind the gesture of scepticism with which Descartes opens his inquiry lies an unbounded faith in reason, and it takes more than a century for this faith to
dissipate itself in the genuine scepticism of David Hume.

The *Discourse,* the *Meditations,* the *Principles of
Philosophy,* each in its turn repeats the initial gesture
of doubt. Let us first, urges Descartes, put away all
the uncertain rubbish of the Schools which has been

taught us; then let us imagine that what we see or hear, the colors, sounds, shapes, all the appearances of the physical world, are illusions; let us even suppose that a malignant demon tricks us when we are confronted with the seeming truths of mathematics. What remains? The true sceptic would answer, "Nothing." As for "that strange fiction of doubt," remarks Leibniz, "if ever this doubt could be justly raised, it would be absolutely insuperable." Descartes raises the doubt and surmounts it by the famous, "I think, therefore I am." He who doubts cannot doubt that he doubts; he cannot escape his own doubting mind, and here is the foundation on which to build. Thinking and the soul that thinks exist. From then onward the philosophy unfolds, act on act, to the dénouement. The soul exists, God exists, the world of material things exists and all—or nearly all—that has been doubted away in the beginning, except the useless lumber of ancient and mediæval learning, is demonstrated back into existence.

This is the outward form of the system, the order of exposition, calculated to produce an effect like the author's own illumination in the memorable year of the three dreams. But the dramatic order of the exposition is not strictly parallel to the logical order of the ideas.

The strength of Cartesianism as a speculative scaffolding for the new science lies in its simplicity. This philosophy rests, as does its model, analytical geometry, on a few clear and distinct ideas. The basic notion is that of *substance*. A substance is an entity which can have attributes; it is a subject which underlies activities and qualities. In the reply to Hobbes, Descartes makes the statement that "no activity, no accident can be without a substance in which to exist." Now, look within yourself, as the method of doubt bids you do. What do you discover? Thinking, an activity; and therefore there must be a substance which displays itself in this activity. Here we have the first clear and distinct idea. Again, look at the physical world, or merely at the piece of wax, which the philosopher, meditating beside his German stove in winter quarters, has immortalized by way of illustration. The qualities of the wax change continually; now the wax is cold, now it is hot, now it loses its shape and odor. Yet one attribute persists at every stage of the change: the wax continues to fill space, it is always extended, as is the whole physical world, no matter what alteration of quality takes place upon its surface. Extension then is the essential property of that world, just as thinking is the essential property of the mental world; and beneath the changing activities of each of these worlds lies an *it*, a substance.

Moreover, these two realms are utterly diverse. A mind could not be extended, nor could a body think. The author of the *Meditations* would have stirred uneasily at the statement of Thomas Huxley, in the nineteenth century, who writes in defence of Cartesianism: "I am prepared to go with the Materialists wherever the true pursuit of the path of Descartes may lead them. . . . I hold, with the Materialists, that the human body, like all living bodies, is a machine, all the operations of which will, sooner or later be explained on physical principles. I believe that we shall, sooner or later, arrive at a mechanical equivalent of consciousness, just as we have arrived at a mechanical equivalent of heat." A mechanical equivalent of consciousness! Descartes would have laughed the phrase aside as meaningless and self-contradictory, as no less absurd than the statement that a straight line could be curved. The soul stands by itself, independent of the world of matter and co-equal with the body it inhabits.

The Cartesian notion of substance was soon questioned by philosophers. It is not difficult to show, as did Berkeley, that we have no experience of a material substratum in the physical world, but only of qualities —colors, shapes, motions, sounds. And Hume applied the same argument to the mental realm: we have no direct knowledge of the thinking thing, "man's glassy essence", but only of passing ideas and impressions; the mind, faithfully described, is not a substance but a stream of sensations, thoughts, and feelings. Even Leibniz, Descartes' successor in the rationalistic philosophy of the continent, pointed to the difficulties of the Cartesian idea of substance. A substance, he argued, is a center of activity; this activity is not the manifestation of a stuff or matter, but the activity itself *is* the substance, and matter is an appearance on the surface of this activity. The criticism of the concept of substance forms a dominant theme in the philosophy that followed Descartes. But this criticism did not dislodge the idea. Any concept so congruent with natural ways of speech and thought is not easily dislodged. It remained an unquestioned belief in the general mind, despite the protests of philosophers, that matter is a substantial thing with physical qualities, and mind a substantial thing with mental qualities.

But if matter and mind are not entities, the one with physical qualities, and the other with mental qualities, what are they? The thought of the present day has discarded the Cartesian substances. William James, for instance, in his essay *Does Consciousness Exist* (1904), slashes boldly at the substantial soul. He denies that consciousness is a thing, but he adds, "To deny plumply that 'consciousness' exists seems so absurd on the face of it—for undeniably 'thoughts' do exist—that I fear some readers will follow me no farther. Let me immediately explain then that I mean only to deny that the word stands for an entity, but to insist that it does stand for a function." Here is the key to the modern idea—"function." Consciousness is a function, but not a function of an underlying stuff. Functioning or activity is basic, and what we call "a mind" or "a physical object" is a concretion—a more or less permanent pattern—of that basic functioning. M. Henri Bergson and Professor A. N. Whitehead give different, but typical, expressions to this modern point of view; both completely abandon the notion of a matter or a mind which *has* qualities.

"Of course," says Professor Whitehead, "substance and quality . . . are the most natural ideas for the human mind. . . . The only question is, How concretely are we thinking when we consider nature under these conceptions? My point will be, that we are presenting ourselves with simplified editions of immediate matters of fact."[1] The Cartesian idea of substance is oversimple in the place it assigns to process or becoming in nature. It asks us to believe that only the properties of things change; their substance persists. Thus change or becoming is a mere "adjective" of changeless, substantial things. We come closer to "immediate matters of fact" when we repudiate this idea of substance; then we see, as Professor Whitehead puts it, that "nature is a structure of evolving process. The reality is the process." What are called by Descartes "substantial things"—stones, atoms, minds—issue out of the process of becoming, which is more fundamental than the things.

The Cartesian scheme had this great advantage for

[1] A. N. Whitehead, "Science and the Modern World," 1925, p 74.

the mechanical view of nature: it enabled the scientist
to ascribe to the mind all the qualities of the world
which need not be taken account of in framing physical
laws. These were the "secondary qualities." The
"primary qualities" alone, that is, motion, and the
geometrical and mathematical properties of substances,
were accorded physical reality.

The soundless, scentless, colorless world of extended
substance comes third, and last, in Descartes' order of
exposition. Taking his stand, first, on the existence of
his own soul, he finds difficulty in making the transition
to this other world. He cannot do so without an appeal
to the Supreme Being. "I exist; I find in my mind the
idea of God, who must—by his very concept—exist;
God, being good, will not deceive me in my clear and
distinct ideas; hence, my belief in an external world of
extended substance in motion, following mechanical
laws, must be a true idea." This is the course of the
argument. To the modern mind this God appears as a
deus ex machina invoked to solve a metaphysical problem; the philosopher seems to be at desperate shifts to
get from ideas to physical things. If the existence of
the soul is the single premise of the argument, it seems
that the only position Descartes could take, without the
appeal to God, would be that of Locke, "that the mind,
in all its thoughts and reasonings, hath no other immediate object but its own ideas, which it alone does
or can contemplate." Cartesianism here rubs elbows
with the idealism of Berkeley, who pursues Locke's way
of ideas to its conclusion in affirming that ideas, and
the spirits that produce them, are the sole realities.

Thus Cartesianism gives to subsequent thought, not
only a general setting for the mechanical view of nature,
but something very different—a strain of subjectivism.
The axiom, "I think, therefore I am," places the *self*

in high relief as the primary datum of philosophy. It
sets the fashion for philosophizing outward from the
inner world of self-consciousness. Other selves and a
common realm of objects are no longer taken for granted
but must be proved to exist. A strange new problem
enters philosophy—"Is there anything in existence beyond my own mind and its thoughts?"

A whole school of philosophers follows Descartes in
approaching reality from the standpoint of self-consciousness. These are the idealists. The Cartesian
emphasis on the self is reflected in Berkeley and Malebranche, and again in Kant, Fichte, and Hegel at the
close of the eighteenth century and the beginning of
the nineteenth. The discovery of the "I"—the life of the
individual personality with its struggle and destiny—
is pointed to as a distinguishing mark of modern, as
opposed to ancient philosophy. For the Greek mind,
man was a social animal, entering into a community not
only with other men, but with nature. It did not occur
to the Pre-Socratics or to Aristotle to ask whether the
soul could escape its own thoughts and share in a world
of common things. Descartes, with the tradition of
Christianity behind him, definitely set aside this simple
realistic point of view. The objective life of community
with nature and other selves was no longer looked on
as a primary fact; it became necessary to rediscover the
common world from the standpoint of an individual
mind, isolated from external objects and other minds.

Pure subjectivism—in its extreme form, solipsism,
which affirms that "only I and my thoughts exist,"—is
difficult to maintain. "Indeed," says a current writer,
"one can easily imagine the difficulty of a situation in
which two solipsists should happen to meet and the
sheepish manner in which, by averting their eyes, they
would endeavor to escape the mutual refutation which

their co-presence in the world would involve."[1] The idealistic philosophers who followed Descartes in stressing self-consciousness, condemned pure subjectivism. Even Berkeley, who comes nearer to solipsism than any of them, finds a way out by making the common world a system of ideas in God's mind; while for Hegel, and for contemporary idealism in general, the self can know its true nature only by participating in a world of realities beyond itself. Modern idealism has come a long way since Descartes. His "thinking substance" is thin and empty beside the self-consciousness from which the philosophies of Fichte and Hegel unfold; and yet the tone of later idealism, as well as of later materialism (and mechanism), begins to make itself articulate in the Cartesian system.

Descartes does not deduce the physical realm and the Divine Being from his thinking ego, though his argument creates the impression that he is attempting this remarkable feat. The final appeal is to the "natural light" of reason, which attests a whole sheaf of eternal verities, among which the existence of God and of a world of matter in motion is no less axiomatic than the existence of the ego. These truths are immediately perceived by an "inspection" of the reason, just as the axiomatic truths of geometry are perceived.

The Cartesian God is therefore much less a *deus ex machina* than the author causes him to appear in the *Meditations* and the *Discourse*. The entire world and all the eternal truths made evident by the light of reason rest on the will of God. The supreme truth, the basic axiom, is that God exists and wills a world order. But the philosopher's instinct for physical science will not permit him to explain the details of nature through the purposes of God, though he is forced thus to explain

[1] W. P. Montague, "The Ways of Knowing," 1925.

the whole. Final causes, the purposes of God, are not to be considered sufficient reasons for physical occurrences. And yet here again Descartes' caution in religious matters asserts itself. He does not deny the reality of final causes. He has not the rashness, or courage, of Spinoza to sweep aside the purposes of God as figments of the human imagination, which can lead only to error in seeking the causes of natural events. He guards himself by the assertion that God's purposes are inscrutable to man. "Finally we shall not seek for the reason of natural things from the end which God or nature has set before Him in their creation; for we should not take so much upon ourselves as to believe that God could take us into His counsels." Thus "we shall utterly set aside from our philosophy the search for final causes," and confine ourselves to the efficient, that is, the mechanical causes.

The appeal to God, in the *Meditations* and elsewhere, as the guarantor of the truth of clear and distinct ideas, is a statement in brief form of Descartes' doctrine that the truths of mathematics, metaphysics, and physics proceed from the Divine Decree. God, the one true substance, who wills all things, is first in the order of being. Even in the depths of doubt and despair, the awareness of God is present and needs only to be made clear. The self is the reality first known, but God is the first reality.

One of the arguments for God's existence is of great importance for the philosopher's view of nature. Finite things, such as the self, not only lack the power to produce themselves, but also the power to maintain themselves in existence, unless they are continually re-created by God. Nothing could prevent the world from suddenly ceasing to be, at this moment, if God did not, at this very moment, create the next moment. "We cannot doubt the truth of this demonstration," says the *Principles*, "so long as we observe the nature of time or of the duration of things; for this is of such a kind that its parts do not depend one upon another, and never co-exist; and from the fact that we now are, it does not follow that we shall be a moment afterwards, if some cause—the same that first produced us—does not continue to produce us; that is to say, to conserve us."

Descartes finds no genuine continuity in physical occurrences. Nature breaks off at every moment. There is no duration, no power of self-prolongation in natural things. God, who is outside nature, must be invoked to carry the world over to each new moment. Here again is a simplified edition of immediate matters of fact. The world *at an instant* is an abstraction which must not be mistaken for the concrete fact. Transition, passage, flow, are of the essence of nature, yet the mechanical scheme of the seventeenth century science has no place for these facts. The most that Descartes can do to bring real transition into the world is to call upon the Deity.

Descartes is deeply concerned to take the burden of error from the shoulders of God and place it on the free will of man, a thoroughly orthodox position. This leads him to a second dualism, within his dualism of mind and body: he must distinguish man's intellect from his will. Error arises from the unbridled will, which affirms the truth of ideas that are not clear and distinct to the intellect. The intellect is limited in its perception of truths; in this respect man is less than God. But the will is unlimited, it is wholly free; and in this respect man is like God. Hence the will can run into error if it permits itself to believe, for instance, in the unqualified reality of the objects of sense; it may mistake dreaming for waking, heat for cold, and be subject to a thousand other illusions. Deliberate carefully and give your assent only when you have attained absolute clarity in thought—this is the rule for avoiding error.

Once the veracity of the Supreme Being is established, and error is shown to spring from our haste in jumping at unclear and indistinct ideas, the Cartesian mood of doubt rises from the philosophic landscape like a mist before the sun, revealing a world of extended bodies moving in space. We must not suppose that the colors, odors, and sounds which strike our senses belong to this world. They are the effects produced in our minds by the movement of subtle bodies in contact with our organs of sense. Only extension, figure, number, quantity, movement,—the primary qualities—are really inherent in the nature of material substance. The realm of mechanical law is before us.

The Cartesian picture of this world is bold and complete. "Since the creation, the world of extended bodies has been nothing but a vast machine." I quote from a recent study of the growth of scientific ideas.[1] "There is no spontaneity at any point; all continues to move in fixed accordance with the principles of extension and motion. This meant that the universe is to be conceived as an extended *plenum,* the motions of whose several parts are communicated to each other by immediate impact. There is no need of calling in the force or attraction of Galileo to account for specific kinds of motion, still less the 'active powers' of Kepler; all happens in accordance with the regularity, precision, inevitability, of a smoothly running machine.

"How could the facts of astronomy and of terrestrial gravity be accounted for in a way which would not do havoc with this beautifully simple hypothesis? Only by regarding the objects of our study as swimming

[1] E. A. Burtt, "The Metaphysical Foundations of Modern Physical Science," 1925.

helplessly in an infinite ether, or 'first matter,' to use Descartes' own term, which, being vaguely and not at all mathematically conceived, Descartes was able to picture as taking on forms of motion that rendered the phenomena explicable. This primary matter, forced into a certain quantity of motion divinely bestowed, falls into a series of whirlpools or vortices, in which the visible bodies such as planets and terrestrial objects are carried around or impelled toward certain central points by the laws of vortical motion. Hence the bodies thus carried can be conceived as purely mathematical; they possess no qualities but those deducible from extension and free mobility in the surrounding medium ... The world is pictured concretely as material rather than spiritual, as mechanical rather than teleological. The stage is set for the likening of it, in Boyle, Locke, and Leibniz, to a big clock once wound up by the Creator, and since kept in orderly motion by nothing more than his 'general concourse.'"

One problem remains, that of the relation between matter and spirit, the two created substances, which have no attribute in common. The human body is no less a mechanism than the solar whirlpool; and yet the freely-acting soul influences the working of the bodily machine. Descartes regards this fact as inescapable: the will can choose and set the body on the proper way toward carrying out its choices. The physical action itself—as when I move my pen to write this sentence— is mechanical, but the choice is free. For the soul, seated in the pineal gland in the center of the brain, can alter the direction of the animal fluids, and thus determine the body to act in one way rather than another.

Gassendi's objections to Descartes' theory of interaction between soul and body state the difficulty in much the same way that it might be put to-day. If the mind touches and influences the body at some point, at that point the mind must be extended and material. And if the mind is material at one point, it is not different in essence from the body. That is to say, only a physical thing can act on a physical thing. In the same way it can be argued that the body could not act on the mind —as Descartes believed it did in the process of sensation—unless the body were spiritual in nature. There is no way of bringing together a soulless body and a bodiless soul.

Following out Descartes' clue—that God is the only true substance, mind and matter being substances in a different sense from God,—Spinoza (1677) attempts to solve the problem of mind and body by conceiving thought and extension as parallel attributes of the one substance God. The Spinozistic view proceeds readily from Descartes by the elimination of an ambiguity in the term substance. "Really the notion of *substance* is just this," declares Descartes, "that which can exist by itself without the aid of any other substance." And God alone answers to this definition. Mind and matter, in Spinoza's system, are coördinate aspects or essences of a God of infinite aspects, who is the inner substance of all things. For every mental event there is a corresponding physical event, and for every physical event, a corresponding mental event, but no action of the physical on the mental or of the mental on the physical is possible. God is the unity of the two—and of an infinity of other attributes. This solution is too general to be of value in psychology or physiology. It tells us nothing more than that the mental and the physical come together in *some way*, not through causal action of the one on the other.

The occasionalists, represented by Geulincx (died 1669), propose another solution which has its roots in the Cartesian system. Geulincx denies all action of soul on body and body on soul, but—in the spirit of Descartes' argument that God continually intervenes to re-create the world—he gives this answer to the mind-body problem: "God, who manipulates these two instruments (mind and body), brings them into harmony with one another, and thus, according to Geulincx, manifests himself as truly admirable. He causes me to think and perceive; precisely at the same moment, he produces a movement in my organs so that I think and perceive, not by means of this movement, but on the occasion of it, not by an efficacy proper to the movement, but by the efficacy of God, who joins the two (soul and body) together, who moves my soul at exactly the same times and as often as he moves my organs; hence my sensations are the signs of the movements and actions of my body. We *will* these movements; that is the only part we play; but it is God alone who produces them as a consequence of our willing. . . . To make this correspondence (of mind and body) understood, he uses the example of two clocks which agree, although they are independent of one another, because they are both regulated by the course of the sun."[1]

For the psychologist and physiologist this solution of the problem can have no other value than to deny, again, the Cartesian theory of interaction. The two-substance view of mind and matter simplifies physical science, by excluding questions that relate to the soul, at the cost of raising a new problem which can find no solution in the Cartesian framework of thought.

[1] F. C. Bouillier, "Histoire de la Philosophie Cartésienne," Paris, 1868.

IV

Thirteen years after the death of Descartes, his writings were placed on the Index of the Catholic Church at the instigation of the Jesuits, upon whom the philosopher had spent many conciliatory words during his lifetime. Despite the proofs of God and the vindication of the life of the spirit, despite the philosophical justification of the sacrament of the Eucharist, (which Descartes was able to explain as not inconsistent with his physical principles), the Church sensed an enemy in the Cartesian philosophy. The true affiliations of this system with the new physical science that was to sweep away mediævalism were apparent.

Descartes' professions of orthodoxy were undoubtedly sincere. The impress of his early training at La Flèche remained on his mind to the end. But the Church was correct in viewing his philosophy—so far as its defence of Christian doctrines went—as a wolf in sheep's clothing. Cartesianism is thickly sown with the seeds of anti-Christian ideas, a fact which becomes evident in the greatest of the philosophical systems that grew immediately from Cartesianism, the system of Spinoza. The "God-intoxicated" Jew of Amsterdam, born five years after the publication of the *Discourse,* was cursed in his own generation and for more than a hundred years later by Jews and Christians alike for his "hideous hypothesis", which demonstrated with mathematical rigor the necessity of all human actions from the necessity of the divine nature, which denied moral responsibility, the immortality of the soul, the existence of purpose in the universe, and the goodness of God. And yet the author of this philosophy was spoken of at the end of the eighteenth century as a "God-intoxicated man." There is no page of Spinoza's *Ethics* on which the name of God does not appear many times, but this God is the antithesis of the Christian God. It is a Deity without personality or moral attributes, nothing more than the inexorable, indwelling principle of order and necessity in nature. Descartes' mathematically and mechanically ordered cosmos has become God.

Descartes would have repudiated Spinoza, and Spinoza repudiates Descartes at many crucial points. Yet Spinozism was the child of Cartesianism. The French philosopher's universal mathematics is here worked out with unfailing logical consistency. The distrust of the Jesuits for what Cartesianism contained in embryo received an ample justification.

At the distance of three hundred years the Cartesian philosophy looks harmless. Its explosive power is spent, and the rumble of its doctrines has become faint. The science and philosophy of the twentieth century are groping for a new set of fundamental concepts. It is impossible to say what these concepts will be, but this much seems certain—that they will depart widely from the Cartesian idea of bits of substance, mental or physical, with changing qualities. They will set aside the dualism of mind and body, and treat mind as a function, not an entity. They will recognize time and process as essential to nature, rather than think of physical occurrences as a patchwork of static configurations at an instant. They will seek a more complete view of mechanical processes, which may enable them to bring the mechanical and biological (not to mention the psychological) sciences together, without doing violence to the facts of living organisms, as Descartes does in trying to reduce them to simple mechanisms.

But there is one idea of the Cartesian system that will be preserved. The method of mathematics will continue to be the most effective instrument of physical inquiry, for the pattern of rational thinking is mathematical, in a wide sense of that term. This fact is even more apparent to-day than it was in the age of Descartes; logic itself has been shown to be a kind of super-mathematics. All careful analysis—whether it be of space, of numbers, of organic processes, of physical laws—can be assimilated to the type of mathematical analysis. This idea of a rational analysis of the order of nature, following the methods of mathematics, was, more than any other conception, the motive power of Cartesianism and of the science of the seventeenth century in which this philosophy was set.

RALPH M. EATON.

CONTENTS

DESCARTES
SELECTIONS

DISCOURSE ON THE METHOD OF RIGHTLY CONDUCTING THE REASON AND SEEKING FOR TRUTH IN THE SCIENCES

If this Discourse appears too long to be read all at once, it may be separated into six portions. And in the first there will be found various considerations respecting the sciences; in the second, the principal rules regarding the Method which the author has sought out; while in the third are some of the rules of morality which he has derived from this Method. In the fourth are the reasons by which he proves the existence of God and of the human soul, which form the foundation of his Metaphysic. In the fifth, the order of the questions regarding physics which he has investigated, and particularly the explanation of the movement of the heart, and of some other difficulties which pertain to medicine, as also the difference between the soul of man and that of the brutes. And in the last part the questions raised relate to those matters which the author believes to be requisite in order to advance further in the investigation of nature, in addition to the reasons that caused him to write.

PART I - various considerations re the sciences

Good sense is of all things in the world the most equally distributed, for everybody thinks himself so abundantly provided with it, that even those most difficult to please in all other matters do not commonly desire more of it than they already possess. It is

1

unlikely that this is an error on their part; it seems
rather to be evidence in support of the view that the
power of forming a good judgment and of distinguishing
the true from the false, which is properly speaking what
is called Good sense or Reason, is by nature equal in
all men.   Hence too, it will show that the diversity of
our opinions does not proceed from some men being
more rational than others, but solely from the fact that
our thoughts pass through diverse channels and the same
objects are not considered by all.   For to be possessed
of good mental powers is not sufficient; the principal
matter is to apply them well.   The greatest minds are
capable of the greatest vices as well as of the greatest
virtues, and those who proceed very slowly may, provided they always follow the straight road, really
advance much faster than those who, though they run,
forsake it.

For myself I have never ventured to presume that
my mind was in any way more perfect than that of the
ordinary man; I have even longed to possess thought
as quick, or an imagination as accurate and distinct, or
a memory as comprehensive or ready, as some others.
And besides these I do not know any other qualities
that make for the perfection of the human mind.   For
as to reason or sense, inasmuch as it is the only thing
that constitutes us men and distinguishes us from the
brutes, I would fain believe that it is to be found complete in each individual, and in this I follow the common opinion of the philosophers, who say that the question of more or less occurs only in the sphere of the
accidents and does not affect the *forms* or natures of
the *individuals* in the same *species*.

But I shall not hesitate to say that I have had great
good fortune from my youth up, in lighting upon and
pursuing certain paths which have conducted me to

considerations and maxims from which I have formed a Method, by whose assistance it appears to me I have the means of gradually increasing my knowledge and of little by little raising it to the highest possible point which the mediocrity of my talents and the brief duration of my life can permit me to reach. For I have already reaped from it fruits of such a nature that, even though I always try in the judgments I make on myself to lean to the side of self-depreciation rather than to that of arrogance, and though, looking with the eye of a philosopher on the diverse actions and enterprises of all mankind, I find scarcely any which do not seem to me vain and useless, I do not cease to receive extreme satisfaction in the progress which I seem to have already made in the search after truth, and to form such hopes for the future as to venture to believe that, if amongst the occupations of men, simply as men, there is some one in particular that is excellent and important, that is the one which I have selected.

It must always be recollected, however, that possibly I deceive myself, and that what I take to be gold and diamonds is perhaps no more than copper and glass. I know how subject we are to delusion in whatever touches ourselves, and also how much the judgments of our friends ought to be suspected when they are in our favour. But in this Discourse I shall be very happy to show the paths I have followed, and to set forth my life as in a picture, so that everyone may judge of it for himself; and thus in learning from the common talk what are the opinions which are held of it, a new means of obtaining self-instruction will be reached, which I shall add to those which I have been in the habit of using.

Thus my design is not here to teach the Method which everyone should follow in order to promote the good conduct of his Reason, but only to show in what manner I have endeavoured to conduct my own. Those who set about giving precepts must esteem themselves more skilful than those to whom they advance them, and if they fall short in the smallest matter they must, of course, take the blame for it. But regarding this Treatise simply as a history, or, if you prefer it, a fable in which, amongst certain things which may be imitated, there are possibly others also which it would not be right to follow, I hope that it will be of use to some without being hurtful to any, and that all will thank me for my frankness.

I have been nourished on letters since my childhood, and since I was given to believe that by their means a clear and certain knowledge could be obtained of all that is useful in life, I had an extreme desire to acquire instruction. But so soon as I had achieved the entire course of study at the close of which one is usually received into the ranks of the learned, I entirely changed my opinion. For I found myself embarrassed with so many doubts and errors that it seemed to me that the effort to instruct myself had no effect other than the increasing discovery of my own ignorance. And yet I was studying at one of the most celebrated Schools in Europe, where I thought that there must be men of learning if they were to be found anywhere in the world. I learned there all that others learned; and not being satisfied with the sciences that we were taught, I even read through all the books which fell into my hands, treating of what is considered most curious and rare. Along with this I knew the judgments that others had formed of me, and I did not feel that I was esteemed inferior to my fellow-students, although there were amongst them some destined to fill the places of our masters. And finally our century seemed to me as flourishing, and as fertile in great minds, as any which had preceded. And this made me take the liberty of judging all others by myself and of coming to the conclusion that there was no learning in the world such as I was formerly led to believe it to be.

I did not omit, however, always to hold in esteem those exercises which are the occupation of the Schools. I knew that the Languages which one learns there are essential for the understanding of all ancient literature; that fables with their charm stimulate the mind and histories of memorable deeds exalt it; and that, when read with discretion, these books assist in forming a sound judgment. I was aware that the reading of all good books is indeed like a conversation with the noblest men of past centuries who were the authors of them, nay a carefully studied conversation, in which they reveal to us none but the best of their thoughts. I deemed Eloquence to have a power and beauty beyond compare; that Poesy has most ravishing delicacy and sweetness; that in Mathematics there are the subtlest discoveries and inventions which may accomplish much, both in satisfying the curious, and in furthering all the arts, and in diminishing man's labour; that those writings that deal with Morals contain much that is instructive, and many exhortations to virtue which are most useful; that Theology points out the way to Heaven; that Philosophy teaches us to speak with an appearance of truth on all things, and causes us to be admired by the less learned; that Jurisprudence, Medicine and all other sciences bring honour and riches to those who cultivate them; and finally that it is good to have examined all things, even those most full of superstition and falsehood, in order that we may know their just value, and avoid being deceived by them.

But I considered that I had already given sufficient

time to languages and likewise even to the reading of
the literature of the ancients, both their histories and
their fables. For to converse with those of other centuries is almost the same thing as to travel. It is good
to know something of the customs of different people in
order to judge more sanely of our own, and not to
think that everything of a fashion not ours is absurd
and contrary to reason, as do those who have seen
nothing. But when one employs too much time in
travelling, one becomes a stranger in one's own country,
and when one is too curious about things which were
practised in past centuries, one is usually very ignorant
about those which are practised in our own time. Besides, fables make one imagine many events possible
which in reality are not so, and even the most accurate
of histories, if they do not exactly misrepresent or
exaggerate the value of things in order to render them
more worthy of being read, at least omit in them all the
circumstances which are basest and least notable; and
from this fact it follows that what is retained is not
portrayed as it really is, and that those who regulate
their conduct by examples which they derive from such
a source, are liable to fall into the extravagances of
the knights-errant of Romance, and form projects beyond their power of performance.

I esteemed Eloquence most highly and I was
enamoured of Poesy, but I thought that both were gifts
of the mind rather than fruits of study. Those who
have the strongest power of reasoning, and who most
skilfully arrange their thoughts in order to render them
clear and intelligible, have the best power of persuasion even if they can but speak the language of Lower
Brittany and have never learned Rhetoric. And those
who have the most delightful original ideas and who
know how to express them with the maximum of style

and suavity, would not fail to be the best poets even if the art of Poetry were unknown to them.

Most of all was I delighted with Mathematics because of the certainty of its demonstrations and the evidence of its reasoning; but I did not yet understand its true use, and, believing that it was of service only in the mechanical arts, I was astonished that, seeing how firm and solid was its basis, no loftier edifice had been reared thereupon. On the other hand I compared the works of the ancient pagans which deal with Morals to palaces most superb and magnificent, which are yet built on sand and mud alone. They praise the virtues most highly and show them to be more worthy of being prized than anything else in the world, but they do not sufficiently teach us to become acquainted with them, and often that which is called by a fine name is nothing but insensibility, or pride, or despair, or parricide.

I honoured our Theology and aspired as much as anyone to reach to heaven, but having learned to regard it as a most highly assured fact that the road is not less open to the most ignorant than to the most learned, and that the revealed truths which conduct thither are quite above our intelligence, I should not have dared to submit them to the feebleness of my reasonings; and I thought that, in order to undertake to examine them and succeed in so doing, it was necessary to have some extraordinary assistance from above and to be more than a mere man.

I shall not say anything about Philosophy, but that, seeing that it has been cultivated for many centuries by the best minds that have ever lived, and that nevertheless no single thing is to be found in it which is not subject of dispute, and in consequence which is not dubious, I had not enough presumption to hope to fare better there than other men had done. And also, considering how many conflicting opinions there may be regarding the self-same matter, all supported by learned people, while there can never be more than one which is true, I esteemed as well-nigh false all that only went as far as being probable.

Then as to the other sciences, inasmuch as they derive their principles from Philosophy, I judged that one could have built nothing solid on foundations so far from firm. And neither the honour nor the promised gain was sufficient to persuade me to cultivate them, for, thanks be to God, I did not find myself in a condition which obliged me to make a merchandise of science for the improvement of my fortune; and, although I did not pretend to scorn all glory like the Cynics, I yet had very small esteem for what I could not hope to acquire, excepting through fictitious titles. And, finally, as to false doctrines, I thought that I already knew well enough what they were worth to be subject to deception neither by the promises of an alchemist, the predictions of an astrologer, the impostures of a magician, the artifices or the empty boastings of any of those who make a profession of knowing that of which they are ignorant.

This is why, as soon as age permitted me to emerge from the control of my tutors, I entirely quitted the study of letters. And resolving to seek no other science than that which could be found in myself, or at least in the great book of the world, I employed the rest of my youth in travel, in seeing courts and armies, in intercourse with men of diverse temperaments and conditions, in collecting varied experiences, in proving myself in the various predicaments in which I was placed by fortune, and under all circumstances bringing my mind to bear on the things which came before it, so that I might derive some profit from my experience. For it seemed to me that I might meet with much more truth

in the reasonings that each man makes on the matters
that specially concern him, and the issue of which would
very soon punish him if he made a wrong judgment,
than in the case of those made by a man of letters in
his study touching speculations which lead to no result,
and which bring about no other consequences to himself excepting that he will be all the more vain the
more they are removed from common sense, since in
this case it proves him to have employed so much the
more ingenuity and skill in trying to make them seem
probable. And I always had an excessive desire to
learn to distinguish the true from the false, in order to
see clearly in my actions and to walk with confidence
in this life.

It is true that while I only considered the manners
of other men I found in them nothing to give me settled
convictions; and I remarked in them almost as much
diversity as I had formerly seen in the opinions of
philosophers. So much was this the case that the
greatest profit which I derived from their study was
that, in seeing many things which, although they seem
to us very extravagant and ridiculous, were yet commonly received and approved by other great nations, I
learned to believe nothing too certainly of which I had
only been convinced by example and custom. Thus
little by little I was delivered from many errors which
might have obscured our natural vision and rendered
us less capable of listening to Reason. But after I
had employed several years in thus studying the book
of the world and trying to acquire some experience, I
one day formed the resolution of also making myself an
object of study and of employing all the strength of
my mind in choosing the road I should follow. This
succeeded much better, it appeared to me, than if I had
never departed either from my country or my books.

Part II *Principles re method*
Descartes suggests

I was then in Germany, to which country I had been
attracted by the wars which are not yet at an end.
And as I was returning from the coronation of the
Emperor to join the army, the setting in of winter
detained me in a quarter where, since I found no society
to divert me, while fortunately I had also no cares or
passions to trouble me, I remained the whole day shut
up alone in a stove-heated room, where I had complete
leisure to occupy myself with my own thoughts. One
of the first of the considerations that occurred to me
was that there is very often less perfection in works
composed of several portions, and carried out by the
hands of various masters, than in those on which one
individual alone has worked. Thus we see that buildings planned and carried out by one architect alone are
usually more beautiful and better proportioned than
those which many have tried to put in order and
improve, making use of old walls which were built with
other ends in view. In the same way also, those ancient
cities which, originally mere villages, have become in the
process of time great towns, are usually badly constructed in comparison with those which are regularly
laid out on a plain by a surveyor who is free to follow
his own ideas. Even though, considering their buildings
each one apart, there is often as much or more display
of skill in the one case than in the other, the former have
large buildings and small buildings indiscriminately
placed together, thus rendering the streets crooked and
irregular, so that it might be said that it was chance
rather than the will of men guided by reason that led
to such an arrangement. And if we consider that this
happens despite the fact that from all time there have
been certain officials who have had the special duty

of looking after the buildings of private individuals in order that they may be public ornaments, we shall understand how difficult it is to bring about much that is satisfactory in operating only upon the works of others. Thus I imagined that those people who were once half-savage, and who have become civilized only by slow degrees, merely forming their laws as the disagreeable necessities of their crimes and quarrels constrained them, could not succeed in establishing so good a system of government as those who, from the time they first came together as communities, carried into effect the constitution laid down by some prudent legislator. Thus it is quite certain that the constitution of the true Religion whose ordinances are of God alone is incomparably better regulated than any other. And to come down to human affairs, I believe that if Sparta was very flourishing in former times, this was not because of the excellence of each and every one of its laws, seeing that many were very strange and even contrary to good morals, but because, being drawn up by one individual, they all tended towards the same end. And similarly I thought that the sciences found in books—in those at least whose reasonings are only probable and which have no demonstrations, composed as they are of the gradually accumulated opinions of many different individuals—do not approach so near to the truth as the simple reasoning which a man of common sense can quite naturally carry out respecting the things which come immediately before him. Again I thought that since we have all been children before being men, and since it has for long fallen to us to be governed by our appetites and by our teachers (who often enough contradicted one another, and none of whom perhaps counselled us always for the best), it is almost impossible that our judgments should be so

excellent or solid as they should have been had we had
complete use of our reason since our birth, and had we
been guided by its means alone.

It is true that we do not find that all the houses in a
town are rased to the ground for the sole reason that
the town is to be rebuilt in another fashion, with streets
made more beautiful; but at the same time we see that
many people cause their own houses to be knocked down
in order to rebuild them, and that sometimes they are
forced so to do where there is danger of the houses
falling of themselves, and when the foundations are
not secure.   From such examples I argued to myself
that there was no plausibility in the claim of any private
individual to reform a state by altering everything, and
by overturning it throughout, in order to set it right
again.   Nor is it likewise probable that the whole body
of the Sciences, or the order of teaching established by
the Schools, should be reformed.   But as regards all
the opinions which up to this time I had embraced, I
thought I could not do better than endeavour once for
all to sweep them completely away, so that they might
later on be replaced, either by others which were better,
or by the same, when I had made them conform to the
uniformity of a rational scheme.   And I firmly believed
that by this means I should succeed in directing my life
much better than if I had only built on old foundations,
and relied on principles of which I allowed myself
to be in youth persuaded without having inquired into
their truth.   For although in so doing I recognised
various difficulties, these were at the same time not
unsurmountable, nor comparable to those which are
found in reformation of the most insignificant kind in
matters which concern the public.   In the case of great
bodies it is too difficult a task to raise them again when
they are once thrown down, or even to keep them in

their places when once thoroughly shaken; and their fall cannot be otherwise than very violent. Then as to any imperfections that they may possess (and the very diversity that is found between them is sufficient to tell us that these in many cases exist) custom has doubtless greatly mitigated them, while it has also helped us to avoid, or insensibly corrected a number against which mere foresight would have found it difficult to guard. And finally the imperfections are almost always more supportable than would be the process of removing them, just as the great roads which wind about amongst the mountains become, because of being frequented, little by little so well-beaten and easy that it is much better to follow them than to try to go more directly by climbing over rocks and descending to the foot of precipices.

This is the reason why I cannot in any way approve of those turbulent and unrestful spirits who, being called neither by birth nor fortune to the management of public affairs, never fail to have always in their minds some new reforms. And if I thought that in this treatise there was contained the smallest justification for this folly, I should be very sorry to allow it to be published. My design has never extended beyond trying to reform my own opinion and to build on a foundation which is entirely my own. If my work has given me a certain satisfaction, so that I here present to you a draft of it, I do not so do because I wish to advise anybody to imitate it. Those to whom God has been most beneficent in the bestowal of His grace will perhaps form designs which are more elevated; but I fear much that this particular one will seem too venturesome for many. The simple resolve to strip oneself of all opinions and beliefs formerly received is not to be regarded as an example that each man should follow, and the world may be said to be mainly composed of two classes of minds neither of which could prudently adopt it. There are those who, believing themselves to be cleverer than they are, cannot restrain themselves from being precipitate in judgment and have not sufficient patience to arrange their thoughts in proper order; hence, once a man of this description had taken the liberty of doubting the principles he formerly accepted, and had deviated from the beaten track, he would never be able to maintain the path which must be followed to reach the appointed end more quickly, and he would hence remain wandering astray all through his life. Secondly, there are those who having reason or modesty enough to judge that they are less capable of distinguishing truth from falsehood than some others from whom instruction might be obtained, are right in contenting themselves with following the opinions of these others rather than in searching better ones for themselves.

For myself I should doubtless have been of these last if I had never had more than a single master, or had I never known the diversities which have from all time existed between the opinions of men of the greatest learning. But I had been taught, even in my College days, that there is nothing imaginable so strange or so little credible that it has not been maintained by one philosopher or other, and I further recognised in the course of my travels that all those whose sentiments are very contrary to ours are yet not necessarily barbarians or savages, but may be possessed of reason in as great or even a greater degree than ourselves. I also considered how very different the self-same man, identical in mind and spirit, may become, according as he is brought up from childhood amongst the French or Germans, or has passed his whole life amongst

Chinese or cannibals. I likewise noticed how even in the fashions of one's clothing the same thing that pleased us ten years ago, and which will perhaps please us once again before ten years are passed, seems at the present time extravagant and ridiculous. I thus concluded that it is much more custom and example that persuade us than any certain knowledge, and yet in spite of this the voice of the majority does not afford a proof of any value in truths a little difficult to discover, because such truths are much more likely to have been discovered by one man than by a nation. I could not, however, put my finger on a single person whose opinions seemed preferable to those of others, and I found that I was, so to speak, constrained myself to undertake the direction of my procedure.

But like one who walks alone and in the twilight I resolved to go so slowly, and to use so much circumspection in all things, that if my advance was but very small, at least I guarded myself well from falling. I did not wish to set about the final rejection of any single opinion which might formerly have crept into my beliefs without having been introduced there by means of Reason, until I had first of all employed sufficient time in planning out the task which I had undertaken, and in seeking the true Method of arriving at a knowledge of all the things of which my mind was capable.

Among the different branches of Philosophy, I had in my younger days to a certain extent studied Logic; and in those of Mathematics, Geometrical Analysis and Algebra—three arts or sciences which seemed as though they ought to contribute something to the design I had in view. But in examining them I observed in respect to Logic that the syllogisms and the greater part of the other teaching served better in explaining to others those things that one knows (or like the art

of Lully, in enabling one to speak without judgment of
those things of which one is ignorant) than in learning
what is new. And although in reality Logic contains
many precepts which are very true and very good, there
are at the same time mingled with them so many others
which are hurtful or superfluous, that it is almost as
difficult to separate the two as to draw a Diana or a
Minerva out of a block of marble which is not yet
roughly hewn. And as to the Analysis of the ancients
and the Algebra of the moderns, besides the fact that
they embrace only matters the most abstract, such as
appear to have no actual use, the former is always so
restricted to the consideration of symbols that it cannot
exercise the Understanding without greatly fatiguing
the Imagination; and in the latter one is so subjected
to certain rules and formulas that the result is the con-
struction of an art which is confused and obscure, and
which embarrasses the mind, instead of a science which
contributes to its cultivation. This made me feel that
some other Method must be found, which, comprising
the advantages of the three, is yet exempt from their
faults. And as a multiplicity of laws often furnishes
excuses for evil-doing, and as a State is hence much
better ruled when, having but very few laws, these are
most strictly observed; so, instead of the great number
of precepts of which Logic is composed, I believed
that I should find the four which I shall state quite
sufficient, provided that I adhered to a firm and constant
resolve never on any single occasion to fail in their
observance.

The first of these was to accept nothing as true which
I did not clearly recognise to be so: that is to say,
carefully to avoid precipitation and prejudice in judgments, and to accept in them nothing more than what

was presented to my mind so clearly and distinctly that I could have no occasion to doubt it.

The second was to divide up each of the difficulties which I examined into as many parts as possible, and as seemed requisite in order that it might be resolved in the best manner possible.

The third was to carry on my reflections in due order, commencing with objects that were the most simple and easy to understand, in order to rise little by little, or by degrees, to knowledge of the most complex, assuming an order, even if a fictitious one, among those which do not follow a natural sequence relatively to one another.

The last was in all cases to make enumerations so complete and reviews so general that I should be certain of having omitted nothing.

Those long chains of reasoning, simple and easy as they are, of which geometricians make use in order to arrive at the most difficult demonstrations, had caused me to imagine that all those things which fall under the cognisance of man might very likely be mutually related in the same fashion; and that, provided only that we abstain from receiving anything as true which is not so, and always retain the order which is necessary in order to deduce the one conclusion from the other, there can be nothing so remote that we cannot reach to it, nor so recondite that we cannot discover it. And I had not much trouble in discovering which objects it was necessary to begin with, for I already knew that it was with the most simple and those most easy to apprehend. Considering also that of all those who have hitherto sought for the truth in the Sciences, it has been the mathematicians alone who have been able to succeed in making any demonstrations, that is to say producing reasons which are evident and certain, I did not doubt that it had been by means of a similar kind that they carried on their investigations. I did not at the same time hope for any practical result in so doing, except that my mind would become accustomed to the nourishment of truth and would not content itself with false reasoning. But for all that I had no intention of trying to master all those particular sciences that receive in common the name of Mathematics; but observing that, although their objects are different, they do not fail to agree in this, that they take nothing under consideration but the various relationships or proportions which are present in these objects, I thought that it would be better if I only examined these proportions in their general aspect, and without viewing them otherwise than in the objects which would serve most to facilitate a knowledge of them. Not that I should in any way restrict them to these objects, for I might later on all the more easily apply them to all other objects to which they were applicable. Then, having carefully noted that in order to comprehend the proportions I should sometimes require to consider each one in particular, and sometimes merely keep them in mind, or take them in groups, I thought that, in order the better to consider them in detail, I should picture them in the form of lines, because I could find no method more simple nor more capable of being distinctly represented to my imagination and senses. I considered, however, that in order to keep them in my memory or to embrace several at once, it would be essential that I should explain them by means of certain formulas, the shorter the better. And for this purpose it was requisite that I should borrow all that is best in Geometrical Analysis and Algebra, and correct the errors of the one by the other.

As a matter of fact, I can venture to say that the

exact observation of the few precepts which I had chosen gave me so much facility in sifting out all the questions embraced in these two sciences, that in the two or three months which I employed in examining them—commencing with the most simple and general, and making each truth that I discovered a rule for helping me to find others—not only did I arrive at the solution of many questions which I had hitherto regarded as most difficult, but, towards the end, it seemed to me that I was able to determine in the case of those of which I was still ignorant, by what means, and in how far, it was possible to solve them. In this I might perhaps appear to you to be very vain if you did not remember that having but one truth to discover in respect to each matter, whoever succeeds in finding it knows in its regard as much as can be known. It is the same as with a child, for instance, who has been instructed in Arithmetic and has made an addition according to the rule prescribed; he may be sure of having found as regards the sum of figures given to him all that the human mind can know. For, in conclusion, the Method which teaches us to follow the true order and enumerate exactly every term in the matter under investigation contains everything which gives certainty to the rules of Arithmetic.

But what pleased me most in this Method was that I was certain by its means of exercising my reason in all things, if not perfectly, at least as well as was in my power. And besides this, I felt in making use of it that my mind gradually accustomed itself to conceive of its objects more accurately and distinctly; and not having restricted this Method to any particular matter, I promised myself to apply it as usefully to the difficulties of other sciences as I had done to those of Algebra. Not that on this account I dared under-

take to examine just at once all those that might present
themselves; for that would itself have been contrary to
the order which the Method prescribes. But having
noticed that the knowledge of these difficulties must be
dependent on principles derived from Philosophy in
which I yet found nothing to be certain, I thought that
it was requisite above all to try to establish certainty
in it. I considered also that since this endeavour is the
most important in all the world, and that in which
precipitation and prejudice were most to be feared,
I should not try to grapple with it till I had attained
to a much riper age than that of three and twenty, which
was the age I had reached. I thought, too, that I should
first of all employ much time in preparing myself for
the work by eradicating from my mind all the wrong
opinions which I had up to this time accepted, and
accumulating a variety of experiences fitted later on to
afford matter for my reasonings, and by ever exercising
myself in the Method which I had prescribed, in order
more and more to fortify myself in the power of using it.

PART III   Rules of morality derived
for Descartes method

And finally, as it is not sufficient, before commencing
to rebuild the house which we inhabit, to pull it down
and provide materials and an architect (or to act in
this capacity ourselves, and make a careful drawing
of its design), unless we have also provided ourselves
with some other house where we can be comfortably
lodged during the time of rebuilding, so in order that
I should not remain irresolute in my actions while reason obliged me to be so in my judgments, and that I
might not omit to carry on my life as happily as I
could, I formed for myself a code of morals for the
time being which did not consist of more than three

or four maxims, which maxims I should like to enumerate to you.

The first was to obey the laws and customs of my country, adhering constantly to the religion in which by God's grace I had been instructed since my childhood, and in all other things directing my conduct by opinions the most moderate in nature, and the farthest removed from excess in all those which are commonly received and acted on by the most judicious of those with whom I might come in contact. For since I began to count my own opinions as nought, because I desired to place all under examination, I was convinced that I could not do better than follow those held by people on whose judgment reliance could be placed. And although such persons may possibly exist amongst the Personias and Chinese as well as amongst ourselves, it seemed to me that it was most expedient to bring my conduct into harmony with the ideas of those with whom I should have to live; and that, in order to ascertain that these were their real opinions, I should observe what they did rather than what they said, not only because in the corrupt state of our manners there are few people who desire to say all that they believe, but also because many are themselves ignorant of their beliefs. For since the act of thought by which we believe a thing is different from that by which we know that we believe it, the one often exists without the other. And amongst many opinions all equally received, I chose only the most moderate, both because these are always most suited for putting into practice, and probably the best (for all excess has a tendency to be bad), and also because I should have in a less degree turned aside from the right path, supposing that I was wrong, than if, having chosen an extreme course, I found that I had chosen amiss. I also made a point of counting as excess all the engagements by means of which we limit in some degree our liberty. Not that I hold in low esteem those laws which, in order to remedy the inconstancy of feeble souls, permit, when we have a good object in our view, that certain vows be taken, or contracts made, which oblige us to carry out that object. This sanction is even given for security in commerce where designs are wholly indifferent. But because I saw nothing in all the world remaining constant, and because for my own part I promised myself gradually to get my judgments to grow better and never to grow worse, I should have thought that I had committed a serious sin against commonsense if, because I approved of something at one time, I was obliged to regard it similarly at a later time, after it had possibly ceased to meet my approval, or after I had ceased to regard it in favourable light.

My second maxim was that of being as firm and resolute in my actions as I could be, and not to follow less faithfully opinions the most dubious, when my mind was once made up regarding them, than if these had been beyond doubt. In this I should be following the example of travellers, who, finding themselves lost in a forest, know that they ought not to wander first to one side and then to the other, nor, still less, to stop in one place, but understand that they should continue to walk as straight as they can in one direction, not diverging for any slight reason, even though it was possibly chance alone that first determined them in their choice. By this means if they do not go exactly where they wish, they will at least arrive somewhere at the end, where probably they will be better off than in the middle of a forest. And thus since often enough in the actions of life no delay is permissible, it is very certain that, when it is beyond our power to discern the opinions which carry most truth, we should follow the most probable; and even although we notice no greater probability in the one opinion than in the other, we at least should make up our minds to follow a particular one and afterwards consider it as no longer doubtful in its relationship to practice, but as very true and very certain, inasmuch as the reason which caused us to determine upon it is known to be so. And henceforward this principle was sufficient to deliver me from all the penitence and remorse which usually affect the mind and agitate the conscience of those weak and vacillating creatures who allow themselves to keep changing their procedure, and practise as good, things which they afterwards judge to be evil.

My third maxim was to try always to conquer myself rather than fortune, and to alter my desires rather than change the order of the world, and generally to accustom myself to believe that there is nothing entirely within our power but our own thoughts: so that after we have done our best in regard to the things that are without us, our ill-success cannot possibly be failure on our part. And this alone seemed to me sufficient to prevent my desiring anything in the future beyond what I could actually obtain, hence rendering me content; for since our will does not naturally induce us to desire anything but what our understanding represents to it as in some way possible of attainment, it is certain that if we consider all good things which are outside of us as equally outside of our power, we should not have more regret in resigning those goods which appear to pertain to our birth, when we are deprived of them for no fault of our own, than we have in not possessing the kingdoms of China or Mexico. In the same way, making what is called a virtue out of a necessity, we should no more desire to be well if ill, or free. if in prison, than we

now do to have our bodies formed of a substance as
little corruptible as diamonds, or to have wings to fly
with like birds. I allow, however, that to accustom
oneself to regard all things from this point of view
requires long exercise and meditation often repeated;
and I believe that it is principally in this that is to
be found the secret of those philosophers who, in ancient
times, were able to free themselves from the empire of
fortune, or, despite suffering or poverty, to rival their
gods in their happiness. For, ceaselessly occupying
themselves in considering the limits which were prescribed to them by nature, they persuaded themselves
so completely that nothing was within their own power
but their thoughts, that this conviction alone was sufficient to prevent their having any longing for other
things. And they had so absolute a mastery over their
thoughts that they had some reason for esteeming
themselves as more rich and more powerful, and more
free and more happy than other men, who, however
favoured by nature or fortune they might be, if devoid
of this philosophy, never could arrive at all at which
they aim.

And last of all, to conclude this moral code, I felt
it incumbent on me to make a review of the various
occupations of men in this life in order to try to choose
out the best; and without wishing to say anything of
the employment of others I thought that I could not do
better than continue in the one in which I found myself
engaged, that is to say, in occupying my whole life
in cultivating my Reason, and in advancing myself as
much as possible in the knowledge of the truth in accordance with the method which I had prescribed myself. I had experienced so much satisfaction since
beginning to use this method, that I did not believe that
any sweeter or more innocent could in this life be

found,—every day discovering by its means some truths
which seemed to me sufficiently important, although commonly ignored by other men. The satisfaction which I
had so filled my mind that all else seemed of no account. And, besides, the three preceding maxims were
founded solely on the plan which I had formed of
continuing to instruct myself. For since God has given
to each of us some light with which to distinguish
truth from error, I could not believe that I ought for
a single moment to content myself with accepting the
opinions held by others unless I had in view the employment of my own judgment in examining them at
the proper time; and I could not have held myself free
of scruple in following such opinions, if nevertheless
I had not intended to lose no occasion of finding superior
opinions, supposing them to exist; and finally, I should
not have been able to restrain my desires nor to remain
content, if I had not followed a road by which, thinking that I should be certain to be able to acquire all the
knowledge of which I was capable, I also thought I
should likewise be certain of obtaining all the best
things which could ever come within my power. And
inasmuch as our will impels us neither to follow after
nor to flee from anything, excepting as our understanding represents it as good or evil, it is sufficient to judge
wisely in order to act well, and the best judgment brings
the best action—that is to say, the acquisition of all
the virtues and all the other good things that it is
possible to obtain. When one is certain that this point
is reached, one cannot fail to be contented.

Having thus assured myself of these maxims, and
having set them on one side along with the truths of
religion which have always taken the first place in my
creed, I judged that as far as the rest of my opinions
were concerned, I could safely undertake to rid myself

of them. And inasmuch as I hoped to be able to reach my end more successfully in converse with man than in living longer shut up in the warm room where these reflections had come to me, I hardly awaited the end of winter before I once more set myself to travel. And in all the nine following years I did nought but roam hither and thither, trying to be a spectator rather than an actor in all the comedies the world displays. More especially did I reflect in each matter that came before me as to anything which could make it subject to suspicion or doubt, and give occasion for mistake, and I rooted out of my mind all the errors which might have formerly crept in. Not that indeed I imitated the sceptics, who only doubt for the sake of doubting, and pretend to be always uncertain; for, on the contrary, my design was only to provide myself with good ground for assurance, and to reject the quicksand and mud in order to find the rock or clay. In this task it seems to me, I succeeded pretty well, since in trying to discover the error or uncertainty of the propositions which I examined, not by feeble conjectures, but by clear and assured reasonings, I encountered nothing so dubious that I could not draw from it some conclusion that was tolerably secure, if this were no more than the inference that it contained in it nothing that was certain. And just as in pulling down an old house we usually preserve the debris to serve in building up another, so in destroying all those opinions which I considered to be ill-founded, I made various observations and acquired many experiences, which have since been of use to me in establishing those which are more certain. And more than this, I continued to exercise myself in the method which I had laid down for my use; for besides the fact that I was careful as a rule to conduct all my thoughts according to its maxims, I set aside some hours from time to time which I more especially employed in practising myself in the solution of mathematical problems according to the Method, or in the solution of other problems which though pertaining to other sciences, I was able to make almost similar to those of mathematics, by detaching them from all principles of other sciences which I found to be not sufficiently secure. You will see the result in many examples which are expounded in this volume. And hence, without living to all appearance in any way differently from those who, having no occupation beyond spending their lives in ease and innocence, study to separate pleasure from vice, and who, in order to enjoy their leisure without weariness, make use of all distractions that are innocent and good, I did not cease to prosecute my design, and to profit perhaps even more in my study of Truth than if I had done nothing but read books or associate with literary people.

These nine years thus passed away before I had taken any definite part in regard to the difficulties as to which the learned are in the habit of disputing, or had commenced to seek the foundation of any philosophy more certain than the vulgar. And the example of many excellent men who had tried to do the same before me, but, as it appears to me, without success, made me imagine it to be so hard that possibly I should not have dared to undertake the task, had I not discovered that someone had spread abroad the report that I had already reached its conclusion. I cannot tell on what they based this opinion; if my conversation has contributed anything to it, this must have arisen from my confessing my ignorance more ingenuously than those who have studied a little usually do. And perhaps it was also due to my having shown forth my reasons for doubting many things which were held by

others to be certain, rather than from having boasted
of any special philosophic system. But being at heart
honest enough not to desire to be esteemed as different
from what I am, I thought that I must try by every
means in my power to render myself worthy of the
reputation which I had gained. And it is just eight
years ago that this desire made me resolve to remove
myself from all places where any acquaintances were
possible, and to retire to a country such as this,[1] where
the long-continued war has caused such order to be
established that the armies which are maintained seem
only to be of use in allowing the inhabitants to enjoy
the fruits of peace with so much the more security; and
where, in the crowded throng of a great and very active
nation, which is more concerned with its own affairs
than curious about those of others, without missing any
of the conveniences of the most populous towns, I can
live as solitary and retired as in deserts the most remote.

PART IV _Proofs re existence of God & human soul_

I do not know that I ought to tell you of the first
meditations there made by me, for they are so metaphysical and so unusual that they may perhaps not be
acceptable to everyone. And yet at the same time, in
order that one may judge whether the foundations which
I have laid are sufficiently secure, I find myself constrained in some measure to refer to them. For a long
time I had remarked that it is sometimes requisite in
common life to follow opinions which one knows to be
most uncertain, exactly as though they were indisput-
able, as has been said above. But because in this case
I wished to give myself entirely to the search after
Truth, I thought that it was necessary for me to take

---

[1] i.e. Holland, where Descartes settled in 1629.

an apparently opposite course, and to reject as absolutely false everything as to which I could imagine the least ground of doubt, in order to see if afterwards there remained anything in my belief that was entirely certain. Thus, because our senses sometimes deceive us, I wished to suppose that nothing is just as they cause us to imagine it to be; and because there are men who deceive themselves in their reasoning and fall into paralogisms, even concerning the simplest matters of geometry, and judging that I was as subject to error as was any other, I rejected as false all the reasons formerly accepted by me as demonstrations. And since all the same thoughts and conceptions which we have while awake may also come to us in sleep, without any of them being at that time true, I resolved to assume that everything that ever entered into my mind was no more true than the illusions of my dreams. But immediately afterwards I noticed that whilst I thus wished to think all things false, it was absolutely essential that the 'I' who thought this should be somewhat, and remarking that this truth *I think, therefore I am* was so certain and so assured that all the most extravagant suppositions brought forward by the sceptics were incapable of shaking it, I came to the conclusion that I could receive it without scruple as the first principle of the Philosophy for which I was seeking.

And then, examining attentively that which I was, I saw that I could conceive that I had no body, and that there was no world nor place where I might be; but yet that I could not for all that conceive that I was not. On the contrary, I saw from the very fact that I thought of doubting the truth of other things, it very evidently and certainly followed that I was; on the other hand if I had only ceased from thinking, even if all the rest of what I had ever imagined had really existed, I should have no reason for thinking that I had existed. From that I knew that I was a substance the whole essence or nature of which is to think, and that for its existence there is no need of any place, nor does it depend on any material thing; so that this 'me,' that is to say, the soul by which I am what I am, is entirely distinct from body, and is even more easy to know than is the latter; and even if body were not, the soul would not cease to be what it is.

After this I considered generally what in a proposition is requisite in order to be true and certain; for since I had just discovered one which I knew to be such, I thought that I ought also to know in what this certainty consisted. And having remarked that there was nothing at all in the statement '*I think, therefore I am*' which assures me of having thereby made a true assertion, excepting that I see very clearly that to think it is necessary to be, I came to the conclusion that I might assume, as a general rule, that the things which we conceive very clearly and distinctly are all true—remembering, however, that there is some difficulty in ascertaining which are those that we distinctly conceive.

Following upon this, and reflecting on the fact that I doubted, and that consequently my existence was not quite perfect (for I saw clearly that it was a greater perfection to know than to doubt), I resolved to inquire whence I had learnt to think of anything more perfect than I myself was; and I recognised very clearly that this conception must proceed from some nature which was really more perfect. As to the thoughts which I had of many other things outside of me, like the heavens, the earth, light, heat, and a thousand others, I had not so much difficulty in knowing whence they came, because, remarking nothing in them which seemed to render them superior to me, I could believe that, if

they were true, they were dependencies upon my
nature, in so far as it possessed some perfection; and
if they were not true, that I held them from nought,
that is to say, that they were in me because I had something lacking in my nature. But this could not apply
to the idea of a Being more perfect than my own, for
to hold it from nought would be manifestly impossible;
and because it is no less contradictory to say of the more
perfect that it is what results from and depends on
the less perfect, than to say that there is something
which proceeds from nothing, it was equally impossible
that I should hold it from myself. In this way it could
but follow that it had been placed in me by a Nature
which was really more perfect than mine could be, and
which even had within itself all the perfections of which
I could form any idea—that is to say, to put it in a
word, which was God. To which I added that since I
knew some perfections which I did not possess, I was
not the only being in existence (I shall here use freely,
if you will allow, the terms of the School); but that
there was necessarily some other more perfect Being
on which I depended, or from which I acquired all that
I had. For if I had existed alone and independent of
any others, so that I should have had from myself all
that perfection of being in which I participated to
however small an extent, I should have been able for
the same reason to have had all the remainder which
I knew that I lacked; and thus I myself should have
been infinite, eternal, immutable, omniscient, all-powerful, and, finally, I should have all the perfections which
I could discern in God. For, in pursuance of the reasonings which I have just carried on, in order to know
the nature of God as far as my nature is capable of
knowing it, I had only to consider in reference to all
these things of which I found some idea in myself,

whether it was a perfection to possess them or not. And
I was assured that none of those which indicated some
imperfection were in Him, but that all else was present;
and I saw that doubt, inconstancy, sadness, and such
things, could not be in Him considering that I myself
should have been glad to be without them. In addition
to this, I had ideas of many things which are sensible
and corporeal, for, although I might suppose that I
was dreaming, and that all that I saw or imagined was
false, I could not at the same time deny that the ideas
were really in my thoughts. But because I had already
recognised very clearly in myself that the nature of
the intelligence is distinct from that of the body, and
observing that all composition gives evidence of dependency, and that dependency is manifestly an imperfection, I came to the conclusion that it could not
be a perfection in God to be composed of these two
natures, and that consequently He was not so composed.
I judged, however, that if there were any bodies in the
world, or even any intelligences or other natures which
were not wholly perfect, their existence must depend
on His power in such a way that they could not subsist
without Him for a single moment.

After that I desired to seek for other truths, and
having put before myself the object of the geometricians,
which I conceived to be a continuous body, or a space
indefinitely extended in length, breadth, height or depth,
which was divisible into various parts, and which might
have various figures and sizes, and might be moved or
transposed in all sorts of ways (for all this the geometricians suppose to be in the object of their contemplation), I went through some of their simplest demonstrations, and having noticed that this great certainty
which everyone attributes to these demonstrations is
founded solely on the fact that they are conceived of

with clearness, in accordance with the rule which I have just laid down, I also noticed that there was nothing at all in them to assure me of the existence of their object. For, to take an example, I saw very well that if we suppose a triangle to be given, the three angles must certainly be equal to two right angles; but for all that I saw no reason to be assured that there was any such triangle in existence, while on the contrary, on reverting to the examination of the idea which I had of a Perfect Being, I found that in this case existence was implied in it in the same manner in which the equality of its three angles to two right angles is implied in the idea of a triangle; or in the idea of a sphere, that all the points on its surface are equidistant from its centre, or even more evidently still. Consequently it is at least as certain that God, who is a Being so perfect, is, or exists, as any demonstration of geometry can possibly be.

What causes many, however, to persuade themselves that there is difficulty in knowing this truth, and even in knowing the nature of their soul, is the fact that they never raise their minds above the things of sense, or that they are so accustomed to consider nothing excepting by imagining it, which is a mode of thought specially adapted to material objects, that all that is not capable of being imagined appears to them not to be intelligible at all. This is manifest enough from the fact that even the philosophers in the Schools hold it as a maxim that there is nothing in the understanding which has first of all been in the senses, in which there is certainly no doubt that the ideas of God and of the soul have never been. And it seems to me that those who desire to make use of their imagination in order to understand these ideas, act in the same way as if, to hear sounds or smell odours, they should wish to make use of their eyes:

excepting that there is indeed this difference, that the sense of sight does not give us less assurance of the truth of its objects, than do those of scent or of hearing, while neither our imagination nor our senses can ever assure us of anything, if our understanding does not intervene.

If there are finally any persons who are not sufficiently persuaded of the existence of God and of their soul by the reasons which I have brought forward, I wish that they should know that all other things of which they perhaps think themselves more assured (such as possessing a body, and that there are stars and an earth and so on) are less certain. For, although we have a moral assurance of these things which is such that it seems that it would be extravagant in us to doubt them, at the same time no one, unless he is devoid of reason, can deny, when a metaphysical certainty is in question, that there is sufficient cause for our not having complete assurance, by observing the fact that when asleep we may similarly imagine that we have another body, and that we see other stars and another earth, without there being anything of the kind. For how do we know that the thoughts that come in dreams are more false than those that we have when we are awake, seeing that often enough the former are not less lively and vivid than the latter? And though the wisest minds may study the matter as much as they will, I do not believe that they will be able to give any sufficient reason for removing this doubt, unless they presuppose the existence of God. For to begin with, that which I have just taken as a rule, that is to say, that all the things that we very clearly and very distinctly conceive of are true, is certain only because God is or exists, and that He is a Perfect Being, and that all that is in us issues from Him. From this it follows that our ideas or notions, which to the extent of their being clear or distinct are ideas of real things issuing from God, cannot but to that extent be true. So that though we often enough have ideas which have an element of falsity, this can only be the case in regard to those which have in them somewhat that is confused or obscure, because in so far as they have this character they participate in negation—that is, they exist in us as confused only because we are not quite perfect. And it is evident that there is no less repugnance in the idea that error or imperfection, inasmuch as it is imperfection, proceeds from God, than there is in the idea of truth or perfection proceeding from nought. But if we did not know that all that is in us of reality and truth proceeds from a perfect and infinite Being, however clear and distinct were our ideas, we should not have any reason to assure ourselves that they had the perfection of being true.

But after the knowledge of God and of the soul has thus rendered us certain of this rule, it is very easy to understand that the dreams which we imagine in our sleep should not make us in any way doubt the truth of the thoughts which we have when awake. For even if in sleep we had some very distinct idea such as a geometrician might have who discovered some new demonstration, the fact of being asleep would not militate against its truth. And as to the most ordinary error in our dreams, which consists in their representing to us various objects in the same way as do our external senses, it does not matter that this should give us occasion to suspect the truth of such ideas, because we may be likewise often enough deceived in them without our sleeping at all, just as when those who have the jaundice see everything as yellow, or when stars or other bodies which are very remote appear much smaller than they really are. For, finally, whether we are awake or asleep, we should never allow ourselves to be persuaded excepting by the evidence of our Reason. And it must be remarked that I speak of our Reason and not of our imagination nor of our senses; just as though we see the sun very clearly, we should not for that reason judge that it is of the size of which it appears to be; likewise we could quite well distinctly imagine the head of a lion on the body of a goat, without necessarily concluding that a chimera exists. For Reason does not insist that whatever we see or imagine thus is a truth, but it tells us clearly that all our ideas or notions must have some foundation of truth. For otherwise it could not be possible that God, who is all perfection and truth, should have placed them within us. And because our reasonings are never so evident nor so complete during sleep as during wakefulness, although sometimes our imaginations are then just as lively and acute, or even more so, Reason tells us that since our thoughts cannot possibly be all true, because we are not altogether perfect, that which they have of truth must infallibly be met with in our waking experience rather than in that of our dreams.

. . . .

If I write in French which is the language of my country, rather than in Latin which is that of my teachers, that is because I hope that those who avail themselves only of their natural reason in its purity may be better judges of my opinions than those who believe only in the writings of the ancients; and as to those who unite good sense with study, whom alone I crave for my judges, they will not, I feel sure, be so partial to Latin as to refuse to follow my reasoning because I expound it in a vulgar tongue.

For the rest, I do not desire to speak here more particularly of the progress which I hope in the future to make in the sciences, nor to bind myself as regards the public with any promise which I shall not with certainty be able to fulfil. But I will just say that I have resolved not to employ the time which remains to me in life in any other matter than in endeavouring to acquire some knowledge of nature, which shall be of such a kind that it will enable us to arrive at rules for Medicine more assured than those which have as yet been attained; and my inclination is so strongly opposed to any other kind of pursuit, more especially to those which can only be useful to some by being harmful to others, that if certain circumstances had constrained me to employ them, I do not think that I should have been capable of succeeding. In so saying I make a declaration that I know very well cannot help me to make myself of consideration in the world, but to this end I have no desire to attain; and I shall always hold myself to be more indebted to those by whose favour I may enjoy my leisure without hindrance, than I shall be to any who may offer me the most honourable position in all the world.

RULES FOR THE DIRECTION OF THE MIND.

Rule I

The end of study should be to direct the mind towards the enunciation of sound and correct judgments on all matters that come before it.

Whenever men notice some similarity between two things, they are wont to ascribe to each, even in those respects in which the two differ, what they have found to be true of the other. Thus they erroneously compare the sciences, which entirely consist in the cognitive exercise of the mind, with the arts, which depend upon an exercise and disposition of the body. They see that not all the arts can be acquired by the same man, but that he who restricts himself to one, most readily becomes the best executant, since it is not so easy for the same hand to adapt itself both to agricultural operations and to harp-playing, or to the performance of several such tasks as to one alone. Hence they have held the same to be true of the sciences also, and distinguishing them from one another according to their subject matter, they have imagined that they ought tò be studied separately, each in isolation from all the rest. But this is certainly wrong. For since the sciences taken all together are identical with human wisdom, which always remains one and the same, however applied to different subjects, and suffers no more differentiation proceeding from them than the light of the sun experiences from the variety of the things which it illumines, there is no need for minds to be confined at all within limits; for neither does the knowing of one truth have an effect like that of the acquisition of one art and prevent us from finding out another, it rather aids us to do so. Certainly it appears to me strange that so many people should investigate human customs with such care, the virtues of plants, the motions of the stars, the transmutations of metals, and the objects of similar sciences, while at the same time practically none bethink themselves about good understanding, or universal Wisdom, though nevertheless all other studies are to be esteemed not so much for their own value as because they contribute something to this. Consequently we are justified in bringing forward this as the first rule of all, since there is nothing more prone to turn us aside from the correct way of seeking out truth than this directing of our inquiries, not towards their general end, but towards certain special investigations. I do not here refer to perverse and censurable pursuits like empty glory or base gain; obviously counterfeit reasonings and quibbles suited to vulgar understanding open up a much more direct route to such a goal than does a sound apprehension of the truth. But I have in view even honourable and laudable pursuits, because these mislead us in a more subtle fashion. For example take our investigations of those sciences conducive to the conveniences of life or which yield that pleasure which is found in the contemplation of truth, practically the only joy in life that is complete and untroubled with any pain. There we may indeed expect to receive the legitimate fruits of scientific inquiry; but if, in the course of our study, we think of them, they frequently cause us to omit many facts which are necessary to the understanding of other matters, because they seem to be either of slight value or of little interest. Hence we must believe that all the sciences are so inter-connected, that it is much

easier to study them all together than to isolate one
from all the others. If, therefore, anyone wishes to
search out the truth of things in serious earnest, he
ought not to select one special science; for all the
sciences are conjoined with each other and interdepend-
ent: he ought rather to think how to increase the natural
light of reason, not for the purpose of resolving this
or that difficulty of scholastic type, but in order that
his understanding may light his will to its proper choice
in all the contingencies of life. In a short time he will
see with amazement that he has made much more progress than those who are eager about particular ends,
and that he has not only obtained all that they desire,
but even higher results than fall within his expectation.

RULE II

*Only those objects should engage our attention, to
the sure and indubitable knowledge of which our mental
powers seem to be adequate.*

Science in its entirety is true and evident cognition.
He is no more learned who has doubts on many matters
than the man who has never thought of them; nay he
appears to be less learned if he has formed wrong opinions on any particulars. Hence it were better not to
study at all than to occupy one's self with objects of
such difficulty, that, owing to our inability to distinguish
true from false, we are forced to regard the doubtful
as certain; for in those matters any hope of augmenting
our knowledge is exceeded by the risk of diminishing it.
Thus in accordance with the above maxim we reject all
such merely probable knowledge and make it a rule to
trust only what is completely known and incapable of
being doubted. No doubt men of education may persuade themselves that there is but little of such certain

knowledge, because, forsooth, a common failing of human nature has made them deem it too easy and open to everyone, and so led them to neglect to think upon such truths; but I nevertheless announce that there are more of these than they think—truths which suffice to give a rigorous demonstration of innumerable propositions, the discussion of which they have hitherto been unable to free from the element of probability. Further, because they have believed that it was unbecoming for a man of education to confess ignorance on any point, they have so accustomed themselves to trick out their fabricated explanations, that they have ended by gradually imposing on themselves and thus have issued them to the public as genuine.

But if we adhere closely to this rule we shall find left but few objects of legitimate study. For there is scarce any question occurring in the sciences about which talented men have not disagreed. But whenever two men come to opposite decisions about the same matter one of them at least must certainly be in the wrong, and apparently there is not even one of them in the right; for if the reasoning of the second was sound and clear he would be able so to lay it before the other as finally to succeed in convincing *his* understanding also. Hence apparently we cannot attain to a perfect knowledge in any such case of probable opinion, for it would be rashness to hope for more than others have attained to. Consequently if we reckon correctly, of the sciences already discovered, Arithmetic and Geometry alone are left, to which the observance of this rule reduces us.

Yet we do not therefore condemn that method of philosophizing which others have already discovered and those weapons of the schoolmen, probable syllogisms, which are so well suited for polemics. They indeed give practice to the wits of youths and, producing emulation among them, act as a stimulus; and it is much better for their minds to be moulded by opinions of this sort, uncertain though they appear, as being objects of controversy among the learned, than to be left entirely to their own devices. For thus through lack of guidance they might stray into some abyss; but as long as they follow in their masters' footsteps, though they may diverge at times from the truth, they will yet certainly find a path which is at least in this respect safer, that it has been approved of by more prudent people. We ourselves rejoice that we in earlier years experienced this scholastic training; but now, being released from that oath of allegiance which bound us to our old masters, and since, as becomes our riper years, we are no longer subject to the ferule, if we wish in earnest to establish for ourselves those rules which shall aid us in scaling the heights of human knowledge, we must admit assuredly among the primary members of our catalogue that maxim which forbids us to abuse our leisure as many do, who neglect all easy quests and take up their time only with difficult matters; for they, though certainly making all sorts of subtle conjectures and elaborating most plausible arguments with great ingenuity, frequently find too late that after all their labours they have only increased the multitude of their doubts, without acquiring any knowledge whatsoever.

But now let us proceed to explain more carefully our reasons for saying, as we did a little while ago, that of all the sciences known as yet, Arithmetic and Geometry alone are free from any taint of falsity or uncertainty. We must note then that there are two ways by which we arrive at the knowledge of facts, viz, by experience and by deduction. We must further observe that while our inferences from experience are frequently fallacious, deduction, or the pure illation of one thing from another, though it may be passed over, if it is not seen through, cannot be erroneous when performed by an understanding that is in the least degree rational. And it seems to me that the operation is profited but little by those constraining bonds by means of which the Dialecticians claim to control human reason, though I do not deny that that discipline may be serviceable for other purposes. My reason for saying so is that none of the mistakes which men can make (men, I say, not beasts) are due to faulty inference; they are caused merely by the fact that we found upon a basis of poorly comprehended experiences, or that propositions are posited which are hasty and groundless.

This furnishes us with an evident explanation of the great superiority in certitude of Arithmetic and Geometry to other sciences. The former alone deal with an object so pure and uncomplicated, that they need make no assumptions at all which experience renders uncertain, but wholly consist in the rational deduction of consequences. They are on that account much the easiest and clearest of all, and possess an object such as we require, for in them it is scarce humanly possible for anyone to err except by inadvertence. And yet we should not be surprised to find that plenty of people of their own accord prefer to apply their intelligence to other studies, or to Philosophy. The reason for this is that every person permits himself the liberty of making guesses in the matter of an obscure subject with more confidence than in one which is clear, and that it is much easier to have some vague notion about any subject, no matter what, than to arrive at the real truth about a single question however simple that may be.

But one conclusion now emerges out of these considerations, viz. not, indeed, that Arithmetic and Geometry are the sole sciences to be studied, but only that in our search for the direct road towards truth we should busy ourselves with no object about which we cannot attain a certitude equal to that of the demonstrations of Arithmetic and Geometry.

RULE III

In the subjects we propose to investigate, our inquiries should be directed, not to what others have thought, nor to what we ourselves conjecture, but to what we can clearly and perspicuously behold and with certainty deduce; for knowledge is not won in any other way.

To study the writings of the ancients is right, because it is a great boon for us to be able to make use of the labours of so many men; and we should do so, both in order to discover what they have correctly made out in previous ages, and also that we may inform ourselves as to what in the various sciences is still left for investigation. But yet there is a great danger lest in a too absorbed study of these works we should become infected with their errors, guard against them as we may. For it is the way of writers, whenever they have allowed themselves rashly and credulously to take up a position in any controverted matter, to try with the subtlest of arguments to compel us to go along with them. But when, on the contrary, they have happily come upon something certain and evident, in displaying it they never fail to surround it with ambiguities, fearing, it would seem, lest the simplicity of their explanation should make us respect their discovery less, or because they grudge us an open vision of the truth.

Further, supposing now that all were wholly open

and candid, and never thrust upon us doubtful opinions as true, but expounded every matter in good faith, yet since scarce anything has been asserted by any one man the contrary of which has not been alleged by another, we should be eternally uncertain which of the two to believe. It would be no use to total up the testimonies in favour of each, meaning to follow that opinion which was supported by the greater number of authors; for if it is a question of difficulty that is in dispute, it is more likely that the truth would have been discovered by few than by many. But even though all these men agreed among themselves, what they teach us would not suffice for us. For we shall not, e.g., all turn out to be mathematicians though we know by heart all the proofs that others have elaborated, unless we have an intellectual talent that fits us to resolve difficulties of any kind. Neither, though we have mastered all the arguments of Plato and Aristotle, if yet we have not the capacity for passing a solid judgment on these matters, shall we become Philosophers; we should have acquired the knowledge not of a science, but of history.

I lay down the rule also, that we must wholly refrain from ever mixing up conjectures with our pronouncements on the truth of things. This warning is of no little importance. There is no stronger reason for our finding nothing in the current Philosophy which is so evident and certain as not to be capable of being controverted, than the fact that the learned, not content with the recognition of what is clear and certain, in the first instance hazard the assertion of obscure and ill-comprehended theories, at which they have arrived merely by probable conjecture. Then afterwards they gradually attach complete credence to them, and mingling them promiscuously with what is true and evident, they finish by being unable to deduce any conclusion which does not appear to depend upon some proposition of the doubtful sort, and hence is not uncertain.

But lest we in turn should slip into the same error, we shall here take note of all those mental operations by which we are able, wholly without fear of illusion, to arrive at the knowledge of things. Now I admit only two, viz., intuition and deduction.

By *intuition* I understand, not the fluctuating testimony of the senses, nor the misleading judgment that proceeds from the blundering constructions of imagination, but the conception which an unclouded and attentive mind gives us so readily and distinctly that we are wholly freed from doubt about that which we understand. Or, what comes to the same thing, *intuition* is the undoubting conception of an unclouded and attentive mind, and springs from the light of reason alone; it is more certain than deduction itself, in that it is simpler, though deduction, as we have noted above, cannot by us be erroneously conducted. Thus each individual can mentally have intuition of the fact that he exists, and that he thinks; that the triangle is bounded by three lines only, the sphere by a single superficies, and so on. Facts of such a kind are far more numerous than many people think, disdaining as they do to direct their attention upon such simple matters.

But in case anyone may be put out by this new use of the term intuition and of other terms which in the following pages I am similarly compelled to dissever from their current meaning, I here make the general announcement that I pay no attention to the way in which particular terms have of late been employed in the schools, because it would have been difficult to employ the same terminology while my theory was wholly different. All that I take note of is the meaning of the Latin of each word, when, in cases where an appropriate term is lacking, I wish to transfer to the vocabulary that expresses my own meaning those that I deem most suitable.

This evidence and certitude, however, which belongs to intuition, is required not only in the enunciation of propositions, but also in discursive reasoning of whatever sort. For example consider this consequence: 2 and 2 amount to the same as 3 and 1. Now we need to see intuitively not only that 2 and 2 make 4, and that likewise 3 and 1 make 4, but further that the third of the above statements is a necessary conclusion from these two.

Hence now we are in a position to raise the question as to why we have, besides intuition, given this supplementary method of knowing, viz., knowing by _deduction_, by which we understand all necessary inference from other facts that are known with certainty. This, however, we could not avoid, because many things are known with certainty, though not by themselves evident, but only deduced from true and known principles by the continuous and uninterrupted action of a mind that has a clear vision of each step in the process. It is in a similar way that we know that the last link in a long chain is connected with the first, even though we do not take in by means of one and the same act of vision all the intermediate links on which that connection depends, but only remember that we have taken them successively under review and that each single one is united to its neighbour, from the first even to the last. Hence we distinguish this mental intuition from deduction by the fact that into the conception of the latter there enters a certain movement or succession, into that of the former there does not. Further deduction does not require an immediately presented evidence such as intuition possesses; its certitude is rather conferred upon it in some way by memory. The upshot of the matter is that it is possible to say that those propositions indeed which are immediately deduced from first principles are known now by intuition, now by deduction, i.e., in a way that differs according to our point of view. But the first principles themselves are given by intuition alone, while, on the contrary, the remote conclusions are furnished only by deduction.

These two methods are the most certain routes to knowledge, and the mind should admit no others. All the rest should be rejected as suspect of error and dangerous. But this does not prevent us from believing matters that have been divinely revealed as being more certain than our surest knowledge, since belief in these things, as all faith in obscure matters, is an action not of our intelligence, but of our will. They should be heeded also since, if they have any basis in our understanding, they can and ought to be, more than all things else, discovered by one or other of the ways abovementioned, as we hope perhaps to show at greater length on some future opportunity.

to Rule XI

RULE IV

There is need of a method for finding out the truth.

So blind is the curiosity by which mortals are possessed, that they often conduct their minds along unexplored routes, having no reason to hope for success, but merely being willing to risk the experiment of finding whether the truth they seek lies there. As well might a man burning with an unintelligent desire to find treasure, continuously roam the streets, seeking to find something that a passerby might have chanced to drop. This is the way in which most Chemists, many

Geometricians, and Philosophers not a few prosecute their studies. I do not deny that sometimes in these wanderings they are lucky enough to find something true. But I do not allow that this argues greater industry on their part, but only better luck. But, however that may be, it were far better never to think of investigating truth at all, than to do so without a method. For it is very certain that unregulated inquiries and confused reflections of this kind only confound the natural light and blind our mental powers. Those who so become accustomed to walk in darkness weaken their eye-sight so much that afterwards they cannot bear the light of day. This is confirmed by experience; for how often do we not see that those who have never taken to letters, give a sounder and clearer decision about obvious matters than those who have spent all their time in the schools? Moreover by a method I mean certain and simple rules, such that, if a man observe them accurately, he shall never assume what is false as true, and will never spend his mental efforts to no purpose, but will always gradually increase his knowledge and so arrive at a true understanding of all that does not surpass his powers.

These two points must be carefully noted, viz., never to assume what is false as true, and to arrive at a knowledge which takes in all things. For, if we are without the knowledge of any of the things which we are capable of understanding, that is only because we have never perceived any way to bring us to this knowledge, or because we have fallen into the contrary error. But if our method rightly explains how our mental vision should be used, so as not to fall into the contrary error, and how deductions should be discovered in order that we may arrive at the knowledge of all things, I do not see what else is needed to make it complete; for I have already said that no science is acquired except by mental intuition or deduction. There is besides no question of extending it further in order to show how these said operations ought to be effected, because they are the most simple and primary of all. Consequently, unless our understanding were already able to employ them, it could comprehend none of the precepts of that very method, not even the simplest. But as for the other mental operations, which Dialectic does its best to direct by making use of these prior ones, they are quite useless here; rather they are to be accounted impediments, because nothing can be added to the pure light of reason which does not in some way obscure it.

Since then the usefulness of this method is so great that without it study seems to be harmful rather than profitable, I am quite ready to believe that the greater minds of former ages had some knowledge of it, nature even conducting them to it. For the human mind has in it something that we may call divine, wherein are scattered the first germs of useful modes of thought. Consequently it often happens that however much neglected and choked by interfering studies they bear fruit of their own accord. Arithmetic and Geometry, the simplest sciences, give us an instance of this; for we have sufficient evidence that the ancient Geometricians made use of a certain analysis which they extended to the resolution of all problems, though they grudged the secret to posterity. At the present day also there flourishes a certain kind of Arithmetic, called Algebra, which designs to effect, when dealing with numbers, what the ancients achieved in the matter of figures. These two methods are nothing else than the spontaneous fruit sprung from the inborn principles of the discipline here in question; and I do not wonder that these sciences with their very simple subject matter should have yielded results so much more satisfactory than others in which greater obstructions choke all growth. But even in the latter case, if only we take care to cultivate them assiduously, fruits will certainly be able to come to full maturity.

This is the chief result which I have had in view in writing this treatise. For I should not think much of these rules, if they had no utility save for the solution of the empty problems with which Logicians and Geometers have been wont to beguile their leisure; my only achievement thus would have seemed to be an ability to argue about trifles more subtly than others. Further, though much mention is here made of numbers and figures, because no other sciences furnish us with illustrations of such self-evidence and certainty, the reader who follows my drift with sufficient attention will easily see that nothing is less in my mind than ordinary Mathematics, and that I am expounding quite another science, of which these illustrations are rather the outer husk than the constituents. Such a science should contain the primary rudiments of human reason, and its province ought to extend to the eliciting of true results in every subject. To speak freely, I am convinced that it is a more powerful instrument of knowledge than any other that has been bequeathed to us by human agency, as being the source of all others. But as for the outer covering I mentioned, I mean not to employ it to cover up and conceal my method for the purpose of warding off the vulgar; rather I hope so to clothe and embellish it that I may make it more suitable for presentation to the human mind.

When first I applied my mind to Mathematics I read straight away most of what is usually given by the mathematical writers, and I paid special attention to

Arithmetic and Geometry, because they were said to be
the simplest and so to speak the way to all the rest.
But in neither case did I then meet with authors
who fully satisfied me. I did indeed learn in their
works many propositions about numbers which I found
on calculation to be true. As to figures, they in a sense
exhibited to my eyes a great number of truths and
drew conclusions from certain consequences. But they
did not seem to make it sufficiently plain to the mind
itself why those things are so, and how they discovered
them. Consequently I was not surprised that many
people, even of talent and scholarship, should, after
glancing at these sciences, have either given them up as
being empty and childish or, taking them to be very
difficult and intricate, been deterred at the very outset
from learning them. For really there is nothing more
futile than to busy one's self with bare numbers and
imaginary figures in such a way as to appear to rest
content with such trifles, and so to resort to those super-
ficial demonstrations, which are discovered more frequently by chance than by skill, and are a matter more
of the eyes and the imagination than of the understanding, that in a sense one ceases to make use of one's
reason. I might add that there is no more intricate task
than that of solving by this method of proof new difficulties that arise, involved as they are with numerical
confusions. But when I afterwards bethought myself
how it could be that the earliest pioneers of Philosophy
in bygone ages refused to admit to the study of wisdom
any one who was not versed in Mathematics, evidently
believing that this was the easiest and most indispens-
able mental exercise and preparation for laying hold of
other more important sciences, I was confirmed in my
suspicion that they had knowledge of a species of
Mathematics very different from that which passes

current in our time. I do not indeed imagine that they had a perfect knowledge of it, for they plainly show how little advanced they were by the insensate rejoicings they display and the pompous thanksgivings they offer for the most trifling discoveries. I am not shaken in my opinion by the fact that historians make a great deal of certain machines of theirs. Possibly these machines were quite simple, and yet the ignorant and wonder-loving multitude might easily have lauded them as miraculous. But I am convinced that certain primary germs of truth implanted by nature in human minds—though in our case the daily reading and hearing of innumerable diverse errors stifle them—had a very great vitality in that rude and unsophisticated age of the ancient world. Thus the same mental illumination which let them see that virtue was to be preferred to pleasure, and honour to utility, although they knew not why this was so, made them recognise true notions in Philosophy and Mathematics, although they were not yet able thoroughly to grasp these sciences. Indeed I seem to recognise certain traces of this true Mathematics in Pappus and Diophantus, who though not belonging to the earliest age, yet lived many centuries before our own times. But my opinion is that these writers then with a sort of low cunning, deplorable indeed, suppressed this knowledge. Possibly they acted just as many inventors are known to have done in the case of their discoveries, i.e., they feared that their method being so easy and simple would become cheapened on being divulged, and they preferred to exhibit in its place certain barren truths, deductively demonstrated with show enough of ingenuity, as the results of their art, in order to win from us our admiration for these achievements, rather than to disclose to us that method itself which would have wholly annulled the

admiration accorded. Finally there have been certain
men of talent who in the present age have tried to revive
this same art. For it seems to be precisely that science
known by the barbarous name Algebra, if only we
could extricate it from that vast array of numbers and
inexplicable figures by which it is overwhelmed, so
that it might display the clearness and simplicity which,
we imagine, ought to exist in a genuine Mathematics.
It was these reflections that recalled me from the particular studies of Arithmetic and Geometry to a general
investigation of Mathematics, and thereupon I sought
to determine what precisely was universally meant by
that term, and why not only the above mentioned
sciences, but also Astronomy, Music, Optics, Mechanics
and several others are styled parts of Mathematics.
Here indeed it is not enough to look to the origin of
the word; for since the name 'Mathematics' means
exactly the same thing as 'scientific study,' these other
branches could, with as much right as Geometry itself,
be called Mathematics. Yet we see that almost anyone
who has had the slightest schooling, can easily distinguish
what relates to Mathematics in any question from that
which belongs to the other sciences. But as I considered the matter carefully it gradually came to light
that all those matters only were referred to Mathematics in which order and measurement are investigated, and that it makes no difference whether it be
in numbers, figures, stars, sounds or any other object
that the question of measurement arises. I saw consequently that there must be some general science to
explain that element as a whole which gives rise to
problems about order and measurement, restricted as
these are to no special subject matter. This, I perceived, was called 'Universal Mathematics,' not a far-
fetched designation, but one of long standing which has

passed into current use, because in this science is contained everything on account of which the others are called parts of Mathematics. We can see how much it excels in utility and simplicity the sciences subordinate to it, by the fact that it can deal with all the objects of which they have cognisance and many more besides, and that any difficulties it contains are found in them as well, added to the fact that in them fresh difficulties arise due to their special subject matter which in it do not exist. But now how comes it that though everyone knows the name of this science and understands what is its province even without studying it attentively, so many people laboriously pursue the other dependent sciences, and no one cares to master this one? I should marvel indeed were I not aware that everyone thinks it to be so very easy, and had I not long since observed that the human mind passes over what it thinks it can easily accomplish, and hastens straight away to new and more imposing occupations.

I, however, conscious as I am of my inadequacy, have resolved that in my investigation into truth I shall follow obstinately such an order as will require me first to start with what is simplest and easiest, and never permit me to proceed farther until in the first sphere there seems to be nothing further to be done. This is why up to the present time to the best of my ability I have made a study of this universal Mathematics; consequently I believe that when I go on to deal in their turn with more profound sciences, as I hope to do soon, my efforts will not be premature. But before I make this transition I shall try to bring together and arrange in an orderly manner, the facts which in my previous studies I have noted as being more worthy of attention. Thus I hope both that at a future date, when through advancing years my memory is enfeebled, I shall, if need be, conveniently be able to recall them by looking in this little book, and that having now disburdened my memory of them I may be free to concentrate my mind on my future studies.

Rule V

Method consists entirely in the order and disposition of the objects towards which our mental vision must be directed if we would find out any truth. We shall comply with it exactly if we reduce involved and obscure propositions step by step to those that are simpler, and then starting with the intuitive apprehension of all those that are absolutely simple, attempt to ascend to the knowledge of all others by precisely similar steps.

In this alone lies the sum of all human endeavour, and he who would approach the investigation of truth must hold to this rule as closely as he who enters the labyrinth must follow the thread which guided Theseus. But many people either do not reflect on the precept at all, or ignore it altogether, or presume not to need it. Consequently they often investigate the most difficult questions with so little regard to order, that, to my mind, they act like a man who should attempt to leap with one bound from the base to the summit of a house, either making no account of the ladders provided for his ascent or not noticing them. It is thus that all Astrologers behave, who, though in ignorance of the nature of the heavens, and even without having made proper observations of the movements of the heavenly bodies, expect to be able to indicate their effects. This is also what many do who study Mechanics apart from Physics, and readily set about devising new instruments for producing motion. Along with them go also those Philosophers who, neglecting experience, imagine that truth will spring from their brain like Pallas from the head of Zeus.

Now it is obvious that all such people violate the present rule. But since the order here required is often so obscure and intricate that not everyone can make it out, they can scarcely avoid error unless they diligently observe what is laid down in the following proposition.

Rule VI

In order to separate out what is quite simple from what is complex, and to arrange these matters methodically, we ought, in the case of every series in which we have deduced certain facts the one from the other, to notice which fact is simple, and to mark the interval, greater, less, or equal, which separates all the others from this.

Although this proposition seems to teach nothing very new, it contains, nevertheless, the chief secret of method, and none in the whole of this treatise is of greater utility. For it tells us that all facts can be arranged in certain series, not indeed in the sense of being referred to some ontological genus such as the categories employed by Philosophers in their classification, but in so far as certain truths can be known from others; and thus, whenever a difficulty occurs we are able at once to perceive whether it will be profitable to examine certain others first, and which, and in what order.

Further, in order to do that correctly, we must note first that for the purpose of our procedure, which does not regard things as isolated realities, but compares them with one another in order to discover the dependence in knowledge of one upon the other, all things can be said to be either absolute or relative.

I call that absolute which contains within itself the
pure and simple essence of which we are in quest.
Thus the term will be applicable to whatever is considered as being independent, or a cause, or simple,
universal, one, equal, like, straight, and so forth; and
the absolute I call the simplest and the easiest of all,
so that we can make use of it in the solution of questions.

But the relative is that which, while participating
in the same nature, or at least sharing in it to some
degree which enables us to relate it to the absolute and
to deduce it from that by a chain of operations, involves in addition something else in its concept which
I call relativity. Examples of this are found in whatever is said to be dependent, or an effect, composite,
particular, many, unequal, unlike, oblique, etc. These
relatives are the further removed from the absolute,
in proportion as they contain more elements of relativity subordinate the one to the other. We state in
this rule that these should all be distinguished and their
correlative connection and natural order so observed,
that we may be able by traversing all the intermediate
steps to proceed from the most remote to that which
is in the highest degree absolute.

Herein lies the secret of this whole method, that in
all things we should diligently mark that which is most
absolute. For some things are from one point of view
more absolute than others, but from a different standpoint are more relative. Thus though the universal is
more absolute than the particular because its essence
is simpler, yet it can be held to be more relative than
the latter, because it depends upon individuals for its
existence, and so on. Certain things likewise are truly
more absolute than others, but yet are not the most
absolute of all. Thus relatively to individuals, species
is something absolute, but contrasted with genus it is

relative. So too, among things that can be measured, extension is something absolute, but among the various aspects of extension it is length that is absolute, and so on. Finally also, in order to bring out more clearly that we are considering here not the nature of each thing taken in isolation, but the series involved in knowing them, we have purposely enumerated cause and equality among our absolutes, though the nature of these terms is really relative. For though Philosophers make cause and effect correlative, we find that here even, if we ask what the effect is, we must first know the cause and not conversely. Equals too mutually imply one another, but we can know unequals only by comparing them with equals and not *per contra.*

Secondly we must note that there are but few pure and simple essences, which either our experiences or some sort of light innate in us enable us to behold as primary and existing *per se,* not as depending on any others. These we say should be carefully noticed, for they are just those facts which we have called the simplest in any single series. All the others can only be perceived as deductions from these, either immediate and proximate, or not to be attained save by two or three or more acts of inference. The number of these acts should be noted in order that we may perceive whether the facts are separated from the primary and simplest proposition by a greater or smaller number of steps. And so pronounced is everywhere the inter-connection of ground and consequence, which gives rise, in the objects to be examined, to those series to which every inquiry must be reduced, that it can be investi-gated by a sure method. But because it is not easy to make a review of them all, and besides, since they have not so much to be kept in the memory as to be detected by a sort of mental penetration, we must seek for something which will so mould our intelligence as to let it perceive these connected sequences immediately whenever it needs to do so. For this purpose I have found nothing so effectual as to accustom ourselves to turn our attention with a sort of penetrative insight on the very minutest of the facts which we have already discovered.

Finally we must in the third place note that our inquiry ought not to start with the investigation of difficult matters. Rather, before setting out to attack any definite problem, it behooves us first, without making any selection, to assemble those truths that are obvious as they present themselves to us, and afterwards, proceeding step by step, to inquire whether any others can be deduced from these, and again any others from these conclusions and so on, in order. This done, we should attentively think over the truths we have discovered and mark with diligence the reasons why we have been able to detect some more easily than others, and which these are. Thus, when we come to attack some definite problem we shall be able to judge what previous questions it were best to settle first. For example, if it comes into my thought that the number 6 is twice 3, I may then ask what is twice 6, viz., 12; again, perhaps I seek for the double of this, viz., 24, and again of this, viz., 48. Thus I may deduce that there is the same proportion between 3 and 6, as between 6 and 12, and likewise 12 and 24, and so on, and hence that the numbers 3, 6, 12, 24, 48, etc., are in continued proportion. But though these facts are all so clear as to seem almost childish, I am now able by attentive reflection to understand what is the form involved by all questions that can be propounded about the proportions or relations of things, and the order in which they should be investigated; and this discovery embraces the sum of the entire science of Pure Mathematics.

RULE VII

If we wish our science to be complete, those matters which promote the end we have in view must one and all be scrutinized by a movement of thought which is continuous and nowhere interrupted; they must also be included in an enumeration which is both adequate and methodical.

It is necessary to obey the injunctions of this rule if we hope to gain admission among the certain truths for those which, we have declared above, are not immediate deductions from primary and self-evident principles. For this deduction frequently involves such a long series of transitions from ground to consequent that when we come to the conclusion we have difficulty in recalling the whole of the route by which we have arrived at it. This is why I say that there must be a continuous movement of thought to make good this weakness of the memory. Thus, e.g., if I have first found out by separate mental operations what the relation is between the magnitudes A and B, then what between B and C, between C and D, and finally between D and E, that does not entail my seeing what the relation is between A and E, nor can the truths previously learnt give me a precise knowledge of it unless I recall them all. To remedy this I would run them over from time to time, keeping the imagination moving continuously in such a way that while it is intuitively perceiving each fact it simultaneously passes on to the next; and this I would do until I had learned to pass from the first to the last so quickly, that no stage in the process was left to the care of the memory, but I seemed to have the

whole in intuition before me at the same time. This
method will both relieve the memory, diminish the slug-
gishness of our thinking, and definitely enlarge our
mental capacity.

But we must add that this movement should nowhere
be interrupted. Often people who attempt to deduce a
conclusion too quickly and from remote principles do
not trace the whole chain of intermediate conclusions
with sufficient accuracy to prevent them from passing
over many steps without due consideration. But it is
certain that wherever the smallest link is left out the
chain is broken and the whole of the certainty of the
conclusion falls to the ground.

Here we maintain that an enumeration [of the steps
in a proof] is required as well, if we wish to make our
science complete. For resolving most problems other
precepts are profitable, but enumeration alone will
secure our always passing a true and certain judgment
on whatsoever engages our attention; by means of it
nothing at all will escape us, but we shall evidently
have some knowledge of every step.

This enumeration or induction is thus a review or
inventory of all those matters that have a bearing on
the problem raised, which is so thorough and accurate
that by its means we can clearly and with confidence
conclude that we have omitted nothing by mistake.
Consequently as often as we have employed it, if the
problem defies us, we shall at least be wiser in this
respect, viz., that we are quite certain that we know
of no way of resolving it. If it chance, as often it does,
that we have been able to scan all the routes leading to
it which lie open to the human intelligence, we shall be
entitled boldly to assert that the solution of the problem
lies outside the reach of human knowledge.

Furthermore we must note that by adequate enu-

meration or induction is only meant that method by
which we may attain surer conclusion than by any other
type of proof, with the exception of simple intuition.
But when the knowledge of some matter cannot be
reduced to this, we must cast aside all syllogistic fetters
and employ induction, the only method left us, but one
in which all confidence should be reposed. For whenever single facts have been immediately deduced the
one from the other, they have been already reduced, if
the inference was evident, to a true intuition. But if we
infer any single thing from various and disconnected
facts, often our intellectual capacity is not so great as
to be able to embrace them all in a single intuition; in
which case our mind should be content with the certitude attaching to this operation. It is in precisely
similar fashion that though we cannot with one single
gaze distinguish all the links of a lengthy chain, yet
if we have seen the connection of each with its neighbour, we shall be entitled to say that we have seen how
the first is connected with the last.

I have declared that this operation ought to be adequate, because it is often in danger of being defective
and consequently exposed to error. For sometimes,
even though in our enumeration we scrutinise many facts
which are highly evident, yet if we omit the smallest
step the chain is broken and the whole of the certitude
of the conclusion falls to the ground. Sometimes also,
even though all the facts are included in an accurate
enumeration, the single steps are not distinguished from
one another, and our knowledge of them all is thus
only confused.

Further, while now the enumeration ought to be complete, now distinct, there are times when it need have
neither of these characters; it was for this reason that
I said only that it should be adequate. For if I want

to prove by enumeration how many genera there are of corporeal things, or of those that in any way fall under the senses, I shall not assert that they are just so many and no more, unless I previously have become aware that I have included them all in my enumeration, and have distinguished them each separately from all the others. But if in the same way I wish to prove that the rational soul is not corporeal, I do not need a complete enumeration; it will be sufficient to include all bodies in certain collections in such a way as to be able to demonstrate that the rational soul has nothing to do with any of these. If, finally, I wish to show by enumeration that the area of a circle is greater than the area of all other figures whose perimeter is equal, there is no need for me to call in review all other figures; it is enough to demonstrate this of certain others in particular, in order to get thence by induction the same conclusion about all the others.

I added also that the enumeration ought to be methodical. This is both because we have no more serviceable remedy for the defects already instanced, than to scan all things in an orderly manner; and also because it often happens that if each single matter which concerns the quest in hand were to be investigated separately, no man's life would be long enough for the purpose, whether because they are far too many, or because it would chance that the same things had to be repeated too often. But if all these facts are arranged in the best order, they will for the most part be reduced to determine classes, out of which it will be sufficient to take one example for exact inspection, or some one feature in a single case, or certain things rather than others, or at least we shall never have to waste our time in traversing the same ground twice. The advantage of this course is so great that often many particulars can, owing to a well devised arrangement, be gone over in a short space of time and with little trouble, though at first view the matter looked immense.

But this order which we employ in our enumerations can for the most part be varied and depends upon each man's judgment. For this reason, if we would elaborate it in our thought with greater penetration, we must remember what was said in our fifth proposition. There are also many of the trivial things of man's devising, in the discovery of which the whole method lies in the disposal of this order. Thus if you wish to construct a perfect anagram by the transposition of the letters of a name, there is no need to pass from the easy to the difficult, nor to distinguish absolute from relative. Here there is no place for these operations; it will be sufficient to adopt an order to be followed in the transpositions of the letters which we are to examine, such that the same arrangements are never handled twice over. The total number of transpositions should, e.g., be split up into definite classes, so that it may immediately appear in which there is the best hope of finding what is sought. In this way the task is often not tedious but merely child's play.

However, these three propositions should not be separated, because for the most part we have to think of them together, and all equally tend towards the perfecting of our method. There was no great reason for treating one before the other, and we have expounded them but briefly here. The reason for this is that in the rest of the treatise we have practically nothing else left for consideration. Therefore we shall then exhibit in detail what here we have brought together in a general way.

Rule VIII

If in the matters to be examined we come to a step in the series of which our understanding is not sufficiently well able to have an intuitive cognition, we must stop short there. We must make no attempt to examine what follows; thus we shall spare ourselves superfluous labour.

The three preceding rules prescribe and explain the order to be followed. The present rule, on the other hand, shows when it is wholly necessary and when it is merely useful. Thus it is necessary to examine whatever constitutes a single step in that series, by which we pass from relative to absolute, or conversely, before discussing what follows from it. But if, as often happens, many things pertain to the same step, though it is indeed always profitable to review them in order, in this case we are not forced to apply our method of observation so strictly and rigidly. Frequently it is permissible to proceed farther, even though we have not clear knowledge of all the facts it involves, but know only a few or a single one of them.

This rule is a necessary consequence of the reasons brought forward in support of the second. But it must not be thought that the present rule contributes nothing fresh towards the advancement of learning, though it seems only to bid us refrain from further discussion, and apparently does not unfold any truth. For beginners, indeed, it has no further value than to teach them how not to waste time, and it employs nearly the same arguments in doing so as Rule II. But it shows those who have perfectly mastered the seven preceding maxims, how in the pursuit of any science so to satisfy themselves as not to desire anything further.

For the man who faithfully complies with the former rules in the solution of any difficulty, and yet by the present rule is bidden desist at a certain point, will then know for certainty that no amount of application will enable him to attain to the knowledge desired, and that not owing to a defect in his intelligence, but because the nature of the problem itself, or the fact that he is human, prevents him. But this knowledge is not the less science than that which reveals the nature of the thing itself; in fact he would seem to have some mental defect who should extend his curiosity farther.

. . . .

But let us give the most splendid example of all. If a man proposes to himself the problem of examining all the truths for the knowledge of which human reason suffices—and I think that this is a task which should be undertaken once at least in his life by every person who seriously endeavours to attain equilibrium of thought—he will, by the rules given above, certainly discover that nothing can be known prior to the understanding, since the knowledge of all things else depends upon this and not conversely. Then, when he has clearly grasped all those things which follow proximately on the knowledge of the naked understanding, he will enumerate among other things whatever instruments of thought we have other than the understanding; and these are only two, viz., imagination and sense. He will therefore devote all his energies to the distinguishing and examining of these three modes of cognition, and seeing that in the strict sense truth and falsity can be a matter of the understanding alone, though often it derives its origin from the other two faculties, he will attend carefully to every source of deception in order that he may be on his guard. He will also enu-

merate exactly all the ways leading to truth which lie
open to us, in order that he may follow the right way.
They are not so many that they cannot all be easily
discovered and embraced in an adequate enumeration.
And though this will seem marvellous and incredible
to the inexpert, as soon as in each matter he has distinguished those cognitions which only fill and embellish the memory, from those which cause one to be
deemed really more instructed, which it will be easy for
him to do . . . [1]; he will feel assured that any absence of
further knowledge is not due to lack of intelligence or
of skill, and that nothing at all can be known by anyone else which he is not capable of knowing, provided
only that he gives to it his utmost mental application.   And though many problems may present themselves, from the solution of which this rule prohibits
him, yet because he will clearly perceive that they pass
the limits of human intelligence, he will deem that he
is not the more ignorant on that account; rather, if he
is reasonable, this very knowledge, that the solution can
be discovered by no one, will abundantly satisfy his
curiosity.

But lest we should always be uncertain as to the
powers of the mind, and in order that we may not labour
wrongly and at random before we set ourselves to think
out things in detail, we ought once in our life to inquire
diligently what the thoughts are of which the human
mind is capable.   In order the better to attain this
end we ought, when two sets of inquiries are equally
simple, to choose the more useful.

This method of ours resembles indeed those devices
employed by the mechanical crafts, which do not need

---

[1] The Amsterdam ed. of 1701 indicates an omission here

the aid of anything outside of them, but themselves
supply the directions for making their own instruments.
Thus if a man wished to practise any one of them,
e.g., the craft of a smith, and were destitute of all instruments, he would be forced to use at first a hard
stone or a rough lump of iron as an anvil, take a piece
of rock in place of a hammer, make pieces of wood
serve as tongs, and provide himself with other such
tools as necessity required. Thus equipped, he would
not then at once attempt to forge swords or helmets
or any manufactured articles of iron for others to use.
He would first of all fashion hammer, anvil, tongs, and
the other tools useful for himself. This example teaches
us that, since thus at the outset we have been able to
discover only some rough precepts, apparently the
innate possession of our mind, rather than the product
of technical skill, we should not forthwith attempt to
settle the controversies of Philosophers, or solve the
puzzles of the Mathematicians, by their help. We must
first employ them for searching out with our utmost
attention all the other things that are more urgently
required in the investigation of truth. And this since
there is no reason why it should appear more difficult
to discover these than any of the answers which the
problems propounded by Geometry or Physics or the
other sciences are wont to demand.

Now no more useful inquiry can be proposed than
that which seeks to determine the nature and the scope
of human knowledge. This is why we state this very
problem succinctly in the single question, which we
deem should be answered at the very outset with the
aid of the rules which we have already laid down. This
investigation should be undertaken once at least in his
life by anyone who has the slightest regard for truth,
since in pursuing it the true instruments of knowledge

and the whole method of inquiry come to light. But
nothing seems to me more futile than the conduct of
those who boldly dispute about the secrets of nature,
the influence of the heavens on these lower regions, the
predicting of future events and similar matters, as
many do, without yet having ever asked even whether
human reason is adequate to the solution of these problems. Neither ought it to seem such a toilsome and
difficult matter to define the limits of that understanding of which we are directly aware as being within us,
when we often have no hesitation in passing judgment
even on things that are without us and quite foreign to
us. Neither is it such an immense task to attempt to
grasp in thought all the objects comprised within this
whole of things, in order to discover how they singly
fall under our mental scrutiny. For nothing can prove
to be so complex or so vague as to defeat the efforts of
the method of enumeration above described, directed
towards restraining it within certain limits or arranging
it under certain categories. But to put this to the test
in the matter of the question above propounded, we first
of all divide the whole problem relative to it into two
parts; for it ought either to relate to us who are capable
of knowledge, or to the things themselves which can be
known: and these two factors we discuss separately.

In ourselves we notice that while it is the understanding alone which is capable of knowing, it yet is either
helped or hindered by three other faculties, namely,
imagination, sense, and memory. We must therefore
examine these faculties in order, with a view to finding
out where each may prove to be an impediment, so
that we may be on our guard; or where it may profit
us, so that we may use to the full the resources of these
powers. This first part of our problem will accordingly

be discussed with the aid of a sufficient enumeration, as will be shown in the succeeding proposition.

We come secondly to the things themselves which must be considered only in so far as they are the objects of the understanding. From this point of view we divide them into the class (1) of those whose nature is of the extremest simplicity and (2) of the complex and composite. Simple natures must be either spiritual or corporeal or at once spiritual and corporeal. Finally among the composites there are some which the understanding realises to be complex before it judges that it can determine anything about them; but there are also others which it itself puts together. All these matters will be expounded at greater length in the twelfth proposition, where it will be shown that there can be no falsity save in the last class—that of the compounds made by the understanding itself. This is why we further subdivide these into the class of those which are deducible from natures which are of the maximum simplicity and are known *per se,* of which we shall treat in the whole of the succeeding book; and into those which presuppose the existence of others which the facts themselves show us to be composite. To the exposition of these we destine the whole of the third[1] book.

But we shall indeed attempt in the whole of this treatise to follow so accurately the paths which conduct men to the knowledge of the truth and to make them so easy, that anyone who has perfectly learned the whole of this method, however moderate may be his talent, may see that no avenue to the truth is closed to him from which everyone else is not also excluded, and that his ignorance is due neither to a deficiency in his

---

1 Apparently not even begun.

capacity nor to his method of procedure. But as often as he applies his mind to the understanding of some matter, he will either be entirely successful, or he will realise that success depends upon a certain experiment which he is unable to perform, and in that case he will not blame his mental capacity although he is compelled to stop short there. Or finally he may show that the knowledge desired wholly exceeds the limits of the human intelligence; and consequently he will believe that he is none the more ignorant on that account. For to have discovered this is knowledge in no less degree than the knowledge of anything else.

Rule IX

We ought to give the whole of our attention to the most insignificant and most easily mastered facts, and remain a long time in contemplation of them until we are accustomed to behold the truth clearly and distinctly.

We have now indicated the two operations of our understanding, intuition and deduction, on which alone we have said we must rely in the acquisition of knowledge. Let us therefore in this and in the following proposition proceed to explain how we can render ourselves more skilful in employing them, and at the same time cultivate the two principal faculties of the mind, to wit, perspicacity, by viewing single objects distinctly, and sagacity, by the skilful deduction of certain facts from others.

Truly we shall learn how to employ our mental intuition from comparing it with the way in which we employ our eyes. For he who attempts to view a multitude of objects with one and the same glance, sees none of them distinctly; and similarly the man who is wont to attend to many things at the same time by means of a single act of thought is confused in mind. But just as workmen, who are employed in very fine and delicate operations and are accustomed to direct their eyesight attentively to separate points, by practice have acquired a capacity for distinguishing objects of extreme minuteness and subtlety; so likewise do people who do not allow their thought to be distracted by various objects at the same time, but always concentrate it in attending to the simplest and easiest particulars, are clear-headed.

But it is a common failing of mortals to deem the more difficult the fairer; and they often think that they have learned nothing when they see a very clear and simple cause for a fact, while at the same time they are lost in admiration of certain sublime and profound philosophical explanations, even though these for the most part are based upon foundations which no one has adequately surveyed—a mental disorder which prizes the darkness higher than the light. But it is notable that those who have real knowledge discern the truth with equal facility whether they evolve it from matter that is simple or that is obscure; they grasp each fact by an act of thought that is similar, single, and distinct, after they have once arrived at the point in question. The whole of the difference between the apprehension of the simple and of the obscure lies in the route taken, which certainly ought to be longer if it conducts us from our initial and most absolute principles to a truth that is somewhat remote.

Everyone ought therefore to accustom himself to grasp in his thought at the same time facts that are at once so few and so simple, that he shall never believe that he has knowledge of anything which he does not mentally behold with a distinctness equal to that of the objects which he knows most distinctly of all. It is

true that some men are born with a much greater apti-
tude for such discernment than others, but the mind
can be made much more expert at such work by art and
exercise.   But there is one fact which I should here
emphasize above all others; and that is that everyone
should firmly persuade himself that none of the sciences,
however abstruse, is to be deduced from lofty and
obscure matters, but that they all proceed only from
what is easy and more readily understood.

For example if I wish to examine whether it is
possible for a natural force to pass at one and the
same moment to a spot at a distance and yet to traverse
the whole space in between, I shall not begin to study
the force of magnetism or the influence of the stars, not
even the speed of light, in order to discover whether
actions such as these occur instantaneously; for the
solution of this question would be more difficult than
the problem proposed.   I should rather bethink myself
of the spatial motions of bodies, because nothing in the
sphere of motion can be found more obvious to sense
than this.   I shall observe that while a stone cannot
pass to another place in one and the same moment,
because it is a body, yet a force similar to that
which moves the stone can only be communicated
instantaneously if it passes unencumbered from one
object to another.   For instance, if I move one end of a
stick of whatever length, I easily form a notion of the
power by which both that part of the stick and all its
other parts are at the same moment necessarily moved,
because then the force passes unencumbered and is not
imprisoned in any body, e.g., a stone, which bears it
along.

In the same way if I wish to understand how one and
the same simple cause can produce contrary effects at
the same time, I shall not cite the drugs of the doctors

which expel certain humours and retain others; nor
shall I romance about the moon's power of warming
with its light and chilling by means of some occult
power. I shall rather cast my eyes upon the balance
in which the same weight raises one arm at the same
time as it depresses the other, or take some other
familiar instance.

RULE X

*In order that it may acquire sagacity the mind should
be exercised in pursuing just those inquiries of which
the solution has already been found by others; and it
ought to traverse in a systematic way even the most
trifling of men's inventions, though those ought to be
preferred in which order is explained or implied.*

I confess that my natural disposition is such that I
have always found, not the following of the arguments
of others, but the discovery of reasons by my own proper
efforts, to yield me the highest intellectual satisfaction.
It was this alone that attracted me, when I was still
a young man, to the study of science. And whenever
any book by its title promised some new discovery,
before I read further, I tried whether I could achieve
something similar by means of some inborn faculty of
invention, and I was careful lest a premature perusal
of the book might deprive me of this harmless pleasure.
So often was I successful that at length I perceived that
I no longer came upon the truth by proceeding as others
commonly do, viz., by pursuing vague and blind inquiries and relying more on good fortune than on skill.
I saw that by long experience I had discovered certain
rules which are of no little help in this inquiry, and
which I used afterwards in resolving many difficulties.

Thus it was that I diligently elaborated the whole of this method and came to the conclusion that I had followed that plan of study which was the most fruitful of all.

But because not all minds are so much inclined to puzzle things out unaided, this proposition announces that we ought not immediately to occupy ourselves with the more difficult and arduous problems, but first should discuss those disciplines which are easiest and simplest, and those above all in which order most prevails. Such are the arts of the craftsmen who weave webs and tapestry, or of women who embroider or use in the same work threads with infinite modification of texture. With these are ranked all play with numbers and everything that belongs to Arithmetic, and the like. It is wonderful how all these studies discipline our mental powers, provided that we do not know the solutions from others, but invent them ourselves. For since nothing in these arts remains hidden, and they are wholly adjusted to the capacity of human cognition, they reveal to us with the greatest distinctness innumerable orderly systems, all different from each other, but none the less conforming to rule, in the proper observance of which systems of order consists the whole of human sagacity.

It was for this reason that we insisted that method must be employed in studying those matters; and this in those arts of less importance consists wholly in the close observation of the order which is found in the object studied, whether that be an order existing in the thing itself, or due to subtle human devising. Thus if we wish to make out some writing in which the meaning is disguised by the use of a cypher, though the order here fails to present itself, we yet make up an imaginary one, for the purpose both of testing all the conjectures we may make about single letters, words or sentences, and in order to arrange them so that when we sum them up we shall be able to tell all the inferences that we can deduce from them. We must principally beware of wasting our time in such cases by proceeding at random and unmethodically; for even though the solution can often be found without method, and by lucky people sometimes quicker, yet such procedure is likely to enfeeble the faculties and to make people accustomed to the trifling and the childish, so that for the future their minds will stick on the surface of things, incapable of penetrating beyond it. But meanwhile we must not fall into the error of those who, having devoted themselves solely to what is lofty and serious, find that after many years of toil they have acquired, not the profound knowledge they hoped for, but only mental confusion. Hence we must give ourselves practice first in those easier disciplines, but methodically, so that by open and familiar ways we may ceaselessly accustom ourselves to penetrate as easily as though we were at play into the very heart of these subjects. For by this means we shall afterwards gradually feel (and in a space of time shorter than we could at all hope for) that we are in a position with equal facility to deduce from evident first principles many propositions which at first sight are highly intricate and difficult.

It may perhaps strike some with surprise that here, where we are discussing how to improve our power of deducing one truth from another, we have omitted all the precepts of the dialecticians, by which they think to control the human reason. They prescribe certain formulae of argument, which lead to a conclusion with such necessity that, if the reason commits itself to their trust, even though it slackens its interest and no longer pays a heedful and close attention to the very proposition inferred, it can nevertheless at the same time come to a sure conclusion by virtue of the form of the argument alone. Exactly so; the fact is that frequently we notice that often the truth escapes away out of these imprisoning bonds, while the people themselves who have used them in order to capture it remain entangled in them. Other people are not so frequently entrapped; and it is a matter of experience that the most ingenious sophisms hardly ever impose on anyone who uses his unaided reason, while they are wont to deceive the sophists themselves.

Wherefore as we wish here to be particularly careful lest our reason should go on holiday while we are examining the truth of any matter, we reject those formulae as being opposed to our project, and look out rather for all the aids by which our thought may be kept attentive, as will be shown in the sequel. But, to say a few words more, that it may appear still more evident that this style of argument contributes nothing at all to the discovery of the truth, we must note that the Dialecticians are unable to devise any syllogism which has a true conclusion, unless they have first secured the material out of which to construct it, i.e., unless they have already ascertained the very truth which is deduced in that syllogism. Whence it is clear that from a formula of this kind they can gather nothing that is new, and hence the ordinary Dialectic is quite valueless for those who desire to investigate the truth of things. Its only possible use is to serve to explain at times more easily to others the truths we have already ascertained; hence it should be transferred from Philosophy to Rhetoric.

RULE XI

If, after we have recognized intuitively a number of simple truths, we wish to draw any inference from them, it is useful to run them over in a continuous and uninterrupted act of thought, to reflect upon their relations to one another, and to grasp together distinctly a number of these propositions so far as is possible at the same time. For this is a way of making our knowledge much more certain, and of greatly increasing the power of the mind.

Here we have an opportunity of expounding more clearly what has been already said of mental intuition in the third and seventh rules. In one passage we opposed it to deduction, while in the other we distinguished it from enumeration only, which we defined as an inference drawn from many and diverse things. But the simple deduction of one thing from another, we said in the same passage, was effected by intuition.

It was necessary to do this, because two things are requisite for mental intuition. Firstly the proposition intuited must be clear and distinct; secondly it must be grasped in its totality at the same time and not successively. As for deduction, if we are thinking of how the process works, as we were in Rule III, it appears not to occur all at the same time, but involves a sort of movement on the part of our mind when it infers one thing from another. We were justified therefore in distinguishing deduction in that rule from intuition. But if we wish to consider deduction as an accomplished fact, as we did in what we said relatively to the seventh rule, then it no longer designates a movement, but rather the completion of a movement, and therefore we suppose that it is presented to us by intuition when it is simple and clear, but not when it is

complex and involved. When this is the case we give
it the name of enumeration or induction, because
it cannot then be grasped as a whole at the same time
by the mind, and its certainty depends to some extent
on the memory, in which our judgments about the
various matters enumerated must be retained, if from
their assemblage a single fact is to be inferred.

All these distinctions had to be made if we were to
elucidate this rule. We treated of mental intuition
solely in Rule IX; the tenth dealt with enumeration
alone; but now the present rule explains how these two
operations aid and complete each other. In doing so
they seem to grow into a single process by virtue of a
sort of motion of thought which has an attentive and
vision-like knowledge of one fact and yet can pass at
the very same moment to another.

Now to this co-operation we assign a two-fold advantage. Firstly it promotes a more certain knowledge
of the conclusion with which we are concerned, and
secondly it makes the mind readier to discover fresh
truths. In fact the memory, on which we have said
depends the certainty of the conclusions which embrace
more than we can grasp in a single act of intuition,
though weak and liable to fail us, can be renewed and
made stronger by this continuous and constantly repeated process of thought. Thus if diverse mental acts
have led me to know what is the relation between a first
and a second magnitude, next between the second and
a third, then between the third and a fourth, and
finally the fourth and a fifth, that need not lead me
to see what is the relation between the first and the
fifth, nor can I deduce it from what I already know,
unless I remember all the other relations. Hence what
I have to do is to run over them all repeatedly in my
mind, until I pass so quickly from the first to the last

that practically no step is left to the memory, and I seem to view the whole all at the same time.

Everyone must see that this plan does much to counteract the slowness of the mind and to enlarge its capacity. But in addition we must note that the greatest advantage of this rule consists in the fact that, by reflecting on the mutual dependence of two propositions, we acquire the habit of distinguishing at a glance what is more or less relative, and what the steps are by which a relative fact is related to something absolute. For example, if I run over a number of magnitudes that are in continued proportion, I shall reflect upon all the following facts: viz., that the mental act is entirely similar—and not easier in the one case, more difficult in another—by which I grasp the relation between the first and the second, the second and third, third and fourth, and so on; while yet it is more difficult for me to conceive what the relation of the second is to the first and to the third at the same time, and much more difficult still to tell its relation to the first and fourth, and so on. These considerations then lead me to see why, if the first and second alone are given, I can easily find the third and fourth, and all the others; the reason being that this process requires only single and distinct acts of thought. But if only the first and the third are given, it is not so easy to recognize the mean, because this can only be accomplished by means of a mental operation in which two of the previous acts are involved. If the first and the fourth magnitudes alone are given, it is still more difficult to present to ourselves the two means, because here three acts of thought come in simultaneously. It would seem likely as a consequence that it would be even more difficult to discover the three means between the first and the fifth. The reason why this is not so is due to a fresh fact; viz., even though here four mental acts come together they can yet be disjoined, since four can be divided by another number. Thus I can discover the third by itself from the first and fifth, then the second from the first and third, and so on. If one accustoms one's self to reflect on these and similar problems, as often as a new question arises, at once one recognizes what produces its special difficulty, and what is the simplest method of dealing with all cases; and to be able to do so is a valuable aid to the discovery of the truth.

RULE XII

Finally we ought to employ all the aids of understanding, imagination, sense and memory, first for the purpose of having a distinct intuition of simple propositions; partly also in order to compare the propositions to be proved with those we know already, so that we may be able to recognize their truth; partly also in order to discover the truths, which should be compared with each other so that nothing may be left lacking on which human industry may exercise itself.

This rule states the conclusion of all that we said before, and shows in general outline what had to be explained in detail, in this wise.

In the matter of the cognition of facts two things alone have to be considered, ourselves who know and the objects themselves which are to be known. Within us there are four faculties only which we can use for this purpose, viz., understanding, imagination, sense and memory. The understanding is indeed alone capable of perceiving the truth, but yet it ought to be aided by imagination, sense and memory, lest perchance we omit any expedient that lies within our power. On the side of the facts to be known it is enough to examine three things; first that which presents itself spontaneously, secondly how we learn one thing by means of another, and thirdly the precise fact with which each conclusion is connected. This enumeration appears to me to be complete, and to omit nothing to which our human powers can apply.

SYNOPSIS OF THE SIX FOLLOWING MEDITATIONS

In the first Meditation I set forth the reasons for which we may, generally speaking, <u>doubt</u> about all things and especially about material things, at least so long as we have no other foundations for the sciences than those which we have hitherto possessed. But although the utility of a Doubt which is so general does not at first appear, it is at the same time very great, inasmuch as it <u>delivers us from every kind of prejudice</u>, and sets out for us a very simple way by which the mind may detach itself from the senses; and finally <u>it makes it impossible for us ever to doubt those things which we have once discovered to be true.</u>

In the <u>second Meditation, mind</u>, which making use of the liberty which pertains to it, takes for granted that all those things of whose existence it has the least doubt, are non-existent, recognises that <u>it is however absolutely impossible that it does not itself exist. This point is likewise of the greatest moment, inasmuch as by this</u> means a distinction is easily drawn between the things which pertain to mind—that is to say to the intellectual nature—and those which pertain to body.

But because it may be that some expect from me in this place a statement of the reasons establishing the immortality of the soul, I feel that I should here make known to them that having aimed at writing nothing in all this Treatise of which I do not possess very exact demonstrations, I am obliged to follow a similar order

*to that made use of by the geometers, which is to begin
by putting forward as premises all those things upon
which the proposition that we seek depends, before
coming to any conclusion regarding it.   Now the first
and principal matter which is requisite for thoroughly
understanding the immortality of the soul is to form the
clearest possible conception of it, and one which will
be entirely distinct from all the conceptions which we
may have of body; and in this Meditation this has been
done.   In addition to this it is requisite that we may be
assured that all the things which we conceive clearly
and distinctly are true in the very way in which we
think them; and this could not be proved previously
to the Fourth Meditation.   Further we must have a distinct conception of corporeal nature, which is given
partly in this second, and partly in the Fifth and
Sixth Meditations.   And finally we should conclude
from all this, that those things which we conceive
clearly and distinctly as being diverse substances, as
we regard mind and body to be, are really substances
essentially distinct one from the other; and this is
the conclusion of the Sixth Meditation.   This is further confirmed in this same Meditation by the fact that
we cannot conceive of body excepting in so far as it is
divisible, while the mind cannot be conceived of excepting as indivisible.   For we are not able to conceive of
the half of a mind as we can do of the smallest of all
bodies; so that we see that not only are their natures
different but even in some respects contrary to one another.   I have not however dealt further with this matter in this treatise, both because what I have said is
sufficient to show clearly enough that the extinction of
the mind does not follow from the corruption of the body,
and also to give men the hope of another life after
death, as also because the premises from which the im-*

mortality of the soul may be deduced depend on an elucidation of a complete system of Physics. This would mean to establish in the first place that all substances generally—that is to say all things which cannot exist without being created by God—are in their nature incorruptible, and that they can never cease to exist unless God, in denying to them his concurrence, reduce them to nought; and secondly that body, regarded generally, is a substance, which is the reason why it also cannot perish, but that the human body, inasmuch as it differs from other bodies, is composed only of a certain configuration of members and of other similar accidents, while the human mind is not similarly composed of any accidents, but is a pure substance. For although all the accidents of mind be changed, although, for instance, it think certain things, will others, perceive others, etc., despite all this it does not emerge from these changes another mind; the human body on the other hand becomes a different thing from the sole fact that the figure or form of any of its portions is found to be changed. From this it follows that the human body may indeed easily enough perish, but the mind [or soul of man (I make no distinction between them)] is owing to its nature immortal.

In the third Meditation it seems to me that I have explained at sufficient length the principal argument of which I make use in order to prove the existence of God. But none the less, because I did not wish in that place to make use of any comparisons derived from corporeal things, so as to withdraw as much as I could the minds of readers from the senses, there may perhaps have remained many obscurities which, however, will, I hope, be entirely removed by the Replies which I have made to the Objections which have been set before me. Amongst others there is, for example, this one, 'How the

*idea in us of being supremely perfect possesses so much
objective reality [that is to say participates by representation in so many degrees of being and perfection]
that it necessarily proceeds from a cause which is absolutely perfect. This is illustrated in these Replies
by the comparison of a very perfect machine, the idea
of which is found in the mind of some workman. For
as the objective contrivance of this idea must have some
cause, i.e. either the science of the workman or that of
some other from whom he has received the idea, it is
similarly impossible that the idea of God which is in us
should not have God himself as its cause.*

*In the fourth Meditation it is shown that all these
things which we very clearly and distinctly perceive are
true, and at the same time it is explained in what the
nature of error or falsity consists. This must of necessity be known both for the confirmation of the preceding
truths and for the better comprehension of those that
follow. (But it must meanwhile be remarked that I do
not in any way there treat of sin—that is to say of the
error which is committed in the pursuit of good and evil,
but only of that which arises in the deciding between
the true and the false. And I do not intend to speak
of matters pertaining to the Faith or the conduct of life,
but only of those which concern speculative truths, and
which may be known by the sole aid of the light of
nature.)*

*In the fifth Meditation corporeal nature generally is
explained, and in addition to this the existence of God
is demonstrated by a new proof in which there may
possibly be certain difficulties also, but the solution
of these will be seen in the Replies to the Objections.
And further I show in what sense it is true to say that
the certainty of geometrical demonstrations is itself
dependent on the knowledge of God.*

Finally in the Sixth I distinguish the action of the understanding from that of the imagination; the marks by which this distinction is made are described. I here show that the mind of man is really distinct from the body, and at the same time that the two are so closely joined together that they form, so to speak, a single thing. All the errors which proceed from the senses are then surveyed, while the means of avoiding them are demonstrated, and finally all the reasons from which we may deduce the existence of material things are set forth. Not that I judge them to be very useful in establishing that which they prove, to wit, that there is in truth a world, that men possess bodies, and other such things which never have been doubted by anyone of sense; but because in considering these closely we come to see that they are neither so strong nor so evident as those arguments which lead us to the knowledge of our mind and of God; so that these last must be the most certain and most evident facts which can fall within the cognisance of the human mind. And this is the whole matter that I have tried to prove in these Meditations, for which reason I here omit to speak of many other questions with which I dealt incidentally in this discussion.

MEDITATIONS ON THE FIRST PHILOSOPHY IN WHICH THE EXISTENCE OF GOD AND THE DISTINCTION BETWEEN MIND AND BODY ARE DEMONSTRATED

MEDITATION I

Of the things which may be brought within the sphere of the doubtful.

It is now some years since I detected how many were the false beliefs that I had from my earliest youth admitted as true, and how doubtful was everything I had since constructed on this basis; and from that time I was convinced that I must once for all seriously undertake to rid myself of all the opinions which I had formerly accepted, and commence to build anew from the foundation, if I wanted to establish any firm and permanent structure in the sciences. But as this enterprise appeared to be a very great one, I waited until I had attained an age so mature that I could not hope that at any later date I should be better fitted to execute my design. This reason caused me to delay so long that I should feel that I was doing wrong were I to occupy in deliberation the time that yet remains to me for action. To-day, then, since very opportunely for the plan I have in view I have delivered my mind from every care [and am happily agitated by no passions] and since I have procured for myself an assured leisure in a peaceable retirement, I shall at last seriously and freely address myself to the general upheaval of all my former opinions.

Now for this object it is not necessary that I should show that all of these are false—I shall perhaps never arrive at this end. But inasmuch as reason already persuades me that I ought no less carefully to withhold my assent from matters which are not entirely certain and indubitable than from those which appear to me manifestly to be false, if I am able to find in each one some reason to doubt, this will suffice to justify my rejecting the whole. And for that end it will not be requisite that I should examine each in particular, which would be an endless undertaking; for owing to the fact that the destruction of the foundations of necessity brings with it the downfall of the rest of the edifice, I shall only in the first place attack those principles upon which all my former opinions rested.

All that up to the present time I have accepted as
most true and certain I have learned either from the
senses or through the senses; but it is sometimes proved
to me that these senses are deceptive, and it is wiser
not to trust entirely to any thing by which we have
once been deceived.

But it may be that although the senses sometimes
deceive us concerning things which are hardly perceptible, or very far away, there are yet many others to be
met with as to which we cannot reasonably have any
doubt, although we recognise them by their means. For
example, there is the fact that I am here, seated by the
fire, attired in a dressing gown, having this paper in my
hands and other similar matters. And how could I
deny that these hands and this body are mine, were it
not perhaps that I compare myself to certain persons,
devoid of sense, whose cerebella are so troubled and
clouded by the violent vapours of black bile, that they
constantly assure us that they think they are kings
when they are really quite poor, or that they are clothed
in purple when they are really without covering, or who
imagine that they have an earthenware head or are
nothing but pumpkins or are made of glass. But they
are mad, and I should not be any the less insane were I
to follow examples so extravagant.

At the same time I must remember that I am a man,
and that consequently I am in the habit of sleeping,
and in my dreams representing to myself the same
things or sometimes even less probable things, than do
those who are insane in their waking moments. How
often has it happened to me that in the night I dreamt
that I found myself in this particular place, that I was
dressed and seated near the fire, whilst in reality I was
lying undressed in bed! At this moment it does indeed
seem to me that it is with eyes awake that I am looking

at this paper; that this head which I move is not asleep,
that it is deliberately and of set purpose that I extend
my hand and perceive it; what happens in sleep does
not appear so clear nor so distinct as does all this.   But
in thinking over this I remind myself that on many occasions I have in sleep been deceived by similar illusions,
and in dwelling carefully on this reflection I see so manifestly that there are no certain indications by which we
may clearly distinguish wakefulness from sleep that I
am lost in astonishment.   And my astonishment is such
that it is almost incapable of persuading me that I now
dream.

Now let us assume that we are asleep and that all
these particulars, e.g. that we open our eyes, shake our
head, extend our hands, and so on, are but false de-
lusions; and let us reflect that possibly neither our hands
nor our whole body are such as they appear to us to be.
At the same time we must at least confess that the things
which are represented to us in sleep are like painted
representations which can only have been formed as the
counterparts of something real and true, and that in this
way those general things at least, i.e. eyes, a head,
hands, and a whole body, are not imaginary things, but
things really existent.   For, as a matter of fact, painters,
even when they study with the greatest skill to represent sirens and satyrs by forms the most strange and
extraordinary, cannot give them natures which are entirely new, but merely make a certain medley of the
members of different animals; or if their imagination is
extravagant enough to invent something so novel that
nothing similar has ever before been seen, and that then
their work represents a thing purely fictitious and absolutely false, it is certain all the same that the colours
of which this is composed are necessarily real.   And
for the same reason, although these general things, to

wit, [a body], eyes, a head, and such like, may be imaginary, we are bound at the same time to confess that there are at least some other objects yet more simple and more universal, which are real and true; and of these just in the same way as with certain real colours, all these images of things which dwell in our thoughts, whether true and real or false and fantastic, are formed.

To such a class of things pertains corporeal nature in general, and its extension, the figure of extended things, their quantity or magnitude and number, as also the place in which they are, the time which measures their duration, and so on.

That is possibly why our reasoning is not unjust when we conclude from this that Physics, Astronomy, Medicine and all other sciences which have as their end the consideration of composite things, are very dubious and uncertain; but that Arithmetic, Geometry and other sciences of that kind which only treat of things that are very simple and very general, without taking great trouble to ascertain whether they are actually existent or not, contain some measure of certainty and an element of the indubitable. For whether I am awake or asleep, two and three together always form five, and the square can never have more than four sides, and it does not seem possible that truths so clear and apparent can be suspected of any falsity [or uncertainty].

Nevertheless I have long had fixed in my mind the belief that an all-powerful God existed by whom I have been created such as I am. But how do I know that He has not brought it to pass that there is no earth, no heaven, no extended body, no magnitude, no place, and that nevertheless [I possess the perceptions of all these things and that] they seem to me to exist just exactly as I now see them? And, besides, as I sometimes imagine that others deceive themselves in the things which they think they know best, how do I know that I am not deceived every time that I add two and three, or count the sides of a square, or judge of things yet simpler, if anything simpler can be imagined? But possibly God has not desired that I should be thus deceived, for He is said to be supremely good. If, however, it is contrary to His goodness to have made me such that I constantly deceive myself, it would also appear to be contrary to His goodness to permit me to be sometimes deceived, and nevertheless I cannot doubt that He does permit this.

There may indeed be those who would prefer to deny the existence of a God so powerful, rather than believe that all other things are uncertain. But let us not oppose them for the present, and grant that all that is said of a God is a fable; nevertheless in whatever way they suppose that I have arrived at the state of being that I have reached—whether they attribute it to fate or to accident, or make out that it is by a continual succession of antecedents, or by some other method—since to err and deceive oneself is a defect, it is clear that the greater will be the probability of my being so imperfect as to deceive myself ever, as is the Author to whom they assign my origin the less powerful. To these reasons I have certainly nothing to reply, but at the end I feel constrained to confess that there is nothing in all that I formerly believed to be true, of which I cannot in some measure doubt, and that not merely through want of thought or through levity, but for reasons which are very powerful and maturely considered; so that henceforth I ought not the less carefully to refrain from giving credence to these opinions than to that which is manifestly false, if I desire to arrive at any certainty [in the sciences].

But it is not sufficient to have made these remarks, we must also be careful to keep them in mind. For these ancient and commonly held opinions still revert frequently to my mind, long and familiar custom having given them the right to occupy my mind against my inclination and rendered them almost masters of my belief; nor will I ever lose the habit of deferring to them or of placing my confidence in them, so long as I consider them as they really are, i.e. opinions in some measure doubtful, as I have just shown, and at the same time highly probable, so that there is much more reason to believe than to deny them. That is why I consider that I shall not be acting amiss, if, taking of set purpose a contrary belief, I allow myself to be deceived, and for a certain time pretend that all these opinions are entirely false and imaginary, until at last, having thus balanced my former prejudices with my latter [so that they cannot divert my opinions more to one side than to the other], my judgment will no longer be dominated by bad usage or turned away from the right knowledge of the truth. For I am assured that there can be neither peril nor error in this course, and that I cannot at present yield too much to distrust, since I am not considering the question of action, but only of knowledge.

I shall then suppose, not that God who is supremely good and the fountain of truth, but some evil genius not less powerful than deceitful, has employed his whole energies in deceiving me; I shall consider that the heavens, the earth, colours, figures, sound, and all other external things are nought but the illusions and dreams of which this genius has availed himself in order to lay traps for my credulity; I shall consider myself as having no hands, no eyes, no flesh, no blood, nor any senses, yet falsely believing myself to possess all these things;

start w. utter scepticism

I shall remain obstinately attached to this idea, and if by this means it is not in my power to arrive at the knowledge of any truth, I may at least do what is in my power [i.e. suspend my judgment], and with firm purpose avoid giving credence to any false thing, or being imposed upon by this arch deceiver, however powerful and deceptive he may be. But this task is a laborious one, and insensibly a certain lassitude leads me into the course of my ordinary life. And just as a captive who in sleep enjoys imaginary liberty, when he begins to suspect that his liberty is but a dream, fears to awaken, and conspires with these agreeable illusions that the deception may be prolonged, so insensibly of my own accord I fall back into my former opinions, and I dread awakening from this slumber, lest the laborious wakefulness which would follow the tranquillity of this repose should have to be spent not in daylight, but in the excessive darkness of the difficulties which have just been discussed.

MEDITATION II - summary p. 84

Of the Nature of the Human Mind; and that it is more easily known than the Body.

The Meditation of yesterday filled my mind with so many doubts that it is no longer in my power to forget them. And yet I do not see in what manner I can resolve them; and, just as if I had all of a sudden fallen into very deep water, I am so disconcerted that I can neither make certain of setting my feet on the bottom, nor can I swim and so support myself on the surface. I shall nevertheless make an effort and follow anew the same path as that on which I yesterday entered, i.e. I shall proceed by setting aside all that in which the least doubt could be supposed to exist, just as if I

cf Hobbes' criticism, p. 194-202

had discovered that it was absolutely false; and I shall ever follow in this road until I have met with something which is certain, or at least, if I can do nothing else, until I have learned for certain that there is nothing in the world that is certain. Archimedes, in order that he might draw the terrestrial globe out of its place, and transport it elsewhere, demanded only that one point should be fixed and immoveable; in the same way I shall have the right to conceive high hopes if I am happy enough to discover one thing only which is certain and indubitable.

I suppose, then, that all the things that I see are false; I persuade myself that nothing has ever existed of all that my fallacious memory represents to me. I consider that I possess no senses; I imagine that body, figure, extension, movement and place are but the fictions of my mind. What, then, can be esteemed as true? Perhaps nothing at all, unless that there is nothing in the world that is certain.

But how can I know there is not something different from those things that I have just considered, of which one cannot have the slightest doubt? Is there not some God, or some other being by whatever name we call it, who puts these reflections into my mind? That is not necessary, for is it not possible that I am capable of producing them myself? I myself, am I not at least something? But I have already denied that I had senses and body. Yet I hesitate, for what follows from that? Am I so independent on body and senses that I cannot exist without these? But I was persuaded that there was nothing in all the world, that there was no heaven, no earth, that there were no minds, nor any bodies: was I not then likewise persuaded that I did not exist? Not at all; of a surety I myself did exist since I persuaded myself of something [or merely because

I thought of something]. But there is some deceiver
or other, very powerful and very cunning, who ever
employs his ingenuity in deceiving me. Then without
doubt I exist also if he deceives me, and let him deceive
me as much as he will, he can never cause me to be
nothing so long as I think that I am something. So
that after having reflected well and carefully examined
all things, we must come to the definite conclusion that
this proposition: I am, I exist, is necessarily true each
time that I pronounce it, or that I mentally conceive it.

But I do not yet know clearly enough what I am, I
who am certain that I am; and hence I must be careful
to see that I do not imprudently take some other object
in place of myself, and thus that I do not go astray
in respect of this knowledge that I hold to be the most
certain and most evident of all that I have formerly
learned. That is why I shall now consider anew what I
believed myself to be before I embarked upon these
last reflections; and of my former opinions I shall withdraw all that might even in a small degree be invali-
dated by the reasons which I have just brought forward,
in order that there may be nothing at all left beyond
what is absolutely certain and indubitable.

What then did I formerly believe myself to be? Undoubtedly I believed myself to be a man. But what is
a man? Shall I say a reasonable animal? Certainly
not; for then I should have to inquire what an animal
is, and what is reasonable; and thus from a single question I should insensibly fall into an infinitude of others
more difficult; and I should not wish to waste the little
time and leisure remaining to me in trying to unravel
subtleties like these. But I shall rather stop here to
consider the thoughts which of themselves spring up in
my mind, and which were not inspired by anything beyond my own nature alone when I applied myself to

the consideration of my being. In the first place, then, I considered myself as having a face, hands, arms, and all that system of members composed of bones and flesh as seen in a corpse which I designated by the name of body. In addition to this I considered that I was nourished, that I walked, that I felt, and that I thought, and I referred all these actions to the soul: but I did not stop to consider what the soul was, or if I did stop, I imagined that it was something extremely rare and subtle like a wind, a flame, or an ether, which was spread throughout my grosser parts. As to body I had no manner of doubt about its nature, but thought I had a very clear knowledge of it; and if I had desired to explain it according to the notions that I had then formed of it, I should have described it thus: By the body I understand all that which can be defined by a certain figure: something which can be confined in a certain place, and which can fill a given space in such a way that every other body will be excluded from it; which can be perceived either by touch, or by sight, or by hearing, or by taste, or by smell: which can be moved in many ways not, in truth, by itself, but by something which is foreign to it, by which it is touched [and from which it receives impressions]: for to have the power of self-movement, as also of feeling or of thinking, I did not consider to appertain to the nature of body: on the contrary, I was rather astonished to find that faculties similar to them existed in some bodies.

But what am I, now that I suppose that there is a certain genius which is extremely powerful, and, if I may say so, malicious, who employs all his powers in deceiving me? Can I affirm that I possess the least of all those things which I have just said pertain to the nature of body? I pause to consider, I resolve all these things in my mind, and find none of which I can say that it pertains to me. It would be tedious to stop to enumerate them. Let us pass to the attributes of soul and see if there is any one which is in me? What of nutrition or walking [the first mentioned]? But if it is so that I have no body it is also true that I can neither walk nor take nourishment. Another attribute is sensation. But one cannot feel without body, and besides I have thought I perceived many things during sleep that I recognised in my waking moments as not having been experienced at all. What of thinking? I find here that thought is an attribute that belongs to me; it alone cannot be separated from me. I am, I exist, that is certain. But how often? Just when I think; for it might possibly be the case if I ceased entirely to think, that I should likewise cease altogether to exist. I do not now admit anything which is not necessarily true: to speak accurately I am not more than a thing which thinks, that is to say a mind or a soul, or an understanding, or a reason, which are terms whose significance was formerly unknown to me. I am, however, a real thing and really exist; but what thing? I have answered: a thing which thinks.

And what more? I shall exercise my imagination [in order to see if I am not something more]. I am not a collection of members which we call the human body: I am not a subtle air distributed through these members, I am not a wind, a fire, a vapour, a breath, nor anything at all which I can imagine or conceive; because I have assumed that all these were nothing. Without changing that supposition I find that I only leave myself certain of the fact that I am somewhat. But perhaps it is true that these same things which I supposed were non-existent because they are unknown to me, are really not different from the self which I know.

I am not sure about this, I shall not dispute about it now; I can only give judgment on things that are known to me. I know that I exist, and I inquire what I am, I whom I know to exist. But it is very certain that the knowledge of my existence taken in its precise significance does not depend on things whose existence is not yet known to me; consequently it does not depend on those which I can feign in imagination. And indeed the very term *feign* in imagination proves to me my error, for I really do this if I image myself a something, since to imagine is nothing else than to contemplate the figure or image of a corporeal thing. But I already know for certain that I am, and that it may be that all these images, and, speaking generally, all things that relate to the nature of body are nothing but dreams [and chimeras]. For this reason I see clearly that I have as little reason to say, 'I shall stimulate my imagination in order to know more distinctly what I am,' than if I were to say, 'I am now awake, and I perceive somewhat that is real and true: but because I do not yet perceive it distinctly enough, I shall go to sleep of express purpose, so that my dreams may represent the perception with greatest truth and evidence.' And, thus, I know for certain that nothing of all that I can understand by means of my imagination belongs to this knowledge which I have of myself, and that it is necessary to recall the mind from this mode of thought with the utmost diligence in order that it may be able to know its own nature with perfect distinctness.

But what then am I? A thing which thinks. What is a thing which thinks? It is a thing which doubts, understands, [conceives], affirms, denies, wills, refuses, which also imagines and feels.

Certainly it is no small matter if all these things pertain to my nature. But why should they not so pertain? Am I not that being who now doubts nearly everything, who nevertheless understands certain things, who affirms that one only is true, who denies all the others, who desires to know more, is averse from being deceived, who imagines many things, sometimes indeed despite his will, and who perceives many likewise, as by the intervention of the bodily organs? Is there nothing in all this which is as true as it is certain that I exist, even though I should always sleep and though he who has given me being employed all his ingenuity in deceiving me? Is there likewise any one of these attributes which can be distinguished from my thought, or which might be said to be separated from myself? For it is so evident of itself that it is I who doubts, who understands, and who desires, that there is no reason here to add anything to explain it. And I have certainly the power of imagining likewise; for although it may happen (as I formerly supposed) that none of the things which I imagine are true, nevertheless this power of imagining does not cease to be really in use, and it forms part of my thought. Finally, I am the same who feels, that is to say, who perceives certain things, as by the organs of sense, since in truth I see light, I hear noise, I feel heat. But it will be said that these phenomena are false and that I am dreaming. Let it be so; still it is at least quite certain that it seems to me that I see light, that I hear noise and that I feel heat. That cannot be false; properly speaking it is what is in me called feeling; and used in this precise sense that is no other thing than thinking.

From this time I begin to know what I am with a little more clearness and distinction than before; but nevertheless it still seems to me, and I cannot prevent myself from thinking, that corporeal things, whose images are framed by thought, which are tested by the senses, are much more distinctly known than that obscure part of me which does not come under the imagination. Although really it is very strange to say that I know and understand more distinctly these things whose existence seems to me dubious, which are unknown to me, and which do not belong to me, than others of the truth of which I am convinced, which are known to me and which pertain to my real nature, in a word, than myself. But I see clearly how the case stands: my mind loves to wander, and cannot yet suffer itself to be retained within the just limits of truth. Very good, let us once more give it the freest rein, so that, when afterwards we seize the proper occasion for pulling up, it may the more easily be regulated and controlled.

Let us begin by considering the commonest matters, those which we believe to be the most distinctly comprehended, to wit, the bodies which we touch and see; not indeed bodies in general, for these general ideas are usually a little more confused, but let us consider one body in particular. Let us take for example, this piece of wax: it has been taken quite freshly from the hive, and it has not yet lost the sweetness of the honey which it contains; it still retains somewhat of the odour of the flowers from which it has been culled; its colour, its figure, its size are apparent; it is hard, cold, easily handled, and if you strike it with the finger, it will emit a sound. Finally all the things which are requisite to cause us distinctly to recognise a body, are met with in it. But notice that while I speak and approach the fire what remained of the taste is exhaled, the smell evaporates, the colour alters, the figure is destroyed, the size increases, it becomes liquid, it heats, scarcely can one handle it, and when one strikes it, no sound is emitted. Does the same wax remain after this change?

We must confess that it remains; none would judge otherwise. What then did I know so distinctly in this piece of wax? It could certainly be nothing of all that the senses brought to my notice, since all these things which fall under taste, smell, sight, touch, and hearing, are found to be changed, and yet the same wax remains.

Perhaps it was what I now think, viz. that this wax was not that sweetness of honey, nor that agreeable scent of flowers, nor that particular whiteness, nor that figure, nor that sound, but simply a body which a little before appeared to me as perceptible under these forms, and which is now perceptible under others. But what, precisely, is it that I imagine when I form such conceptions? Let us attentively consider this, and, abstracting from all that does not belong to the wax, let us see what remains. Certainly nothing remains excepting a certain extended thing which is flexible and movable. But what is the meaning of flexible and movable? Is it not that I imagine that this piece of wax being round is capable of becoming square and of passing from a square to a triangular figure? No, certainly it is not that, since I imagine it admits of an infinitude of similar changes, and I nevertheless do not know how to compass the infinitude by my imagination, and consequently this conception which I have of the wax is not brought about by the faculty of imagination. What now is this extension? Is it not also unknown? For it becomes greater when the wax is melted, greater when it is boiled, and greater still when the heat increases; and I should not conceive [clearly] according to truth what wax is, if I did not think that even this piece that we are considering is capable of receiving more variations in extension than I have ever imagined. We must then grant that I could not even understand through the imagination what this piece of wax is, and that it is my mind alone which perceives it. I say this piece of wax in particular, for as to wax in general it is yet clearer. But what is this piece of wax which cannot be understood excepting by the [understanding or] mind? It is certainly the same that I see, touch, imagine, and finally it is the same which I have always believed it to be from the beginning. But what must particularly be observed is that its perception is neither an act of vision, nor of touch, nor of imagination, and has never been such although it may have appeared formerly to be so, but only an intuition of the mind, which may be imperfect and confused as it was formerly, or clear and distinct as it is at present, according as my attention is more or less directed to the elements which are found in it, and of which it is composed.

Yet in the meantime I am greatly astonished when I consider [the great feebleness of mind] and its proneness to fall [insensibly] into error; for although without giving expression to my thoughts I consider all this in my own mind, words often impede me and I am almost deceived by the terms of ordinary language. For we say that we see the same wax, if it is present, and not that we simply judge that it is the same from its having the same colour and figure. From this I should conclude that I knew the wax by means of vision and not simply by the intuition of the mind; unless by chance I remember that, when looking from a window and saying I see men who pass in the street, I really do not see them, but infer that what I see is men, just as I say that I see wax. And yet what do I see from the window but hats and coats which may cover automatic machines? Yet I judge these to be men. And similarly solely by the faculty of judgment which rests in my mind, I comprehend that which I believed I saw with my eyes.

A man who makes it his aim to raise his knowledge above the common should be ashamed to derive the occasion for doubting from the forms of speech invented by the vulgar; I prefer to pass on and consider whether I had a more evident and perfect conception of what the wax was when I first perceived it, and when I believed I knew it by means of the external senses or at least by the common sense as it is called, that is to say by the imaginative faculty, or whether my present conception is clearer now that I have most carefully examined what it is, and in what way it can be known. It would certainly be absurd to doubt as to this. For what was there in this first perception which was distinct? What was there which might not as well have been perceived by any of the animals? But when I distinguish the wax from its external forms, and when, just as if I had taken from it its vestments, I consider it quite naked, it is certain that although some error may still be found in my judgment, I can nevertheless not perceive it thus without a human mind.

But finally what shall I say of this mind, that is, of myself, for up to this point I do not admit in myself anything but mind? What then, I who seem to perceive this piece of wax distinctly, do I not know myself, not only with much more truth and certainty, but also with much more distinctness and clearness? For if I judge that the wax is or exists from the fact that I see it, it certainly follows much more clearly that I am or that I exist myself from the fact that I see it. For it may be that what I see is not really wax, it may also be that I do not possess eyes with which to see anything; but it cannot be that when I see, or (for I no

longer take account of the distinction) when I think
see, that I myself who think am nought. So if I judg
that the wax exists from the fact that I touch it, th
same thing will follow, to wit, that I am; and if
judge that my imagination, or some other cause, what
ever it is, persuades me that the wax exists, I shal
still conclude the same. And what I have here remarke
of wax may be applied to all other things which ar
external to me [and which are met with outside of me]
And further, if the [notion or] perception of wax ha
seemed to me clearer and more distinct, not only afte
the sight or the touch, but also after many other cause
have rendered it quite manifest to me, with how mucl
more [evidence] and distinctness must it be said tha
I now know myself, since all the reasons which contribute to the knowledge of wax, or any other body whatever, are yet better proofs of the nature of my mind
And there are so many other things in the mind itself
which may contribute to the elucidation of its nature,
that those which depend on body such as these just
mentioned, hardly merit being taken into account.

But finally here I am, having insensibly reverted to
the point I desired, for, since it is now manifest to me
that even bodies are not properly speaking known by
the senses or by the faculty of imagination, but by the
understanding only, and since they are not known from
the fact that they are seen or touched, but only because
they are understood, I see clearly that there is nothing
which is easier for me to know than my mind. But
because it is difficult to rid oneself so promptly of an
opinion to which one was accustomed for so long, it will
be well that I should halt a little at this point, so that
by the length of my meditation I may more deeply im-
print on my memory this new knowledge.

MEDITATION III - *summary p. 80*

Of God: that He exists.

I shall now close my eyes, I shall stop my ears, I shall call away all my senses, I shall efface even from my thoughts all the images of corporeal things, or at least (for that is hardly possible) I shall esteem them as vain and false; and thus holding converse only with myself and considering my own nature, I shall try little by little to reach a better knowledge of and a more familiar acquaintanceship with myself. <u>I am a thing that thinks</u>, that is to say, that doubts, affirms, denies, that knows a few things, that is ignorant of many [that loves, that hates], that wills, that desires, that also imagines and perceives; for as I remarked before, although the things which I perceive and imagine are perhaps nothing at all apart from me and in themselves, I am nevertheless assured that these modes of thought that I call perceptions and imaginations, inasmuch only as they are modes of thought, certainly reside [and are met with] in me.

And in the little that I have just said, <u>I think I have summed up all that I really know</u>, or at least all that hitherto I was aware that I knew. In order to try to extend my knowledge further, I shall now look around more carefully and see whether I cannot still discover in myself some other things which I have not hitherto perceived. I am certain that I am a thing which thinks; but do I not then likewise know what is requisite to render me certain of a truth? Certainly in this first knowledge there is nothing that assures me of its truth, excepting the clear and distinct perception of that which I state, which would not indeed suffice to assure me that what I say is true, if it could ever happen that a thing which I conceived so clearly and distinctly could

cf Hobbes Repetitions, p. 133

be false; and accordingly it seems to me that already I can establish as a general rule that all things which I perceive very clearly and very distinctly are true.

At the same time I have before received and admitted many things to be very certain and manifest, which yet I afterwards recognised as being dubious. What then were these things? They were the earth, sky, stars and all other objects which I apprehended by means of the senses. But what did I clearly [and distinctly] perceive in them? Nothing more than that the ideas or thoughts of these things were presented to my mind. And not even now do I deny that these ideas are met with in me. But there was yet another thing which I affirmed, and which, owing to the habit which I had formed of believing it, I thought I perceived very clearly, although in truth I did not perceive it at all, to wit, that there were objects outside of me from which these ideas proceeded, and to which they were entirely similar. And it was in this that I erred, or, if perchance my judgment was correct, this was not due to any knowledge arising from my perception.

But when I took anything very simple and easy in the sphere of arithmetic or geometry into consideration, e.g. that two and three together made five, and other things of the sort, were not these present to my mind so clearly as to enable me to affirm that they were true? Certainly if I judged that since such matters could be doubted, this would not have been so for any other reason than that it came into my mind that perhaps a God might have endowed me with such a nature that I may have been deceived even concerning things which seemed to me most manifest. But every time that this preconceived opinion of the sovereign power of a God presents itself to my thought, I am constrained to confess that it is easy to Him, if He wishes it, to cause

me to err, even in matters in which I believe myself
to have the best evidence. And, on the other hand,
always when I direct my attention to things which I
believe myself to perceive very clearly, I am so persuaded of their truth that I let myself break out into
words such as these: Let who will deceive me, He can
never cause me to be nothing while I think that I am,
or some day cause it to be true to say that I have never
been, it being true now to say that I am, or that two
and three make more or less than five, or any such thing
in which I see no reason to believe that there is a God
who is a deceiver, and as I have not yet satisfied myself
that there is a God at all, the reason for doubt which depends on this opinion alone is very slight, and so to speak
metaphysical. But in order to be able altogether to remove it, I must inquire whether there is a God as soon as
the occasion presents itself; and if I find that there is a
God, I must also inquire whether He may be a deceiver;
for without a knowledge of these two truths I do not
see that I can ever be certain of anything.

And in order that I may have an opportunity of
inquiring into this in an orderly way [without interrupt-
ing the order of meditation which I have proposed to
myself, and which is little by little to pass from the
notions which I find first of all in my mind to those which
I shall later on discover in it] it is requisite that I
should consider in which of these kinds there is, properly
speaking, truth or error to be found. Of my thoughts
some are, so to speak, images of the things, and to these
alone is the title 'idea' properly applied; examples are
my thought of a man or of a chimera, of heaven, of an
angel, or [even] of God. But other thoughts possess
other forms as well. For example in willing, fearing,
approving, denying, though I always perceive something as the subject of the action of my mind, yet by

this action I always add something else to the idea which I have of that thing; and of the thoughts of this kind some are called volitions or affections, and others judgments.

Now as to what concerns ideas, if we consider them only in themselves and do not relate them to anything else beyond themselves, they cannot properly speaking be false; for whether I imagine a goat or a chimera, it is not the less true that I imagine the one than the other. We must not fear likewise that falsity can enter into will and into affections, for although I may desire evil things, or even things that never existed, it is not the less true that I desire them. Thus there remains no more than the judgments which we make, in which I must take the greatest care not to deceive myself. But the principal error and the commonest which we may meet with in them, consists in my judging that the ideas which are in me are similar or conformable to the things which are outside me; for without doubt if I considered the ideas only as certain modes of my thoughts, without trying to relate them to anything beyond, they could scarcely give me material for error.

But among these ideas, some appear to me to be innate, some adventitious, and others to be formed [or invented] by myself; for, as I have the power of understanding what is called a thing, or a truth, or a thought, it appears to me that I hold this power from no other source than my own nature. But if I now hear some sound, if I see the sun, or feel the heat, I have hitherto judged that these sensations proceeded from certain things that exist outside of me; and finally it appears to me that sirens, hippogryphs, and the like, are formed out of my own mind. But again I may possibly persuade myself that all these ideas are of the nature of those which I term adventitious, or else they are all innate, or all fictitious: for I have not yet clearly discovered their true origin.

And my principal task in this place is to consider, in respect to those ideas which appear to me to proceed from certain objects that are outside me, what are the reasons which cause me to think them similar to these objects. It seems indeed in the first place that I am taught this lesson by nature; and, secondly, I experience in myself that these ideas do not depend on my will nor therefore on myself—for they often present themselves to my mind in spite of my will. Just now, for instance, whether I will or whether I do not will, I feel heat, and thus I persuade myself that this feeling, or at least this idea of heat, is produced in me by something which is different from me, i.e. by the heat of the fire near which I sit. And nothing seems to me more obvious than to judge that this object imprints its likeness rather than anything else upon me.

Now I must discover whether these proofs are sufficiently strong and convincing. When I say that I am so instructed by nature, I merely mean a certain spontaneous inclination which impels me to believe in this connection, and not a natural light which makes me recognise that it is true. But these two things are very different; for I cannot doubt that which the natural light causes me to believe to be true, as, for example, it has shown me that I am from the fact that I doubt, or other facts of the same kind. And I possess no other faculty whereby to distinguish truth from falsehood, which can teach me that what this light shows me to be true is not really true, and no other faculty that is equally trustworthy. But as far as [apparently] natural impulses are concerned, I have frequently remarked, when I had to make active choice between virtue and vice, that they often enough led me to the

part that was worse; and this is why I do not see any
reason for following them in what regards truth and
error.

2) And as to the other reason, which is that these ideas
must proceed from objects outside me, since they do
not depend on my will, I do not find it any more convincing. For just as these impulses of which I have
spoken are found in me, notwithstanding that they do
not always concur with my will, so perhaps there is in
me some faculty fitted to produce these ideas without
the assistance of any external things, even though it is
not yet known by me; just as, apparently, they have
hitherto always been found in me during sleep without
the aid of any external objects.

3) And finally, though they did proceed from objects
different from myself, it is not a necessary consequence
that they should resemble these. On the contrary, I
have noticed that in many cases there was a great
difference between the object and its idea. I find, for
example, two completely diverse ideas of the sun in my
mind; the one derives its origin from the senses, and
should be placed in the category of adventitious ideas,
according to this idea the sun seems to be extremely
small; but the other is derived from astronomical reasonings, i.e. is elicited from certain notions that are innate
in me, or else it is formed by me in some other manner;
in accordance with it the sun appears to be several
times greater than the earth. These two ideas cannot,
indeed, both resemble the same sun, and reason makes me
believe that the one which seems to have originated
directly from the sun itself, is the one which is most
dissimilar to it.

All this causes me to believe that until the present
time it has not been by a judgment that was certain
[or premeditated], but only by a sort of blind impulse

that I believed that things existed outside of, and different from me, which, by the organs of my senses, or by some other method whatever it might be, conveyed these ideas or images to me [and imprinted on me their similitudes].

But there is yet another method of inquiring whether any of the objects of which I have ideas within me exist outside of me. If ideas are only taken as certain modes of thought, I recognise amongst them no difference or inequality, and all appear to proceed from me in the same manner; but when we consider them as images, one representing one thing and the other another, it is clear that they are very different one from the other. There is no doubt that those which represent to me substances are something more, and contain so to speak more objective reality within them [that is to say, by representation participate in a higher degree of being or perfection] than those that simply represent modes or accidents; and that idea again by which I understand a supreme God, eternal, infinite, [immutable], omniscient, omnipotent, and Creator of all things which are outside of Himself, has certainly more objective reality in itself than those ideas by which finite substances are represented.

Now it is manifest by the natural light that there must at least be as much reality in the efficient and total cause as in its effect. For, pray, whence can the effect derive its reality, if not from its cause? And in what way can this cause communicate this reality to it, unless it possessed it in itself? And from this it follows, not only that something cannot proceed from nothing, but likewise that what is more perfect—that is to say, which has more reality within itself—cannot proceed from the less perfect. And this is not only evidently true of those effects which possess actual or formal reality, but also of the ideas in which we consider merely what is termed objective reality. To take an example, the stone which has not yet existed not only cannot now commence to be unless it has been produced by something which possesses within itself, either formally or eminently, all that enters into the composition of the stone [i.e. it must possess the same things or other more excellent things than those which exist in the stone] and heat can only be produced in a subject in which it did not previously exist by a cause that is of an order [degree or kind] at least as perfect as heat, and so in all other cases. But further, the idea of heat, or of a stone, cannot exist in me unless it has been placed within me by some cause which possesses within it at least as much reality as that which I conceive to exist in the heat or the stone. For although this cause does not transmit anything of its actual or formal reality to my idea, we must not for that reason imagine that it is necessarily a less real cause; we must remember that [since every idea is a work of the mind] its nature is such that it demands of itself no other formal reality than that which it borrows from my thought, of which it is only a mode [i.e. a manner or way of thinking]. But in order that an idea should contain some one certain objective reality rather than another, it must without doubt derive it from some cause in which there is at least as much formal reality as this idea contains of objective reality. For if we imagine that something is found in an idea which is not found in the cause, it must then have been derived from nought; but however imperfect may be this mode of being by which a thing is objectively [or by representation] in the understanding by its idea, we cannot certainly say that this mode of being is nothing, nor, consequently, that the idea derives its origin from nothing.

Nor must I imagine that, since the reality that I consider in these ideas is only objective, it is not essential that this reality should be formally in the causes of my ideas, but that it is sufficient that it should be found objectively. For just as this mode of objective existence pertains to ideas by their proper nature, so does the mode of formal existence pertain to the causes of those ideas (this is at least true of the first and principal) by the nature peculiar to them. And although it may be the case that one idea gives birth to another idea, that cannot continue to be so indefinitely; for in the end we must reach an idea whose cause shall be so to speak an archtype, in which the whole reality [or perfection] which is so to speak objectively [or by representation] in these ideas is contained formally [and really]. Thus the light of nature causes me to know clearly that the ideas in me are like [pictures or] images which can, in truth, easily fall short of the perfection of the objects from which they have been derived, but which can never contain anything greater or more perfect.

And the longer and the more carefully that I investigate these matters, the more clearly and distinctly do I recognise their truth. But what am I to conclude from it all in the end? It is this, that if the objective reality of any one of my ideas is of such a nature as clearly to make me recognise that it is not in me either formally or eminently, and that consequently I cannot myself be the cause of it, it follows of necessity that I am not alone in the world, but that there is another being which exists, or which is the cause of this idea. On the other hand, had no such an idea existed in me, I should have had no sufficient argument to convince me of the existence of any being beyond myself; for I have made very careful investigation everywhere and up to the present time have been able to find no other ground.

But of my ideas, beyond that which represents me to myself, as to which there can here be no difficulty, there is another which represents a God, and there are others representing corporeal and inanimate things, others angels, others animals, and others again which represent to me men similar to myself.

As regards the ideas which represent to me other men or animals, or angels, I can however easily conceive that they might be formed by an admixture of the other ideas which I have of myself, of corporeal things, and of God, even although there were apart from me neither men nor animals, nor angels, in all the world.

And in regard to the ideas of corporeal objects, I do not recognise in them anything so great or so excellent that they might not have possibly proceeded from myself; for if I consider them more closely, and examine them individually, as I yesterday examined the idea of wax, I find that there is very little in them which I perceive clearly and distinctly. Magnitude or extension in length, breadth, or depth, I do so perceive; also figure which results from a termination of this extension, the situation which bodies of different figure preserve in relation to one another, and movement or change of situation; to which we may also add substance, duration and number. As to other things such as light, colours, sounds, scents, tastes, heat, cold and the other tactile qualities, they are thought by me with so much obscurity and confusion that I do not even know if they are true or false, i.e. whether the ideas which I form of these qualities are actually the ideas of real objects or not [or whether they only represent chimeras which cannot exist in fact]. For although I have before remarked that it is only in judgments that falsity, properly speaking, or formal falsity, can be met with, a certain material falsity may nevertheless be found in ideas, i.e. when these ideas represent what is nothing as though it were something. For example, the ideas which I have of cold and heat are so far from clear and distinct that by their means I cannot tell whether cold is merely a privation of heat, or heat a privation of cold, or whether both are real qualities, or are not such. And inasmuch as [since ideas resemble images] there cannot be any ideas which do not appear to represent some things, if it is correct to say that cold is merely a privation of heat, the idea which represents it to me as something real and positive will not be improperly termed false, and the same holds good of other similar ideas.

To these it is certainly not necessary that I should attribute any author other than myself. For if they are false, i.e. if they represent things which do not exist, the light of nature shows me that they issue from nought, that is to say, that they are only in me in so far as something is lacking to the perfection of my nature. But if they are true, nevertheless because they exhibit so little reality to me that I cannot even clearly distinguish the thing represented from non-being, I do not see any reason why they should not be produced by myself.

As to the clear and distinct idea which I have of corporeal things, some of them seem as though I might have derived them from the idea which I possess of myself, as those which I have of substance, duration, number, and such like. For [even] when I think that a stone is a substance, or at least a thing capable of existing of itself, and that I am a substance also, although I conceive that I am a thing that thinks and not one that is extended, and that the stone on the other hand is an extended thing which does not think, and that thus there is a notable difference between the two conceptions—they seem, nevertheless, to agree in this, that both represent substances. In the same way, when I perceive that I now exist and further recollect that I have in former times existed, and when I remember that I have various thoughts of which I can recognise the number, I acquire ideas of duration and number which I can afterwards transfer to any object that I please. But as to all the other qualities of which the ideas of corporeal things are composed, to wit, extension, figure, situation and motion, it is true that they are not formally in me, since I am only a thing that thinks; but because they are merely certain modes of substance [and so to speak the vestments under which corporeal substance appears to us] and because I myself am also a substance, it would seem that they might be contained in me eminently.

Hence there remains alone the idea of God, concerning which we must consider whether it is not something that is capable of proceeding from me myself. By the name God I understand a substance that is infinite [eternal, immutable], independent, all-knowing, all-powerful, and by which I myself and everything else, if anything else does exist, have been created. Now all these characteristics are such that the more diligently I attend to them, the less do they appear capable of proceeding from me alone; hence, from what has already been said, we must conclude that God necessarily exists.

For although the idea of substance is within me owing to the fact that I am substance, nevertheless I should not have the idea of an infinite substance—since I am finite—if it had not proceeded from some substance which was veritably infinite.

Nor should I imagine that I do not perceive the infinite by a true idea, but only by the negation of the finite, just as I perceive repose and darkness by the negation of movement and of light; for, on the contrary, I see that there is manifestly more reality in infinite substance than in finite, and therefore that in some way I have in me the notion of the infinite earlier than the finite—to wit, the notion of God before that of myself. For how would it be possible that I should know that I doubt and desire, that is to say, that something is lacking to me, and that I am not quite perfect, unless I had within me some idea of a Being more perfect than myself, in comparison with which I should recognise the deficiencies of my nature?

And we cannot say that this idea of God is perhaps materially false and that consequently I can derive it from nought [i.e. that possibly it exists in me because I am imperfect], as I have just said is the case with ideas of heat, cold and other such things; for, on the contrary, as this idea is very clear and distinct and contains within it more objective reality than any other, there can be none which is of itself more true, nor any in which there can be less suspicion of falsehood. The idea, I say, of this Being who is absolutely perfect and infinite, is entirely true; for although, perhaps, we can imagine that such a Being does not exist, we cannot nevertheless imagine that His idea represents nothing real to me, as I have said of the idea of cold. This idea is also very clear and distinct; since all that I conceive clearly and distinctly of the real and the true, and of what conveys some perfection, is in its entirety contained in this idea. And this does not cease to be true although I do not comprehend the infinite, or though in God there is an infinitude of things which I cannot comprehend, nor possibly even reach in any way by thought; for it is of the nature of the infinite that my nature, which is finite and limited, should not comprehend it; and it is sufficient that I should understand

this, and that I should judge that all things which I
clearly perceive and in which I know that there is some
perfection, and possibly likewise an infinitude of properties of which I am ignorant, are in God formally or
eminently, so that the idea which I have of Him may
become the most true, most clear, and most distinct of
all the ideas that are in my mind.

*possible
objection*

But possibly I am something more than I suppose
myself to be, and perhaps all those perfections which
I attribute to God are in some way potentially in me,
although they do not yet disclose themselves, or issue
in action. As a matter of fact I am already sensible
that my knowledge increases [and perfects itself] little
by little, and I see nothing which can prevent it from
increasing more and more into infinitude; nor do I see,
after it has thus been increased [or perfected], anything to prevent my being able to acquire by its means
all the other perfections of the Divine nature; nor
finally why the power I have of acquiring these perfections, if it really exists in me, shall not suffice to
produce the ideas of them.

*objection
answered*

1)

At the same time I recognise that this cannot be.
For, in the first place, although it were true that every
day my knowledge acquired new degrees of perfection,
and that there were in my nature many things potentially which are not yet there actually, nevertheless
these excellences do not pertain to [or make the smallest
approach to] the idea which I have of God in whom
there is nothing merely potential [but in whom all is
present really and actually]; for it is an infallible
token of imperfection in my knowledge that it increases

2)

little by little. And further, although my knowledge
grows more and more, nevertheless I do not for that
reason believe that it can ever be actually infinite, since
it can never reach a point so high that it will be unable

to attain to any greater increase. But I understand God to be actually infinite, so that He can add nothing to His supreme perfection. And finally I perceive that the objective being of an idea cannot be produced by a being that exists potentially only, which properly speaking is nothing, but only by a being which is formal or actual.

To speak the truth, I see nothing in all that I have just said which by the light of nature is not manifest to anyone who desires to think attentively on the subject; but when I slightly relax my attention, my mind, finding its vision somewhat obscured and so to speak blinded by the images of sensible objects, I do not easily recollect the reason why the idea that I possess of a being more perfect than I, must necessarily have been placed in me by a being which is really more perfect; and this is why I wish here to go on to inquire whether I, who have this idea, can exist if no such being exists.

And I ask, from whom do I then derive my existence? Perhaps from myself or from my parents, or from some other source less perfect than God; for we can imagine nothing more perfect than God, or even as perfect as He is.

But [were I independent of every other and] were I myself the author of my being, I should doubt nothing and I should desire nothing, and finally no perfection would be lacking to me; for I should have bestowed on myself every perfection of which I possessed any idea and should thus be God. And it must not be imagined that those things that are lacking to me are perhaps more difficult of attainment than those which I already possess; for, on the contrary, it is quite evident that it was a matter of much greater difficulty to bring to pass that I, that is to say, a thing or a substance that thinks, should emerge out of nothing, than it would be to attain

to the knowledge of many things of which I am ignorant, and which are only the accidents of this thinking
substance. But it is clear that if I had of myself
possessed this greater perfection of which I have just
spoken [that is to say, if I had been the author of my
own existence], I should not at least have denied myself the things which are the more easy to acquire [to
wit, many branches of knowledge of which my nature
is destitute] ; nor should I have deprived myself of the
things contained in the idea which I form of God, because there are none of them which seem to me specially
difficult to acquire: and if there were any that were
more difficult to acquire, they would certainly appear to
me to be such (supposing I myself were the origin of
the other things which I possess) since I should discover in them that my powers were limited.

But though I assume that perhaps I have always
existed just as I am at present, neither can I escape
the force of this reasoning, and imagine that the conclusion to be drawn from this is, that I need not seek
for any author of my existence. For all the course of
my life may be divided into an infinite number of parts,
none of which is in any way dependent on the other;
and thus from the fact that I was in existence a short
time ago it does not follow that I must be in existence
now, unless some cause at this instant, so to speak,
produces me anew, that is to say, conserves me. It is
as a matter of fact perfectly clear and evident to all
those who consider with attention the nature of time,
that, in order to be conserved in each moment in which
it endures, a substance has need of the same power and
action as would be necessary to produce and create it
anew, supposing it did not yet exist; so that the light
of nature shows us clearly that the distinction between

creation and conservation is solely a distinction of the reason.

All that I thus require here is that I should interrogate myself, if I wish to know whether I possess a power which is capable of bringing it to pass that I who now am shall still be in the future; for since I am nothing but a thinking thing, or at least since thus far it is only this portion of myself which is precisely in question at present, if such power did reside in me, I should certainly be conscious of it. But I am conscious of nothing of the kind, and by this I know clearly that I depend on some being different from myself.

Possibly, however, this being on which I depend is not that which I call God, and I am created either by my parents or by some other cause less perfect than God. This cannot be, because, as I have just said, it is perfectly evident that there must be at least as much reality in the cause as in the effect; and thus since I am a thinking thing, and possess an idea of God within me, whatever in the end be the cause assigned to my existence, it must be allowed that it is likewise a thinking thing and that it possesses in itself the idea of all the perfections which I attribute to God. We may again inquire whether this cause derives its origin from itself or from some other thing. For if from itself, it follows by the reasons before brought forward, that this cause must itself be God; for since it possesses the virtue of self-existence, it must also without doubt have the power of actually possessing all the perfections of which it has the idea, that is, all those which I conceive as existing in God. But if it derives its existence from some other cause than itself, we shall again ask, for the same reason, whether this second cause exists by itself or through another, until from one step to another, we finally arrive at an ultimate cause, which will be God.

And it is perfectly manifest that in this there can be <u>no regression into infinity</u>, since what is in question is not so much the cause which formerly created me, as that which conserves me at the present time.

Nor can we suppose that several causes may have concurred in my production, and that from one I have received the idea of one of the perfections which I attribute to God, and from another the idea of some other, so that all these perfections indeed exist somewhere in the universe, but not as complete in one unity which is God. On the contrary, the unity, the simplicity or the inseparability of all things which are in God is one of the principal perfections which I conceive to be in Him. And certainly the idea of this unity of all Divine perfections cannot have been placed in me by any cause from which I have not likewise received the ideas of all the other perfections; for this cause could not make me able to comprehend them as joined together in an inseparable unity without having at the same time caused me in some measure to know what they are [and in some way to recognise each one of them].

Finally, so far as my parents [from whom it appears I have sprung] are concerned, although all that I have ever been able to believe of them were true, that does not make it follow that it is they who conserve me, nor are they even the authors of my being in any sense, in so far as I am a thinking being; since what they did was merely to implant certain disposition in that matter in which the self—i.e. the mind, which alone I at present identify with myself—is by me deemed to exist. And thus there can be no difficulty in their regard, but we must of necessity conclude from the fact alone that I exist, or that the idea of a Being supremely perfect— that is of God—is in me, that the proof of God's existence is grounded on the highest evidence.

It only remains to me to examine into the manner in which I have acquired this idea from God; for I have not received it through the senses, and it is never presented to me unexpectedly, as is usual with the ideas of sensible things when these things present themselves, or seem to present themselves, to the external organs of my senses; nor is it likewise a fiction of my mind, for it is not in my power to take from or to add anything to it; and consequently the only alternative is that it is innate in me, just as the idea of myself is innate in me.

And one certainly ought not to find it strange that God, in creating me, placed this idea within me to be like the mark of the workman imprinted on his work; and it is likewise not essential that the mark shall be something different from the work itself. For from the sole fact that God created me it is most probable that in some way he has placed his image and similitude upon me, and that I perceive this similitude (in which the idea of God is contained) by means of the same faculty by which I perceive myself—that is to say, when I reflect on myself I not only know that I am something [imperfect], incomplete and dependent on another, which incessantly aspires after something which is better and greater than myself, but I also know that He on whom I depend possesses in Himself all the great things towards which I aspire [and the ideas of which I find within myself], and that not indefinitely or potentially alone, but really, actually and infinitely; and that thus He is God. And the whole strength of the argument which I have here made use of to prove the existence of God consists in this, that I recognise that it is not possible that my nature should be what it is, and indeed that I should have in myself the idea of a God, if God did not veritably exist—a God, I say, whose idea is in me, i.e. who possesses all those supreme perfections of which our mind may indeed have some idea but without understanding them all, who is liable to no errors or defect [and who has none of all those marks which denote imperfection]. From this it is manifest that He cannot be a deceiver, since the light of nature teaches us that fraud and deception necessarily proceed from some defect.

But before I examine this matter with more care, and pass on to the consideration of other truths which may be derived from it, it seems to me right to pause for a while in order to contemplate God Himself, to ponder at leisure his marvellous attributes, to consider, and admire, and adore, the beauty of his light so resplendent, at least so far as the strength of my mind, which is in some measure dazzled by the sight, will allow me to do so. For just as faith teaches us that supreme felicity of the other life consists only in this contemplation of the Divine Majesty, so we continue to learn by experience that a similar meditation, though incomparably less perfect, causes us to enjoy the greatest satisfaction of which we are capable in this life.

MEDITATION IV - summary p. 87

Of the True and the False.

I have been well accustomed these past days to detach my mind from my senses, and I have accurately observed that there are very few things that one knows with certainty respecting corporeal objects, that there are many more which are known to us respecting the human mind, and yet more still regarding God Himself; so that I shall now without any difficulty abstract my thoughts from the consideration of [sensible or] imaginable objects, and carry them to those which, being withdrawn from all contact with matter, are purely intelligible. And certainly the idea which I possess of the human mind inasmuch as it is a thinking thing, and not extended in length, width and depth, nor participating in anything pertaining to body, is incomparably more distinct than is the idea of any corporeal thing. And when I consider that I doubt, that is to say, that I am an incomplete and dependent being, the idea of a being that is complete and independent, that is of God, presents itself to my mind with so much distinctness and clearness—and from the fact alone that this idea is found in me, or that I who possess this idea exist, I conclude so certainly that God exists, and that my existence depends entirely on Him in every moment of my life—that I do not think that the human mind is capable of knowing anything with more evidence and certitude. And it seems to me that I now have before me a road which will lead us from the contemplation of the true God (in whom all the treasures of science and wisdom are contained) to the knowledge of the other objects of the universe.

For, first of all, I recognise it to be impossible that He should ever deceive me; for in all fraud and deception some imperfection is to be found, and although it may appear that the power of deception is a mark of subtilty or power, yet the desire to deceive without doubt testifies to malice or feebleness, and accordingly cannot be found in God.

In the next place I experienced in myself a certain capacity for judging which I have doubtless received from God, like all the other things that I possess; and as He could not desire to deceive me it is clear that He has not given me a faculty that will lead me to err if I use it aright.

And no doubt respecting this matter could remain, if it were not that the consequence would seem to follow that I can thus never be deceived; for if I hold all that I possess from God, and if He has not placed in me the capacity for error, it seems as though I could never fall into error. And it is true that when I think only of God [and direct my mind wholly to Him], I discover [in myself] no cause of error, or falsity; yet directly afterwards, when recurring to myself, experience shows me that I am nevertheless subject to an infinitude of errors, as to which, when we come to investigate them more closely, I notice that not only is there a real and positive idea of God or of a Being of supreme perfection present to my mind, but also, so to speak, a certain negative idea of nothing, that is, of that which is infinitely removed from any kind of perfection; and that I am in a sense something intermediate between God and nought, i.e. placed in such a manner between the supreme Being and non-being, that there is in truth nothing in me that can lead to error in so far as a sovereign Being has formed me; but that, as I in some degree participate likewise in nought or in non-being, i.e. in so far as I am not myself the supreme Being, and as I find myself subject to an infinitude of imperfections, I ought not to be astonished if I should fall into error. Thus do I recognise that error, in so far as it is such, is not a real thing depending on God, but simply a defect; and therefore, in order to fall into it, that I have no need to possess a special faculty given me by God for this very purpose, but that I fall into error from the fact that the power given me by God for the purpose of distinguishing truth from error is not infinite.

Nevertheless this does not quite satisfy me; for error is not a pure negation [i.e. is not the simple defect or want of some perfection which ought not to be mine], but it is a lack of some knowledge which it seems that I ought to possess. And on considering the nature of

God it does not appear to me possible that He should have given me a faculty which is not perfect of its kind, that is, which is wanting in some perfection due to it. For if it is true that the more skilful the artizan, the more perfect is the work of his hands, what can have been produced by this supreme Creator of all things that is not in all its parts perfect? And certainly there is no doubt that God could have created me so that I could never have been subject to error; it is also certain that He ever wills what is best; is it then better that I should be subject to err than that I should not?

In considering this more attentively, it occurs to me in the first place that I should not be astonished if my intelligence is not capable of comprehending why God acts as He does; and that there is thus no reason to doubt of His existence from the fact that I may perhaps find many other things besides this as to which I am able to understand neither for what reason nor how God has produced them. For, in the first place, knowing that my nature is extremely feeble and limited, and that the nature of God is on the contrary immense, incomprehensible, and infinite, I have no further difficulty in recognising that there is an infinitude of matters in His power, the causes of which transcend my knowledge; and this reason suffices to convince me that the species of cause termed final, finds no useful employment in physical [or natural] things; for it does not appear to me that I can without temerity seek to investigate the [inscrutable] ends of God.

It further occurs to me that we should not consider one single creature separately, when we inquire as to whether the works of God are perfect, but should regard all his creations together. For the same thing which might possibly seem very imperfect with some semblance of reason if regarded by itself, is found to be very perfect if regarded as part of the whole universe; and although, since I resolved to doubt all things, I as yet have only known certainly my own existence and that of God, nevertheless since I have recognised the infinite power of God, I cannot deny that He may have produced many other things, or at least that He has the power of producing them, so that I may obtain a place as a part of a great universe.

Whereupon, regarding myself more closely, and considering what are my errors (for they alone testify to there being any imperfection in me), I answer that they depend on a combination of two causes, to wit, on the faculty of knowledge that rests in me, and on the power of choice or of free will—that is to say, of the understanding and at the same time of the will. For by the understanding alone I [neither assert nor deny anything, but] apprehend the ideas of things as to which I can form a judgment. But no error is properly speaking found in it, provided the word error is taken in its proper signification; and though there is possibly an infinitude of things in the world of which I have no idea in my understanding, we cannot for all that say that it is deprived of these ideas [as we might say of something which is required by its nature], but simply it does not possess these; because in truth there is no reason to prove that God should have given me a greater faculty of knowledge than He has given me; and however skilful a workman I represent Him to be, I should not for all that consider that He was bound to have placed in each of His works all the perfections which He may have been able to place in some. I likewise cannot complain that God has not given me a free choice or a will which is sufficient, ample and perfect, since as a matter of fact I am conscious of a will so extended as to be subject to no limits. And what seems to me very remarkable in this regard is that of all the qualities which I possess there is no one so perfect and so comprehensive that I do not very clearly recognise that it might be yet greater and more perfect. For, to take an example, if I consider the faculty of comprehension which I possess, I find that it is of very small extent and extremely limited, and at the same time I find the idea of another faculty much more ample and even infinite, and seeing that I can form the idea of it, I recognise from this very fact that it pertains to the nature of God. If in the same way I examine the memory, the imagination, or some other faculty, I do not find any which is not small and circumscribed, while in God it is immense [or infinite]. It is free-will alone or liberty of choice which I find to be so great in me that I can conceive no other idea to be more great; it is indeed the case that it is for the most part this will that causes me to know that in some manner I bear the image and similitude of God. For although the power of will is incomparably greater in God than in me, both by reason of the knowledge and the power which, conjoined with it, render it stronger and more efficacious, and by reason of its object, inasmuch as in God it extends to a great many things; it nevertheless does not seem to me greater if I consider it formally and precisely in itself: for the faculty of will consists alone in our having the power of choosing to do a thing or choosing not to do it (that is, to affirm or deny, to pursue or to shun it), or rather it consists alone in the fact that in order to affirm or deny, pursue or shun those things placed before us by the understanding, we act so that we are unconscious that any outside force constrains us in doing so. For in order that I should be free it is not necessary that I should be indifferent as to the choice of one or the other of two contraries; but contrariwise the more I lean to the one—whether I recognise clearly that the reasons of the good and true are to be found in it, or whether God so disposes my inward thought—the more freely do I choose and embrace it. And undoubtedly both divine grace and natural knowledge, far from diminishing my liberty, rather increase it and strengthen it. Hence this indifference which I feel, when I am not swayed to one side rather than to the other by lack of reason, is the lowest grade of liberty, and rather evinces a lack or negation in knowledge than a perfection of will: for if I always recognised clearly what was true and good, I should never have trouble in deliberating as to what judgment or choice I should make, and then I should be entirely free without ever being indifferent.

From all this I recognise that the power of will which I have received from God is not of itself the source of my errors—for it is very ample and very perfect of its kind—any more than is the power of understanding; for since I understand nothing but by the power which God has given me for understanding, there is no doubt that all that I understand, I understand as I ought, and it is not possible that I err in this. Whence then come my errors? They come from the sole fact that since the will is much wider in its range and compass than the understanding, I do not restrain it within the same bounds, but extend it also to things which I do not understand: and as the will is of itself indifferent to these, it easily falls into error and sin, and chooses the evil for the good, or the false for the true.

For example, when I lately examined whether any world existed, and found that from the very fact that I myself existed, I could not prevent myself from believing that a thing I so clearly conceived was true: not that I found myself compelled to do so by some external

cause, but simply because from great clearness in my
mind there followed a great inclination of my will; and I
believed this with so much the greater freedom or spontaneity as I possessed the less indifference towards it.
Now, on the contrary, I not only know that I exist,
inasmuch as I am a thinking thing, but a certain representation of corporeal nature is also presented to my
mind; and it comes to pass that I doubt whether this
thinking nature which is in me, or rather by which I
am what I am, differs from this corporeal nature, or
whether both are not simply the same thing; and I here
suppose that I do not yet know any reason to persuade
me to adopt the one belief rather than the other. From
this it follows that I am entirely indifferent as to which
of the two I affirm or deny, or even whether I abstain
from forming any judgment in the matter.

And this indifference does not only extend to matters
as to which the understanding has no knowledge, but
also in general to all those which are not apprehended
with perfect clearness at the moment when the will is
deliberating upon them: for, however probable are the
conjectures which render me disposed to form a judgment respecting anything, the simple knowledge that I
have that those are conjectures alone and not certain
and indubitable reasons, suffices to occasion me to judge
the contrary. Of this I have had great experience of
late when I set aside as false all that I had formerly
held to be absolutely true, for the sole reason that I
remarked that it might in some measure be doubted.

But if I abstain from giving my judgment on any
thing when I do not perceive it with sufficient clearness
and distinctness, it is plain that I act rightly and am
not deceived. But if I determine to deny or affirm, I
no longer make use as I should of my free will, and if
I affirm what is not true, it is evident that I deceive

myself; even though I judge according to truth, this comes about only by chance, and I do not escape the blame of misusing my freedom; for the light of nature teaches us that the knowledge of the understanding should always precede the determination of the will. And it is in the misuse of the free will that the privation which constitutes the characteristic nature of error is met with. Privation, I say, is found in the act, in so far as it proceeds from me, but it is not found in the faculty which I have received from God, nor even in the act in so far as it depends on Him.

For I have certainly no cause to complain that God has not given me an intelligence which is more powerful, or a natural light which is stronger than that which I have received from Him, since it is proper to the finite understanding not to comprehend a multitude of things, and it is proper to a created understanding to be finite; on the contrary, I have every reason to render thanks to God who owes me nothing and who has given me all the perfections I possess, and I should be far from charging Him with injustice, and with having deprived me of, or wrongfully withheld from me, these perfections which He has not bestowed upon me.

I have further no reason to complain that He has given me a will more ample than my understanding, for since the will consists only of one single element, and is so to speak indivisible, it appears that its nature is such that nothing can be abstracted from it [without destroying it]; and certainly the more comprehensive it is found to be, the more reason I have to render gratitude to the giver.

And, finally, I must also not complain that God concurs with me in forming the acts of the will, that is the judgment in which I go astray, because these acts are entirely true and good, inasmuch as they depend on

God; and in a certain sense more perfection accrues to my nature from the fact that I can form them, than if I could not do so. As to the privation in which alone the formal reason of error or sin consists, it has no need of any concurrence from God, since it is not a thing [or an existence], and since it is not related to God as to a cause, but should be termed merely a negation [according to the significance given to these words in the Schools]. For in fact it is not an imperfection in God that He has given me the liberty to give or withhold my assent from certain things as to which He has not placed a clear and distinct knowledge in my understanding; but it is without doubt an imperfection in me not to make a good use of my freedom, and to give my judgment readily on matters which I only understand obscurely. I nevertheless perceive that God could easily have created me so that I never should err, although I still remained free, and endowed with a limited knowledge, viz. by giving to my understanding a clear and distinct intelligence of all things as to which I should ever have to deliberate; or simply by His engraving deeply in my memory the resolution never to form a judgment on anything without having a clear and distinct understanding of it, so that I could never forget it. And it is easy for me to understand that, in so far as I consider myself alone, and as if there were only myself in the world, I should have been much more perfect than I am, if God had created me so that I could never err. Nevertheless I cannot deny that in some sense it is a greater perfection in the whole universe that certain parts should not be exempt from error as others are than that all parts should be exactly similar. And I have no right to complain if God, having placed me in the world, has not called upon

me to play a part that excels all others in distinction
and perfection.

And further I have reason to be glad on the ground
that if He has not given me the power of never going
astray by the first means pointed out above, which depends on a clear and evident knowledge of all the things
regarding which I can deliberate, He has at least left
within my power the other means, which is firmly to
adhere to the resolution never to give judgment on matters whose truth is not clearly known to me; for although
I notice a certain weakness in my nature in that I cannot continually concentrate my mind on one single
thought, I can yet, by attentive and frequently repeated
meditation, impress it so forcibly on my memory that I
shall never fail to recollect it whenever I have need of it,
and thus acquire the habit of never going astray.

And inasmuch as it in this that the greatest and
principal perfection of man consists, it seems to me
that I have not gained a little by this day's Meditation,
since I have discovered the source of falsity and error.
And certainly there can be no other source than that
which I have explained; for as often as I so restrain
my will within the limits of my knowledge that it forms
no judgment except on matters which are clearly and
distinctly represented to it by the understanding, I can
never be deceived; for every clear and distinct conception is without doubt something, and hence cannot
derive its origin from what is nought, but must of necessity have God as its author—God, I say, who being
supremely perfect, cannot be the cause of any error;
and consequently we must conclude that such a conception [or such a judgment] is true. Nor have I only
learned to-day what I should avoid in order that I may
not err, but also how I should act in order to arrive at
a knowledge of the truth; for without doubt I shall

arrive at this end if I devote my attention sufficiently to those things which I perfectly understand; and if I separate from these that which I only understand confusedly and with obscurity. To these I shall henceforth diligently give heed.

MEDITATION V. *summary p. 57*

Of the essence of material things, and, again, of God, that He exists.

Many other matters respecting the attributes of God and my own nature or mind remain for consideration; but I shall possibly on another occasion resume the investigation of these. Now (after first noting what must be done or avoided, in order to arrive at a knowledge of the truth) my principal task is to endeavour to emerge from the state of doubt into which I have these last days fallen, and to see whether nothing certain can be known regarding material things.

But before examining whether any such objects as I conceive exist outside of me, I must consider the ideas of them in so far as they are in my thought, and see which of them are distinct and which confused.

In the first place, I am able distinctly to imagine that quantity which philosophers commonly call continuous, or the extension in length, breadth, or depth, that is in this quantity, or rather in the object to which it is attributed. Further, I can number in it many different parts, and attribute to each of its parts many sorts of size, figure, situation and local movement, and, finally, I can assign to each of these movements all degrees of duration.

And not only do I know these things with distinctness when I consider them in general, but, likewise [however little I apply my attention to the matter],

I discover an infinitude of particulars respecting numbers, figures, movements, and other such things, whose truth is so manifest, and so well accords with my nature, that when I begin to discover them, it seems to me that I learn nothing new, or recollect what I formerly knew —that is to say, that I for the first time perceive things which were already present to my mind, although I had not as yet applied my mind to them.

And what I here find to be most important is that I discover in myself an infinitude of ideas of certain things which cannot be esteemed as pure negations, although they may possibly have no existence outside of my thought, and which are not framed by me, although it is within my power either to think or not to think them, but which possess natures which are true and immutable. For example, when I imagine a triangle, although there may nowhere in the world be such a figure outside my thought, or ever have been, there is nevertheless in this figure a certain determinate nature, form, or essence, which is immutable and eternal, which I have not invented, and which in no wise depends on my mind, as appears from the fact that diverse properties of that triangle can be demonstrated, viz. that its three angles are equal to two right angles, that the greatest side is subtended by the greatest angle, and the like, which now, whether I wish it or do not wish it, I recognise very clearly as pertaining to it, although I never thought of the matter at all when I imagined a triangle for the first time, and which therefore cannot be said to have been invented by me.

Nor does the objection hold good that possibly this idea of a triangle has reached my mind through the medium of the senses, since I have sometimes seen bodies triangular in shape; because I can form in my mind an infinitude of other figures regarding which we

cannot have the least conception of their ever having
been objects of sense, and I can nevertheless demonstrate various properties pertaining to their nature as
well as to that of the triangle, and these must certainly
all be true since I conceive them clearly.   Hence they
are something, and not pure negation; for it is perfectly
clear that all that is true is something, and I have already fully demonstrated that all that I know clearly is
true.   And even although I had not demonstrated this,
the nature of my mind is such that I could not prevent
myself from holding them to be true so long as I conceive them clearly; and I recollect that even when I
was still strongly attached to the objects of sense, I
counted as the most certain those truths which I conceived clearly as regards figures, numbers, and the other
matters which pertain to arithmetic and geometry, and,
in general, to pure and abstract mathematics.

But now, if just because I can draw the idea of something from my thought, it follows that all which I
know clearly and distinctly as pertaining to this object
does really belong to it, may I not derive from this an
argument demonstrating the existence of God?   It is
certain that I no less find the idea of God, that is to
say, the idea of a supremely perfect Being, in me, than
that of any figure or number whatever it is; and I do
not know any less clearly and distinctly that an [actual
and] eternal existence pertains to this nature than I
know that all that which I am able to demonstrate of
some figure or number truly pertains to the nature of
this figure or number, and therefore, although all that
I concluded in the preceding Meditations were found to
be false, the existence of God would pass with me as at
least as certain as I have ever held the truths of mathematics (which concern only numbers and figures) to be.

This indeed is not at first manifest, since it would seem

to present some appearance of being a sophism. For being accustomed in all other things to make a distinction between existence and essence, I easily persuade myself that the existence can be separated from the essence of God, and that we can thus conceive God as not actually existing. But, nevertheless, when I think of it with more attention, I clearly see that existence can no more be separated from the essence of God than can its having its three angles equal to two right angles be separated from the essence of a [rectilinear] triangle, or the idea of a mountain from the idea of a valley; and so there is not any less repugnance to our conceiving a God (that is, a Being supremely perfect) to whom existence is lacking (that is to say, to whom a certain perfection is lacking), than to conceive of a mountain which has no valley.

But although I cannot really conceive of a God without existence any more than a mountain without a valley, still from the fact that I conceive of a mountain with a valley, it does not follow that there is such a mountain in the world; similarly although I conceive of God as possessing existence, it would seem that it does not follow that there is a God which exists; for my thought does not impose any necessity upon things, and just as I may imagine a winged horse, although no horse with wings exists, so I could perhaps attribute existence to God, although no God existed.

But a sophism is concealed in this objection; for from the fact that I cannot conceive a mountain without a valley, it does not follow that there is any mountain or any valley in existence, but only that the mountain and the valley, whether they exist or do not exist, cannot in any way be separated one from the other. While from the fact that I cannot conceive God without existence, it follows that existence is inseparable from

Him, and hence that He really exists; not that my thought can bring this to pass, or impose any necessity on things, but, on the contrary, because the necessity which lies in the thing itself, i.e. the necessity of the existence of God determines me to think in this way. For it is not within my power to think of God without existence (that is of a supremely perfect Being devoid of a supreme perfection) though it is in my power to imagine a horse either with wings or without wings.

And we must not here object that it is in truth necessary for me to assert that God exists after having presupposed that He possesses every sort of perfection, since existence is one of these, but that as a matter of fact my original supposition was not necessary, just as it is not necessary to consider that all quadrilateral figures can be inscribed in the circle; for supposing I thought this, I should be constrained to admit that the rhombus might be inscribed in the circle since it is a quadrilateral figure, which, however, is manifestly false. [We must not, I say, make any such allegations because] although it is not necessary that I should at any time entertain the notion of God, nevertheless whenever it happens that I think of a first and a sovereign Being, and, so to speak, derive the idea of Him from the storehouse of my mind, it is necessary that I should attribute to Him every sort of perfection, although I do not get so far as to enumerate them all, or to apply my mind to each one in particular. And this necessity suffices to make me conclude (after having recognised that existence is a perfection) that this first and sovereign Being really exists; just as though it is not necessary for me ever to imagine any triangle, yet, whenever I wish to consider a rectilinear figure composed only of three angles, it is absolutely essential that I should attribute to it all those properties which serve to bring about the conclusior

that its three angles are not greater than two right
angles, even although I may not then be considering
this point in particular. But when I consider which
figures are capable of being inscribed in the circle, it is
in no wise necessary that I should think that all quadri
lateral figures are of this number; on the contrary, I
cannot even pretend that this is the case, so long as I
do not desire to accept anything which I cannot con
ceive clearly and distinctly. And in consequence there
is a great difference between the false supposition
such as this, and the true ideas born within me, the firs
and principal of which is that of God. For really I
discern in many ways that this idea is not something
factitious, and depending solely on my thought, but
that it is the true image of a true and immutable nature
first of all, because I cannot conceive anything but God
himself to whose essence existence [necessarily] per
tains; in the second place because it is not possible for
me to conceive two or more Gods in this same position
and, granted that there is one such God who now exists
I see clearly that it is necessary that He should have
existed from all eternity, and that He must exist eter
nally; and finally, because I know an infinitude of other
properties in God, none of which I can either diminish
or change.

For the rest, whatever proof or argument I avai
myself of, we must always return to the point that it is
only those things which we conceive clearly and dis
tinctly that have the power of persuading me entirely
And although amongst the matters which I conceive or
in this way, some indeed are manifestly obvious to all
while others only manifest themselves to those who
consider them closely and examine them attentively
still, after they have once been discovered, the latter
are not esteemed as any less certain than the former

For example, in the case of every right-angled triangle, although it does not so manifestly appear that the square of the base is equal to the squares of the other two sides as that this base is opposite to the greatest angle; still, when this has once been apprehended, we are just as certain of its truth as of the truth of the other. And as regards God, if my mind were not pre-occupied with prejudices, and if my thought did not find itself on all hands diverted by the continual pressure of sensible things, there would be nothing which I could know more immediately and more easily than Him. For is there anything more manifest than that there is a God, that is to say, a Supreme Being, to whose essence alone existence pertains?

And although for a firm grasp of this truth I have need of a strenuous application of mind, at present I only feel myself to be as assured of it as of all that I hold as most certain, but I also remark that the certainty of all other things depends on it so absolutely, that without this knowledge it is impossible ever to know anything perfectly.

For although I am of such a nature that as long as I understand anything very clearly and distinctly, I am naturally impelled to believe it to be true, yet because I am also of such a nature that I cannot have my mind constantly fixed on the same object in order to perceive it clearly, and as I often recollect having formed a past judgment without at the same time properly recollecting the reasons that led me to make it, it may happen meanwhile that other reasons present themselves to me, which would easily cause me to change my opinion, if I were ignorant of the facts of the existence of God, and thus I should have no true and certain knowledge, but only vague and vacillating opinions. Thus, for example, when I consider the nature of a [rectilinear] triangle,

I who have some little knowledge of the principles of geometry recognise quite clearly that the three angles are equal to two right angles, and it is not possible for me not to believe this so long as I apply my mind to its demonstration; but so soon as I abstain from attending to the proof, although I still recollect having clearly comprehended it, it may easily occur that I come to doubt its truth, if I am ignorant of there being a God. For I can persuade myself of having been so constituted by nature that I can easily deceive myself even in those matters which I believed myself to apprehend with the greatest evidence and certainty, especially when I recollect that I have frequently judged matters to be true and certain which other reasons have afterwards impelled me to judge to be altogether false.

But after I have recognised that there is a God—because at the same time I have also recognised that all things depend upon Him, and that He is not a deceiver, and from that have inferred that what I perceive clearly and distinctly cannot fail to be true—although I no longer pay attention to the reasons for which I have judged this to be true, provided that I recollect having clearly and distinctly perceived it no contrary reason can be brought forward which could ever cause me to doubt of its truth; and thus I have a true and certain knowledge of it. And this same knowledge extends likewise to all other things which I recollect having formerly demonstrated, such as the truths of geometry and the like; for what can be alleged against them to cause me to place them in doubt? Will it be said that my nature is such as to cause me to be frequently deceived? But I already know that I cannot be deceived in the judgment whose grounds I know clearly. Will it be said that I formerly held many things to be true and certain which I have afterwards recognised to be false? But I had not had any clear and distinct knowledge of these things, and not as yet knowing the rule whereby I assure myself of the truth, I had been impelled to give my assent from reasons which I have since recognised to be less strong than I had at the time imagined them to be. What further objection can then be raised? That possibly I am dreaming (an objection I myself made a little while ago), or that all the thoughts which I now have are no more true than the phantasies of my dreams? But even though I slept the case would be the same, for all that is clearly present to my mind is absolutely true.

And so I very clearly recognise that the certainty and truth of all knowledge depends alone on the knowledge of the true God, in so much that, before I knew Him, I could not have a perfect knowledge of any other thing. And now that I know Him I have the means of acquiring a perfect knowledge of an infinitude of things, not only of those which relate to God Himself and other intellectual matters, but also of those which pertain to corporeal nature in so far as it is the object of pure mathematics [which have no concern with whether it exists or not].

MEDITATION VI — summary p. 88

Of the existence of Material Things, and of the real distinction between the Soul and Body of Man.

Nothing further now remains but to inquire whether material things exist. And certainly I at least know that these may exist in so far as they are considered as the objects of pure mathematics, since in this aspect I perceive them clearly and distinctly. For there is no doubt that God possesses the power to produce everything that I am capable of perceiving with distinctness,

and I have never deemed that anything was impossible
for Him, unless I found a contradiction in attempting
to conceive it clearly. Further, the faculty of imagination which I possess, and of which, experience tells
me, I make use when I apply myself to the consideration
of material things, is capable of persuading me of their
existence; for when I attentively consider what imagination is, I find that it is nothing but a certain application of the faculty of knowledge to the body which is
immediately present to it, and which therefore exists.

And to render this quite clear, I remark in the first
place the difference that exists between the imagination
and pure intellection [or conception]. For example
when I imagine a triangle, I do not conceive it only as
a figure comprehended by three lines, but I also apprehend these three lines as present by the power and
inward vision of my mind, and this is what I call imagining. But if I desire to think of a chiliagon, I certainly
conceive truly that it is a figure composed of a thousand
sides, just as easily as I conceive of a triangle that it is
a figure of three sides only; but I cannot in any way
imagine the thousand sides of a chiliagon [as I do the
three sides of a triangle], nor do I, so to speak, regard
them as present [with the eyes of my mind]. And
although in accordance with the habit I have formed of
always employing the aid of my imagination when I
think of corporeal things, it may happen that in imagining a chiliagon I confusedly represent to myself some
figure, yet it is very evident that this figure is not a
chiliagon, since it in no way differs from that which I
represent to myself when I think of a myriagon or any
other many-sided figure; nor does it serve my purpose
in discovering the properties which go to form the distinction between a chiliagon and other polygons. But
if the question turns upon a pentagon, it is quite true

that I can conceive its figure as well as that of a chiliagon without the help of my imagination; but I can also
imagine it by applying the attention of my mind to each
of its five sides, and at the same time to the space which
they enclose. And thus clearly I recognise that I have
need of a particular effort of mind in order to effect
the act of imagination, such as I do not require in order
to understand, and this particular effort of mind clearly
manifests the difference which exists between imagination and pure intellection.

I remark besides that this power of imagination which
is in one, inasmuch as it differs from the power of understanding, is in no wise a necessary element in my nature,
or in [my essence, that is to say, in] the essence of my
mind; for although I did not possess it I should doubtless ever remain the same as I now am, from which it
appears that we might conclude that it depends on
something which differs from me. And I easily conceive that if some body exists with which my mind is
conjoined and united in such a way that it can apply
itself to consider it when it pleases, it may be that by
this means it can imagine corporeal objects; so that
this mode of thinking differs from pure intellection only
inasmuch as mind in its intellectual activity in some
manner turns on itself, and considers some of the ideas
which it possesses in itself; while in imagining it turns
towards the body, and there beholds in it something
conformable to the idea which it has either conceived
of itself or perceived by the senses. I easily understand, I say, that the imagination could be thus constituted if it is true that body exists; and because I can
discover no other convenient mode of explaining it, I
conjecture with probability that body does exist; but
this is only with probability, and although I examine
all things with care, I nevertheless do not find that from

this distinct idea of corporeal nature, which I have in
my imagination, I can derive any argument from which
there will necessarily be deduced the existence of body.

But I am in the habit of imagining many other things
besides this corporeal nature which is the object of pure
mathematics, to wit, the colours, sounds, scents, pain,
and other such things, although less distinctly. And inasmuch as I perceive these things much better through
the senses, by the medium of which, and by the memory,
they seem to have reached my imagination, I believe
that, in order to examine them more conveniently, it is
right that I should at the same time investigate the
nature of sense perception, and that I should see if
from the ideas which I apprehend by this mode of
thought, which I call feeling, I cannot derive some certain proof of the existence of corporeal objects.

And first of all I shall recall to my memory those
matters which I hitherto held to be true, as having perceived them through the senses, and the foundations on
which my belief has rested; in the next place I shall
examine the reasons which have since obliged me to
place them in doubt; in the last place I shall consider
which of them I must now believe.

First of all, then, I perceived that I had a head,
hands, feet, and all other members of which this body—
which I considered as a part, or possibly even as the
whole, of myself—is composed. Further I was sensible
that this body was placed amidst many others, from
which it was capable of being affected in many different
ways, beneficial and hurtful, and I remarked that a certain feeling of pleasure accompanied those that were
beneficial, and pain those which were harmful. And in
addition to this pleasure and pain, I also experienced
hunger, thirst, and other similar appetites, as also certain corporeal inclinations towards joy, sadness, anger

and other similar passions. And outside myself, in addition to extension, figure, and motions of bodies, I remarked in them hardness, heat, and all other tactile qualities, and, further, light and colour, and scents and sounds, the variety of which gave me the means of distinguishing the sky, the earth, the sea, and generally all the other bodies, one from the other. And certainly, considering the ideas of all these qualities which presented themselves to my mind, and which alone I perceived properly or immediately, it was not without reason that I believed myself to perceive objects quite different from my thought, to wit, bodies from which those ideas proceeded; for I found by experience that these ideas presented themselves to me without my consent being requisite, so that I could not perceive any object, however desirous I might be, unless it were present to the organs of sense; and it was not in my power not to perceive it, when it was present. And because the ideas which I received through the senses were much more lively, more clear, and even, in their own way, more distinct than any of those which I could of myself frame in meditation, or than those I found impressed on my memory, it appeared as though they could not have proceeded from my mind, so that they must necessarily have been produced in me by some other things. And having no knowledge of those objects excepting the knowledge which the ideas themselves gave me, nothing was more likely to occur to my mind than that the objects were similar to the ideas which were caused. And because I likewise remembered that I had formerly made use of my senses rather than my reason, and recognised that the ideas which I formed of myself were not so distinct as those which I perceived through the senses, and that they were most frequently even composed of portions of these last, I persuaded

myself easily that I had no idea in my mind which had
not formerly come to me through the senses. Nor was
it without some reason that I believed that this body
(which by a certain special right I call my own) belonged to me more properly and more strictly than any
other; for in fact I could never be separated from it
as from other bodies; I experienced in it and on account
of it all my appetites and affections, and finally I was
touched by the feeling of pain and the titillation of
pleasure in its parts, and not in the parts of other
bodies which were separated from it. But when I inquired, why, from some, I know not what, painful sensation, there follows sadness of mind, and from the
pleasurable sensation there arises joy, or why this
mysterious emotion of the stomach which I call hunger
causes me to desire to eat, and dryness of throat causes
a desire to drink, and so on, I could give no reason excepting that nature taught me so; for there is certainly
no affinity (that I at least can understand) between
the craving of the stomach and the desire to eat, any
more than between the perception of whatever causes
pain and the thought of sadness which arises from this
perception. And in the same way it appeared to me that
I had learned from nature all the other judgments
which I formed regarding the objects of my senses,
since I remarked that these judgments were formed in
me before I had the leisure to weigh and consider any
reasons which might oblige me to make them.

2) But afterwards many experiences little by little destroyed all the faith which I had rested in my senses;
for I from to time to time observed that those towers
which from afar appeared to me to be round, more
closely observed seemed square, and that colossal statues
raised on the summit of these towers, appeared as quite
tiny statues when viewed from the bottom; and so in

an infinitude of other cases I found error in judgments founded on the external senses. And not only in those founded on the external senses, but even in those founded on the internal as well; for is there anything more intimate or more internal than pain? And yet I have learned from some persons whose arms or legs have been cut off, that they sometimes seemed to feel pain in the part which had been amputated, which made me think that I could not be quite certain that it was a certain member which pained me, even although I felt pain in it. And to those grounds of doubt I have lately added two others, which are very general; the first is that I never have believed myself to feel anything in waking moments which I cannot also sometimes believe myself to feel when I sleep, and as I do not think that these things which I seem to find in sleep, proceed from objects outside of me, I do not see any reason why I should have this belief regarding objects which I seem to perceive while awake. The other was that being still ignorant, or rather supposing myself to be ignorant, of the author of my being, I saw nothing to prevent me from having been so constituted by nature that I might be deceived even in matters which seemed to me to be most certain. And as to the grounds on which I was formerly persuaded of the truth of sensible objects, I had not much trouble in replying to them. For since nature seemed to cause me to lean towards many things from which reason repelled me, I did not believe that I should trust much to the teachings of nature. And although the ideas which I receive by the senses do not depend on my will, I did not think that one should for that reason conclude that they proceeded from things different from myself, since possibly some faculty might be discovered in me—though hitherto unknown to me—which produced them.

3)

But now that I begin to know myself better, and to discover more clearly the author of my being, I do not in truth think that I should rashly admit all the matters which the senses seem to teach us, but, on the other hand, I do not think that I should doubt them all universally.

And first of all, because I know that all things which I apprehend clearly and distinctly can be created by God as I apprehend them, it suffices that I am able to apprehend one thing apart from another clearly and distinctly in order to be certain that the one is different from the other, since they may be made to exist in separation at least by the omnipotence of God; and it does not signify by what power this separation is made in order to compel me to judge them to be different: and, therefore, just because I know certainly that I exist, and that meanwhile I do not remark that any other thing necessarily pertains to my nature or essence, excepting that I am a thinking thing, I rightly conclude that my essence consists solely in the fact that I am a thinking thing [or a substance whose whole essence or nature is to think]. And although possibly (or rather certainly, as I shall say in a moment) I possess a body with which I am very intimately conjoined, yet because, on the one side, I have a clear and distinct idea of myself inasmuch as I am only a thinking and unextended thing, and as, on the other, I possess a distinct idea of body, inasmuch as it is only an extended and unthinking thing, it is certain that this I [that is to say, my soul by which I am what I am], is entirely and absolutely distinct from my body, and can exist without it.

I further find in myself faculties employing modes of thinking peculiar to themselves, to wit, the faculties of imagination and feeling, without which I can easily conceive myself clearly and distinctly as a complete being; while, on the other hand, they cannot be so conceived apart from me, that is without an intelligent substance in which they reside, for [in the notion we have of these faculties, or, to use the language of the Schools] in their formal concept, some kind of intellection is comprised, from which I infer that they are distinct from me as its modes are from a thing. I observe also in me some other faculties such as that of change of position, the assumption of different figures and such like, which cannot be conceived, any more than can the preceding, apart from some substance to which they are attached, and consequently cannot exist without it; but it is very clear that these faculties, if it be true that they exist, must be attached to some corporeal or extended substance, and not to an intelligent substance, since in the clear and distinct conception of these there is some sort of extension found to be present, but no intellection at all. There is certainly further in me a certain passive faculty of perception, that is, of receiving and recognising the ideas of sensible things, but this would be useless to me [and I could in no way avail myself of it], if there were not either in me or in some other thing another active faculty capable of forming and producing these ideas. But this active faculty cannot exist in me [inasmuch as I am a thing that thinks] seeing that it does not presuppose thought, and also that those ideas are often produced in me without my contributing in any way to the same, and often even against my will; it is thus necessarily the case that the faculty resides in some substance different from me in which all the reality which is objectively in the ideas that are produced by this faculty is formally or eminently contained, as I remarked before. And this substance is either a body, that is, a corporeal nature in which there is contained formally [and really] all that which is objectively [and by representation] in those ideas, or it is God Himself, or some other creature more noble than body in which that same is contained eminently. But, since God is no deceiver, it is very manifest that He does not communicate to me these ideas immediately and by Himself, nor yet by the intervention of some creature in which their reality is not formally, but only eminently, contained. For since He has given me no faculty to recognise that this is the case, but, on the other hand, a very great inclination to believe [that they are sent to me or] that they are conveyed to me by corporeal objects, I do not see how He could be defended from the accusation of deceit if these ideas were produced by causes other than corporeal objects. Hence we must allow that corporeal things exist. However, they are perhaps not exactly what we perceive by the senses, since this comprehension by the senses is in many instances very obscure and confused; but we must at least admit that all things which I conceive in them clearly and distinctly, that is to say, all things which, speaking generally, are comprehended in the object of pure mathematics, are truly to be recognised as external objects.

As to other things, however, which are either particular only, as, for example, that the sun is of such and such a figure, etc., or which are less clearly and distinctly conceived, such as light, sound, pain and the like, it is certain that although they are very dubious and uncertain, yet on the sole ground that God is not a deceiver, and that consequently He has not permitted any falsity to exist in my opinion which he has not likewise given me the faculty of correcting, I may assuredly hope to conclude that I have within me the means of arriving at the truth even here. And first of all there is no doubt that in all things which nature teaches me there is some truth contained; for by nature, considered in general, I now understand no other thing than either God Himself or else the order and disposition which God has established in created things; and by my nature in particular I understand no other thing than the complexus of all the things which God has given me.

But there is nothing which this nature teaches me more expressly [nor more sensibly] than that I have a body which is adversely affected when I feel pain, which has need of food or drink when I experience the feelings of hunger and thirst, and so on; nor can I doubt there being some truth in all this.

Nature also teaches me by these sensations of pain, hunger, thirst, etc., that I am not only lodged in my body as a pilot in a vessel, but that I am very closely united to it, and so to speak so intermingled with it that I seem to compose with it one whole. For if that were not the case, when my body is hurt, I, who am merely a thinking thing, should not feel pain, for I should perceive this wound by the understanding only, just as the sailor perceives by sight when something is damaged in his vessel; and when my body has need of drink or food, I should clearly understand the fact without being warned of it by confused feelings of hunger and thirst. For all these sensations of hunger, thirst, pain, etc., are in truth none other than certain confused modes of thought which are produced by the union and apparent intermingling of mind and body.

Moreover, nature teaches me that many other bodies exist around mine, of which some are to be avoided, and others sought after. And certainly from the fact that I am sensible of different sorts of colours, sounds, scents, tastes, heat, hardness, etc., I very easily conclude

that there are in the bodies from which all these diverse
sense-perceptions proceed certain variations which answer to them, although possibly these are not really
at all similar to them. And also from the fact that
amongst these different sense-perceptions some are very
agreeable to me and others disagreeable, it is quite certain that my body (or rather myself in my entirety,
inasmuch as I am formed of body and soul) may receive
different impressions agreeable and disagreeable from
the other bodies which surround it.

But there are many other things which nature seems
to have taught me, but which at the same time I have
never really received from her, but which have been
brought about in my mind by a certain habit which I
have of forming inconsiderate judgments on things;
and thus it may easily happen that these judgments
contain some error. Take, for example, the opinion
which I hold that all space in which there is nothing
that affects [or makes an impression on] my senses
is void; that in a body which is warm there is something entirely similar to the idea of heat which is in
me; that in a white or green body there is the same
whiteness or greenness that I perceive; that in a bitter
or sweet body there is the same taste, and so on in other
instances; that the stars, the towers, and all other distant bodies are of the same figure and size as they appear from far off to our eyes, etc. But in order that
in this there should be nothing which I do not conceive
distinctly, I should define exactly what I really understand when I say that I am taught somewhat by nature.
For here I take nature in a more limited signification
than when I term it the sum of all the things given me
by God, since in this sum many things are comprehended
which only pertain to mind (and to these I do not refer
in speaking of nature) such as the notion which I have

of the fact that what has once been done cannot ever be undone and an infinitude of such things which I know by the light of nature [without the help of the body]; and seeing that it comprehends many other matters besides which only pertain to body, and are no longer here contained under the name of nature, such as the quality of weight which it possesses and the like, with which I also do not deal; for in talking of nature I only treat of those things given by God to me as a being composed of mind and body. But the nature here described truly teaches me to flee from things which cause the sensation of pain, and seek after the things which communicate to me the sentiment of pleasure and so forth; but I do not see that beyond this it teaches me that from those diverse sense-perceptions we should ever form any conclusion regarding things outside of us, without having [carefully and maturely] mentally examined them beforehand. For it seems to me that it is mind alone, and not mind and body in conjunction, that is requisite to a knowledge of the truth in regard to such things. Thus, although a star makes no larger an impression on my eye than the flame of a little candle there is yet in me no real or positive propensity impelling me to believe that it is not greater than that flame; but I have judged it to be so from my earliest years, without any rational foundation. And although in approaching fire I feel heat, and in approaching it a little too near I even feel pain, there is at the same time no reason in this which could persuade me that there is in the fire something resembling this heat any more than there is in pain something resembling it; all that I have any reason to believe from this is, that there is something in it, whatever it may be, which excites in me these sensations of heat or of pain. So also, although there are spaces in which I find nothing which

excites my senses, I must not from that conclude that
these spaces contain no body; for I see in this, as in
other similar things, that I have been in the habit of
perverting the order of nature, because these perceptions of sense having been placed within me by nature
merely for the purpose of signifying to my mind what
things are beneficial or hurtful to the composite whole
on which it forms a part, and being up to that point
sufficiently clear and distinct, I yet avail myself of
them as though they were absolute rules by which I
might immediately determine the essence of the bodies
which are outside me, as to which, in fact, they can
teach me nothing but what is most obscure and confused.

But I have already sufficiently considered how, notwithstanding the supreme goodness of God, falsity
enters into the judgments I make. Only here a new
difficulty is presented—one respecting those things the
pursuit or avoidance of which is taught me by nature,
and also respecting the internal sensations which I
possess, and in which I seem to have sometimes detected
error [and thus to be directly deceived by my own
nature]. To take an example, the agreeable taste of
some food in which poison has been intermingled may
induce me to partake of the poison, and thus deceive
me. It is true, at the same time, that in this case nature
may be excused, for it only induces me to desire food
in which I find a pleasant taste, and not to desire the
poison which is unknown to it; and thus I can infer
nothing from this fact, except that my nature is not
omniscient, at which there is certainly no reason to be
astonished, since man, being finite in nature, can only
have knowledge the perfectness of which is limited.

But we not unfrequently deceive ourselves even in
those things to which we are directly impelled by nature,
as happens with those who when they are sick desire

to drink or eat things hurtful to them. It will perhaps be said here that the cause of their deceptiveness is that their nature is corrupt, but that does not remove the difficulty, because a sick man is none the less truly God's creature than he who is in health; and it is therefore as repugnant to God's goodness for the one to have a deceitful nature as it is for the other. And as a clock composed of wheels and counter-weights no less exactly observes the laws of nature when it is badly made, and does not show the time properly, than when it entirely satisfies the wishes of its maker, and as, if I consider the body of a man as being a sort of machine so built up and composed of nerves, muscles, veins, blood and skin, that though there were no mind in it at all, it would not cease to have the same motions as at present, exception being made of those movements which are due to the direction of the will, and in consequence depend upon the mind [as opposed to those which operate by the disposition of its organs], I easily recognise that it would be as natural to this body, supposing it to be, for example, dropsical, to suffer the parchedness of the throat which usually signifies to the mind the feeling of thirst, and to be disposed by this parched feeling to move the nerves and other parts in the way requisite for drinking, and thus to augment its malady and do harm to itself, as it is natural to it, when it has no indisposition, to be impelled to drink for its good by a similar cause. And although, considering the use to which the clock has been destined by its maker, I may say that it deflects from the order of its nature when it does not indicate the hours correctly; and as, in the same way, considering the machine of the human body as having been formed by God in order to have in itself all the movements usually manifested there, I have reason for thinking that it does not follow the order of nature

when, if the throat is dry, drinking does harm to the
conservation of health, nevertheless I recognise at the
same time that this last mode of explaining nature is
very different from the other. For this is but a purely
verbal characterisation depending entirely on my
thought, which compares a sick man and a badly constructed clock with the idea which I have of a healthy
man and a well made clock, and it is hence extrinsic to
the things to which it is applied; but according to the
other interpretation of the term nature I understand
something which is truly found in things and which is
therefore not without some truth.

But certainly although in regard to the dropsical body
it is only so to speak to apply an extrinsic term when
we say that its nature is corrupted, inasmuch as apart
from the need to drink, the throat is parched; yet in
regard to the composite whole, that is to say, to the
mind or soul united to this body, it is not a purely
verbal predicate, but a real error of nature, for it to
have thirst when drinking would be hurtful to it. And
thus it still remains to inquire how the goodness of
God does not prevent the nature of man so regarded
from being fallacious.

In order to begin this examination, then, I here say,
in the first place, that there is a great difference between mind and body, inasmuch as body is by nature
always divisible, and the mind is entirely indivisible.
For, as a matter of fact, when I consider the mind,
that is to say, myself inasmuch as I am only a thinking
thing, I cannot distinguish in myself any parts, but
apprehend myself to be clearly one and entire; and
although the whole mind seems to be united to the whole
body, yet if a foot, or an arm, or some other part, is
separated from my body, I am aware that nothing has
been taken away from my mind. And the faculties of

willing, feeling, conceiving, etc., cannot be properly speaking said to be its parts, for it is one and the same mind which employs itself in willing and in feeling and understanding. But it is quite otherwise with corporeal or extended objects, for there is not one of these imaginable by me which my mind cannot easily divide into parts, and which consequently I do not recognise as being divisible; this would be sufficient to teach me that the mind or soul of man is entirely different from the body, if I have not already learned it from other sources.

I further notice that the mind does not receive the impressions from all parts of the body immediately, but only from the brain, or perhaps even from one of its smallest parts, to wit, from that in which the common sense is said to reside, which, whenever it is disposed in the same particular way, conveys the same thing to the mind, although meanwhile the other portions of the body may be differently disposed, as is testified by innumerable experiments which it is unnecessary here to recount.

I notice, also, that the nature of body is such that none of its parts can be moved by another part a little way off which cannot also be moved in the same way by each one of the parts which are between the two, although this more remote part does not act at all. As, for example, in the cord *ABCD* [which is in tension] if we pull the last part *D,* the first part *A* will not be moved in any way differently from what would be the case if one of the intervening parts *B* or *C* were pulled, and the last part *D* were to remain unmoved. And in the same way, when I feel pain in my foot, my knowledge of physics teaches me that this sensation is communicated by means of nerves dispersed through the foot, which, being extended like cords from there to the brain, when they are contracted in the foot, at the same time contract the inmost portions of the brain which is their extremity and place of origin, and then excite a certain movement which nature has established in order to cause the mind to be affected by a sensation of pain represented as existing in the foot. But because these nerves must pass through the tibia, the thigh, the loins, the back and the neck, in order to reach from the leg to the brain, it may happen that although their extremities which are in the foot are not affected, but only certain ones of their intervening parts [which pass by the loins or the neck], this action will excite the same movement in the brain that might have been excited there by a hurt received in the foot, in consequence of which the mind will necessarily feel in the foot the same pain as if it had received a hurt. And the same holds good of all the other perceptions of our senses.

4) I notice finally that since each of the movements which are in the portion of the brain by which the mind is immediately affected brings about one particular sensation only, we cannot under the circumstances imagine anything more likely than that this movement, amongst all the sensations which it is capable of impressing on it, causes mind to be affected by that one which is best fitted and most generally useful for the conservation of the human body when it is in health. But experience makes us aware that all the feelings with which nature inspires us are such as I have just spoken of; and there is therefore nothing in them which does not give testimony to the power and goodness of the God [who has produced them]. Thus, for example, when the nerves which are in the feet are violently or more than usually moved, their movement, passing through the medulla of the spine to the inmost parts

of the brain, gives a sign to the mind which makes it feel somewhat, to wit, pain, as though in the foot, by which the mind is excited to do its utmost to remove the cause of the evil as dangerous and hurtful to the foot. It is true that God could have constituted the nature of man in such a way that this same movement in the brain would have conveyed something quite different to the mind; for example, it might have produced consciousness of itself either in so far as it is in the brain, or as it is in the foot, or as it is in some other place between the foot and the brain, or it might finally have produced consciousness of anything else whatsoever; but none of all this would have contributed so well to the conservation of the body. Similarly, when we desire to drink, a certain dryness of the throat is produced which moves its nerves, and by their means the internal portions of the brain; and this movement causes in the mind the sensation of thirst, because in this case there is nothing more useful to us than to become aware that we have need to drink for the conservation of our health; and the same holds good in other instances.

From this it is quite clear that, notwithstanding the supreme goodness of God, the nature of man, inasmuch as it is composed of mind and body, cannot be otherwise than sometimes a source of deception. For if there is any cause which excites, not in the foot but in some parts of the nerves which are extended between the foot and the brain, or even the brain itself, the same movement which usually is produced when the foot is detrimentally affected, pain will be experienced as though it were in the foot, and the sense will thus naturally be deceived; for since the same movement in the brain is capable of causing but one sensation in the mind, and this sensation is much more frequently excited by a cause which hurts the foot than by another existing in some other quarter, it is reasonable that it should convey to the mind pain in the foot rather than in any other part of the body. And although the parchedness of the throat does not always proceed, as it usually does, from the fact that drinking is essential for the health of the body, but sometimes comes from quite a different cause, as is the case with dropsical patients, it is yet much better that it should mislead on this occasion than if, on the other hand, it were always to deceive us when the body is in good health; and so on in similar cases.

And certainly this consideration is of great service to me, not only in enabling me to recognise all the errors to which my nature is subject, but also in enabling me to avoid them or to correct them more easily. For knowing that all my senses more frequently indicate to me truth than falsehood respecting the things which concern that which is beneficial to the body, and being able almost always to avail myself of many of them in order to examine one particular thing, and, besides that, being able to make use of my memory in order to connect the present with the past, and of my understanding which already has discovered all the causes of my errors, I ought no longer to fear that falsity may be found in matters every day presented to me by my senses. And I ought to set aside all the doubts of these past days as hyperbolical and ridiculous, particularly that very common uncertainty respecting sleep, which I could not distinguish from the waking state; for at present I find a very notable difference between the two, inasmuch as our memory can never connect our dreams one with the other, or with the whole course of our lives, as it unites events which happen to us while we are awake. And, as a matter of fact, if someone, while I was awake, quite suddenly appeared to me and disappeared as fast as do the images which I see in sleep, so that I could not know from whence the form came nor whither it went, it would not be without reason that I should deem it a spectre or a phantom formed by my brain [and similar to those which I form in sleep], rather than a real man. But when I perceive things as to which I know distinctly both the place from which they proceed, and that in which they are, and the time at which they appeared to me; and when, without any interruption, I can connect the perceptions which I have of them with the whole course of my life, I am perfectly assured that these perceptions occur while I am waking and not during sleep. And I ought in no wise to doubt the truth of such matters, if, after having called up all my senses, my memory, and my understanding, to examine them, nothing is brought to evidence by any one of them which is repugnant to what is set forth by the others. For because God is in no wise a deceiver, it follows that I am not deceived in this. But because the exigencies of action often oblige us to make up our minds before having leisure to examine matters carefully, we must confess that the life of man is very frequently subject to error in respect to individual objects, and we must in the end acknowledge the infirmity of our nature.

SELECTIONS FROM OBJECTIONS URGED BY CERTAIN MEN OF LEARNING AGAINST THE PRECEDING MEDITATIONS: WITH THE AUTHOR'S REPLIES

FROM THE FIRST SET OF OBJECTIONS[1]

The objection

But he *(Descartes) proceeds,* 'Further, I should like to ask, whether "I" who have this idea could exist, if no such being existed,' *i.e.,* if none existed, 'from which the idea of a being more perfect than I proceeds,' *as he says immediately before.* 'For,' *says he,* 'from what should I proceed? From myself, from my parents, or from some other beings? . . . But, if I were self-originated, neither should I doubt, nor should I wish for anything, nor should I suffer lack of anything whatsoever, for I should have given myself all the perfections of which I have any idea, and should thus myself be God.' '*But, if I am derived from something else, the end of the series of beings from which I come will ultimately be one which is self-originated, and hence what would have held good for myself (if self-originated) will be true of this.*' This is an argument that pursues the same path as that taken by St. Thomas, and which he calls the proof from 'the causality of an efficient cause.' *It is derived from Aristotle. But Aristotle and St. Thomas are not concerned with the causes of ideas. Perhaps they had no need to be, for might not the argu-*

[1] The author of these objections of the first group is Caterus, a priest of Alkmaar.

ment take a more direct and less devious course?—I think, hence I exist; nay I am that very thinking mind, that thinking. But that mind, that thought, springs either from itself or from something else. On the latter alternative, from what does that something else come? If it is self-derived, it must be God? for that which is self-originated will have no trouble in conferring all things on itself.

Descartes' Reply

I have not said that it is impossible for anything to be its own efficient cause; for, although that statement is manifestly true when the meaning of efficient cause is restricted to those causes that are prior in time to their effects or different from them, yet it does not seem necessary to confine the term to this meaning in the present investigation. In the first place the question[1] would in such a case be unmeaning, for who does not know that the same thing can neither be prior to nor different from itself? Secondly, the light of nature does not require that the notion of an efficient cause should compel it to be prior to its effect; on the contrary, a thing does not properly conform to the notion of cause except during the time that it produces its effect, and hence is not prior to it. Moreover, the light of nature certainly tells us that nothing exists about which the question, why it exists, cannot be asked, whether we enquire for its efficient cause, or, if it does not possess one, demand why it does not have one. Hence, if I did not believe that anything could in some way be related to itself exactly as an efficient cause

---

[1] The question 'Can a thing be its own efficient cause?'

is related to its effect, so far should I be from concluding that any first cause existed, that, on the contrary,
I should once more ask for the cause of that which had
been called first, and so should never arrive at the first
of all. But I frankly allow that something may exist
in which there is such a great and inexhaustible power
that it has needed no assistance in order to exist, and
requires none for its preservation, and hence is in a
certain way the cause of its own existence; such a cause
I understand God to be. For, even though I had existed from all eternity and hence nothing had preceded
my existence, none the less, seeing that I deem the
various parts of time to be separable from each other,
and hence that it does not follow that, because I now
exist, I shall in future do so, unless some cause were
so to speak to re-create me at each single moment, I
should not hesitate to call that cause which preserves
me an efficient cause. Thus, even though God has never
been non-existent, yet because He is the very Being who
actually preserves Himself in existence, it seems possible to call Him without undue impropriety the *cause
of His own existence*. But it must be noted that here
I do not mean a preservation which is effected by any
positive operation of causal efficiency but one due merely
to this fact, that the essential nature of God is such
that He cannot be otherwise than always existent.

From these remarks it is easy for me to make my
reply to the distinction in the use of the term 'self-
originated' or *per se,* which, according to the counsel of
my learned theological adversary, requires explanation.
For, although those who, confining themselves to the
peculiar and restricted meaning of efficient cause, think
it impossible for a thing to be its own efficient cause,
and do not discern here another species of cause
analogous to an efficient cause, are accustomed

to understand merely, when they say a thing exists *per se,* that it has no cause; yet, if those people would look to the facts rather than the words, they would easily see that the negative meaning of the term 'self-originated' proceeds merely from the imperfection of the human intellect, and has no foundation in reality, and that there is a certain other positive signification which is drawn from the truth of things and from which alone my argument issues. For if, e.g., anyone should imagine that some body was something *per se,* he can only mean that it has no cause, and he affirms this for no positive reason, but merely in a negative manner, because he knows no cause for it. But this shows some imperfection in his judgment, as he will easily recognize if he remembers that the several parts of time are not derived from one another, and that hence, though that body be supposed to have existed up to the present time *per se,* i.e., without any cause, that will not suffice to make it exist in future, unless there be some power contained in it which continually, as it were, re-creates it; for then, when he sees that no such power is comprised in the idea of body, he will at once conclude that that body does not exist *per se,* taking the expression *per se* positively. Similarly when we say that God exists *per se,* we can indeed understand that negatively, our whole meaning being really that He has no cause. But, if we have previously enquired why He is or why He continues in being, and having regard to the immense and incomprehensible power which exists in the idea of Him we recognise that it is so exceedingly great that it is clearly the cause of His continuing to be, and that there can be nothing else besides it, we say that God exists *per se,* no longer negatively but in the highest positive sense. For, although we need not say that God is the efficient cause of His own self, lest, if we do so, we should be involved in a verbal dispute, yet, because we see that the fact of His existing *per se,* or having no cause other than Himself, issues, not from nothing, but from the real immensity of His power, it is quite permissible for us to think that in a certain sense He stands to Himself in the same way, as an efficient cause does to its effect, and that hence He exists *per se* in a positive sense. Each one may also ask himself whether he exists *per se* in the same sense, and, having found no power in himself sufficient to preserve him through even a moment of time, he will rightly conclude that he depends on something else, and indeed on something else which exists *per se,* because since the matter here concerns the present, not the past or the future, there is no room for an infinite regress. Nay, here I will add a statement I have not hitherto made in writing—that we cannot arrive merely at a secondary cause, but that the cause which has power sufficient to conserve a thing external to it must with all the more reason conserve itself by its own proper power, and so exist *per se.*

FROM THE SECOND SET OF OBJECTIONS[1]

The objection

Sir:

Your endeavour to maintain the cause of the Author of all things against a new race of rebellious giants has sped so well, that henceforth men of worth may hope that in future there will be none who, after attentive study of your Meditations, will not confess that an eternal divine Being does exist, on whom all things depend. Hence we have decided to draw your atten-

---

[1] The second set of objections were collected by the Rev. Father Mersenne from the utterances of divers theologians and philosophers.

ion to certain passages noted beneath and to request you to shed such light upon them that nothing will remain in your work which, if at all demonstrable, is not clearly proved. For, since you have for so many years so exercised your mind by continual meditation, that matters which to others seem doubtful and obscure are to you most evident, and you perhaps know them by a simple intuitive act of mind, without noticing the indistinctness that the same facts have for others, it will be well to bring before your notice those things which need to be more clearly and fully explained and demonstrated. This done, there will scarce remain anyone to deny that those arguments of yours, entered upon for the purpose of promoting the greater glory of God and vast benefit to all mankind, have the force of demonstrations.

In the first place, *pray remember that it was not as an actual fact and in reality, but merely by a mental fiction, that you so stoutly resisted the claim of all bodies to be more than phantasms, in order that you might draw the conclusion that you were merely a thinking being; for otherwise there is perhaps a risk you might believe that you could draw the conclusion that you were in truth nothing other than mind, or thought, or a thinking being. This we find worthy of mention only in connection with the first two Meditations, in which you show clearly that it is at least certain that you, who think, exist. But let us pause a little here. Up to this point you know that you are a being that thinks; but you do not know what this thinking thing is. What if that were a body which by its various motions and encounters produces that which we call thought? For, granted that you rejected the claim of every sort of body, you may have been deceived in this, because you did not rule out yourself, who are a body. For how will you prove that a body cannot think, or that its bodily motions are not thought itself? Possibly even, the whole bodily system, which you imagine you have rejected, or some of its parts, say the parts composing the brain, can unite to produce those motions which we call thoughts. 'I am a thinking thing,' you say; but who knows but you are a corporeal motion, or a body in motion?*

Secondly, from the idea of a supreme being, which, you contend, cannot be by you produced, you are bold enough to infer the necessary existence of the supreme being from which alone can come that idea that your mind perceives. Yet we find in our own selves a sufficient basis on which alone to erect that said idea, even though that supreme being did not exist, or we were ignorant of its existence and did not even think of it though it did exist. Do I not see that I, in thinking, have some degree of perfection? And therefore I conclude that others besides me have a similar degree, and hence I have a basis on which to construct the thought of any number of degrees and so to add one degree of perfection to another to infinity, just as, given the existence of a single degree of light or heat, I can add and imagine fresh degrees up to infinity. Why, on similar reasoning, can I not add, to any degree of being that I perceive in myself any other degree I please, and out of the whole number capable of addition construct the idea of a perfect being? 'But,' you say 'an effect can have no degree of perfection or reality which has not previously existed in its cause.' In reply we urge (passing by the fact that experience shows us that flies and other animals, or even plants are produced by the sun, rain and the earth, in which life, a nobler thing than any merely corporeal grade of being, does not exist, and that hence an effect can derive from its cause some reality which yet is not found in the cause) that that idea is nothing but an entity of reason, which has no more nobility than your mind that thinks it. Besides this, how do you know that that idea would have come before your mind if you had not been nurtured among men of culture, but had passed all your life in some desert spot? Have you not derived it from reflections previously entertained, from books, from interchange of converse with your friends, etc., not from your own mind alone or from a supreme being who exists? You must therefore prove more clearly that that idea could not present itself to you unless a supreme being did exist; though when you show this we shall all confess ourselves vanquished. But it seems to be shown clearly that that idea springs from previous notions by the fact that the natives of Canada, the Hurons, and other savages, have no idea in their minds such as this, which is one that you can form from a previous survey of corporeal things, in such a way that your idea refers only to this corporeal world, which embraces all the perfections that you can imagine; hence you would have up to this point no grounds as yet for inferring more than an entirely perfect corporeal Entity, unless you were to add something else conducting us to the [knowledge of the] incorporeal or spiritual. Let us add that you can construct the idea of an angel (just as you can form the notion of a supremely perfect being) without that idea being caused in you by a [really existing] angel; though the angel has more perfection than you have. But you do not possess the idea of God any more than that of an infinite number or of an infinite line; and though you did possess this, yet there could be no such number. Put along with this the contention that the idea of the unity and simplicity of a sole perfection which embraces all other perfections, is merely the product of the reasoning mind, and is formed in the same way as other universal unities, which do not exist in fact but merely in the understanding, as is illustrated by the cases of generic, transcendental and other unities.

Thirdly, *since you are not yet certain of the aforesaid existence of God, and yet according to your statement, cannot be certain of anything or know anything clearly and distinctly unless previously you know certainly and clearly that God exists, it follows that you cannot clearly and distinctly know that you are a thinking thing, since, according to you, that knowledge depends on the clea: knowledge of the existence of God, the proof of which you have not yet reached at that point where you draw the conclusion that you have a clear knowledge of what you are.*

Take this also, that while an Atheist knows clearly and distinctly that the three angles of a triangle are equal to two right, yet he is far from believing in the existence of God; in fact he denies it, because if God existed there would be a supreme existence, a highest good, i.e., an infinite Being. But the infinite in every type of perfection precludes the existence of anything else whatsoever it be, e.g., of every variety of entity and good, nay even every sort of non-entity and evil; whereas there are in existence many entities, many good things, as well as many non-entities and many evil things. We consider that you should give a solution of this objection, lest the impious should still have some case left them.

Descartes' Reply

GENTLEMEN:

I had much pleasure in reading the criticisms you have passed on my little book dealing with First Philosophy; and I recognise the friendly disposition towards me that you display, united as it is with piety towards God and a zeal to promote His glory. I cannot be otherwise than glad not only that you should think my arguments worthy of your scrutiny, but also that you bring forward nothing in opposition to them to which I do not seem to be able quite easily to reply.

FIRSTLY, you warn me *to remember that it was not actually but merely by a mental fiction that I rejected the claim of bodies to be more than phantasms, in order to draw the conclusion that I was merely a thinking being, so as to avoid thinking that it was a consequence of this that I was really nothing more than mind.* But in the Second Meditation I have already shown that I bore this in mind sufficiently; here are the words:—*But perhaps it is the case that these very things, which I thus suppose to be non-existent because they are unknown to me, do not in very truth differ from that self which I know. I cannot tell; this is not the subject I am now discussing, etc.* By these words I meant expressly to warn the reader that in that passage I did not as yet ask whether the mind was distinct from the body, but was merely investigating these properties of mind of which I am able to attain to sure and evident knowledge. And, since I discovered many such properties, I can only in a qualified sense admit what you subjoin, namely, *That I am yet ignorant as to what a thinking thing is.* For though I confess that as yet I have not discovered whether that thinking thing is the same as the body or something diverse from it, I do not, on that account, admit that I have no knowledge of the mind. Who has ever had such an acquaintance with anything as to know that there was absolutely nothing in it of which he was not aware? But in proportion as we perceive more in anything, the better do we say we know it; thus we have more knowledge of those men with whom we have lived a long time, than of those whose face merely we have seen or whose name we have heard, even though they too are not said to be absolutely unknown. It is in this sense that I think I have demonstrated that the mind, considered apart from what is customarily attributed to the body, is better known than the body viewed as separate from the mind; and this alone was what I intended to maintain.

But I see what you hint at, namely, that since I have written only six Meditations on First Philosophy my readers will marvel that in the first two no further conclusion is reached than that I have just now mentioned, and that hence they will think the meditations to be too meagre, and unworthy of publication. To this I reply merely that I have no fear that anyone who reads with judgment what I have written should have occasion to suspect that my matter gave out; and moreover it appeared highly reasonable to confine to separate Meditations matters which demand a particular attention and must be considered apart from others.

Nothing conduces more to the obtaining of a secure knowledge of reality than a previous accustoming of ourselves to entertain doubts especially about corporeal things; and although I had long ago seen several books written by the Academics and Sceptics about this subject and felt some disgust in serving up again this stale dish, I could not for the above reasons refuse to allot to this subject one whole Meditation. I should be pleased also if my readers would expend not merely the little item which is required for reading it, in thinking over the matter of which the Meditation treats, but would give months, or at least weeks, to this, before going on further; for in this way the rest of the work will yield them a much richer harvest.

Further, since our previous ideas of what belongs to the mind have been wholly confused and mixed up with the ideas of sensible objects, and this was the first and chief reason why none of the propositions asserted of God and the soul could be understood with sufficient clearness, I thought I should perform something worth the doing if I showed how the properties or qualities of the soul are to be distinguished from those of the body. For although many have already maintained that, in order to understand the facts of metaphysics, the mind must be abstracted from the senses, no one hitherto, so far as I know, has shown how this is to be done. The true, and in my judgment, the only way to do this is found in my Second Meditation, but such is its nature that it is not enough to have once seen how it goes; much time and many repetitions are required if we would, by forming the contrary habit of distinguishing intellectual from corporeal matters, for at least a few days, obliterate the life-long custom of confounding them. This appeared to me to be a very sound reason for treating of nothing further in the said Meditation.

But besides this you here ask, *how I prove that a body cannot think.* Pardon me if I reply that I have not yet given ground for the raising of this question, for I first treat of it in the Sixth Meditation. Here are the words:—*In order that I may be sure that one thing is diverse from another, it is sufficient that I should be able to conceive the one apart from the other, etc.,* and shortly afterwards I say: *Although I have a body very closely conjoined with me, yet since, on the one hand, I have a clear and distinct idea of myself, in so far as I am a thinking thing and not extended;*

and, on the other hand, I have a distinct idea of the body in so far as it is an extended, not a thinking thing, it is certain that I (that is the mind [or soul, by which I am what I am]) *am really distinct from my body and can exist without it.* It is easy from this to pass to the following:—*everything that can think is mind or is called mind, but, since mind and body are really distinct, no body is a mind; hence no body can think.*

I do not here see what you are able to deny. Do you deny that in order to recognise a real distinctness between objects it is sufficient for us to conceive one of them clearly apart from the other? If so, offer us some surer token of real distinction. I believe that none such can be found. What will you say? That those things are really distinct each of which can exist apart from the other. But once more I ask how you will know that one thing can be apart from the other; this, in order to be a sign of the distinctness, should be known. Perhaps you will say that it is given to you by the senses, since you can see, touch, etc., the one thing while the other is absent. But the trustworthiness of the senses is inferior to that of the intellect, and it is in many ways possible for one and the same thing to appear under various guises or in several places or in different manners, and so to be taken to be two things. And finally if you bear in mind what was said at the end of the Second Meditation about wax, you will see that properly speaking not even are bodies themselves perceived by sense, but that they are perceived by the intellect alone, so that there is no difference between perceiving by sense one thing apart from another, and having an idea of one thing and understanding that the idea is not the same as an idea of something else. Moreover, this knowledge can be drawn from no other source than the fact that the one thing is perceived apart from the other; nor can this be known with certainty unless the ideas in each case are clear and distinct. Hence that sign you offer of real distinctness must be reduced to my criterion in order to be infallible.

But if any people deny that they have distinct ideas of mind and body, I can do nothing further than ask them to give sufficient attention to what is said in the Second Meditation. I beg them to note that the opinion they perchance hold, namely, that the parts of the brain join their forces with the soul to form thoughts, has not arisen from any positive ground, but only from the fact that they have never had experience of separation from the body, and have not seldom been hindered by it in their operations, and that similarly if anyone had from infancy continually worn irons on his legs, he would think that those irons were part of his own body and that he needed them in order to walk.

SECONDLY, when you say that *in ourselves there is a sufficient foundation on which to construct the idea of God,* your assertion in no way conflicts with my opinion. I myself at the end of the Third Meditation have expressly said that *this idea is innate in me,* or alternatively that it comes to me from no other source than myself. I admit that *we could form this very idea, though we did not know that a supreme being existed,* but not that we could do so *if it were in fact non-existent,* for on the contrary I have notified that *the whole force of my argument lies in the fact that the capacity for constructing such an idea could not exist in me, unless I were created by God.*

Neither does what you say about flies, plants, etc., tend to prove that there can be any degree of perfection in the effect which has not antecedently existed in the cause. For it is certain that either there is no perfec-

tion in animals that lack reason, which does not exist
also in inanimate bodies; or that, if such do exist, it
comes to them from elsewhere, and that sun, rain and
earth are not their adequate causes. It would also be
highly irrational for anyone, simply because he did not
notice any cause co-operating in the production of a
fly, which had as many degrees of perfection as the
fly, though meanwhile he was not sure that no cause
beyond those he has noticed is at work, to make this an
occasion for doubting a truth which, as I shall directly
explain in greater detail, the light of Nature itself
makes manifest.

To this I add that what you say by way of objection
about flies, being drawn from a consideration of material things, could not occur to people who, following
my Meditations, withdraw their thoughts from the
things of sense with a view to making a start with
philosophical thinking.

There is also no more force in the objection you
make in calling our idea of God an entity formed by
thinking. For, firstly, it is not true that it is an *ens
rationis* in the sense in which that means something
non-existent, but only in the sense in which every mental
operation is an *ens rationis,* meaning by this something
that issues from thought; this entire world also could be
called an entity formed by the divine thought, i.e., an
entity created by a simple act of the divine mind.
Secondly, I have already sufficiently insisted in various
places that what I am concerned with is only the perfection of the idea or its objective reality which, not
less than the objective artifice in the idea of a machine
of highly ingenious device, requires a cause in which
is actually contained everything that it, though only
objectively, comprises.

I really do not see what can be added to make it

clearer that that idea[1] could not be present in my consciousness unless a supreme being existed, except that the reader might by attending more diligently to what I have written, free himself of the prejudices that perchance overwhelm his natural light, and might accustom his mind to put trust in ultimate principles, than which nothing can be more true or more evident, rather than in the obscure and false opinions which, however, long usage has fixed in his mind.

That *there is nothing in the effect, that has not existed in a similar or in some higher form in the cause,* is a first principle than which none clearer can be entertained. The common truth *'from nothing, nothing comes'* is identical with it. For, if we allow that there is something in the effect which did not exist in the cause, we must grant also that this something has been created by nothing; again the only reason why nothing cannot be the cause of a thing, is that in such a cause there would not be the same thing as existed in the effect.

It is a first principle *that the whole of the reality or perfection that exists only objectively in ideas must exist in them formally or in a superior manner in their causes.* It is on this alone we wholly rely, when believing that things situated outside the mind have real existence; for what should have led us to suspect their existence except the fact that the ideas of them were borne in on the mind by means of the senses?

But it will become clear to those who give sufficient attention to the matter and accompany me far in my reflections, that we possess the idea of a supreme and perfect being, and also that the objective reality of this idea exists in us neither formally nor eminently. A

---

[1] The idea of God.

truth, however, which depends solely on being grasped by another's thought, cannot be forced on a listless mind.

Now, from these arguments we derive it as a most evident conclusion that God exists. But for the sake of those whose natural light is so exceeding small that they do not see this first principle, viz., *that every perfection existing objectively in an idea must exist actually in something that causes that idea,* I have demonstrated in a way more easily grasped an identical conclusion, from the fact that the mind possessing that idea cannot be self-derived; and I cannot in consequence see what more is wanted to secure your admission that I have prevailed.

Moreover there is no force in your plea, that perchance the idea that conveys to me my knowledge of God has come *from notions previously entertained, from books, from conversations with friends, etc., not from my own mind alone.* For the argument takes the same course as it follows in my own case, if I raise the question whether those from whom I am said to have acquired the idea have derived it from themselves or from any one else; the conclusion will be always the same, that it is God from whom it first originated.

The objection you subjoin, *that the idea of God can be constructed out of a previous survey of corporeal things,* seems to be no nearer the truth than if you should say that we have no faculty of hearing, but have attained to a knowledge of sound from seeing colours alone; you can imagine a greater analogy and parity between colours and sounds than between corporeal things and God. When you ask me *to add something conducting us to* [*the knowledge of*] *an incorporeal and spiritual entity,* I can do nothing better than refer you back to my Second Meditation, so that you may at least see that it is not wholly useless. For what could I achieve here in one or two paragraphs, if the longer discourse to be found there, designed as it were with this very matter in view, and one on which I think I have expended as much care as on anything that I have ever written, has been wholly unsuccessful?

There is no drawback in the fact that in that Meditation I dealt only with the human mind; most readily and gladly do I admit that the idea we have, e.g., of the Divine intellect, does not differ from that we have of our own, except merely as the idea of an infinite number differs from that of a number of the second or third power; and the same holds good of the various attributes of God, of which we find some trace in ourselves.

But, besides this, we have in the notion of God absolute immensity, simplicity, and a unity that embraces all other attributes; and of this idea we find no example in us: it is, as I have said before, *like the mark of the workman imprinted on his work*. By means of this, too, we recognise that none of the particular attributes which we, owing to the limitations of our minds, assign piecemeal to God, just as we find them in ourselves, belong to Him and to us in precisely the same sense. Also we recognise that of various particular indefinite attributes of which we have ideas, as e.g., knowledge whether indefinite or infinite, likewise power, number, length, etc., and of various infinite attributes also, some are contained formally in the idea of God, e.g., knowledge and power, others only eminently, as number and length; and this would certainly not be so if that idea were nothing else than a figment in our minds.

If that were so it would not be so constantly conceived by all in the same way. It is most worthy of note that all metaphysicians are unanimous in their description of the attributes of God (those at least which can be grasped by the human mind unaided); and hence there is no physical or sensible object, nothing of which we have the most concrete and comprehensible idea, about the nature of which there is not more dispute among philosophers.

No man could go astray and fail to conceive that idea of God correctly if only he cared to attend to the nature of an all-perfect being. But those who confuse one thing with another, owing to this very fact utter contradictions; and constructing in their imagination a chimerical idea of God, not unreasonably afterwards deny that a God, who is represented by such an idea, exists. So here, when you talk of *a corporeal being of the highest perfection,* if you take the term 'of the highest perfection' absolutely, meaning that the corporeal thing is one in which all perfections are found, you utter a contradiction. For its very bodily nature involves many imperfections, as that a body is divisible into parts, that each of its parts is not the other, and other similar defects. For it is self-evident that it is a greater perfection not to be divided than to be divided, etc. But if you merely understand what is most perfect in the way of body, this will not be God.

I readily grant your further point, that *in the case of the idea of an angel, than which we are less perfect, there is certainly no need for that idea to be produced in us by an angel;* I myself have already in the third Meditation said that *the idea can be constructed out of those that we possess of God and of man.* There is no point against me here.

Further, those who maintain that they do not possess the idea of God, but in place of it form some image, etc., while they refuse the name concede the fact. I certainly do not think that that idea is of a nature akin to the images of material things depicted in the imagination, but that it is something that we are aware of by an apprehension or judgment or inference of the understanding alone. And I maintain that there is a necessary conclusion from the fact alone that, howsoever it come about, by thought or understanding, I attain to the notion of a perfection that is higher than I; a result that may follow merely from the fact that in counting I cannot reach a highest of all numbers, and hence recognise that in enumeration there is something that exceeds my powers. And this conclusion is, not indeed to the effect that an infinite number does exist, nor yet that it implies a contradiction as you say, but that I have received the power of conceiving that a number is thinkable, that is higher than any that can ever be thought by me, and have received it not from myself but from some other entity more perfect than I.

It is of no account whether or not one gives the name idea to this concept of an indefinitely great number. But in order to understand what is that entity more perfect than I am, and to discover whether it is this very infinite number as an actually existing fact, or whether it is something else, we must take into account all the other attributes that can exist in the being from which the idea originates, over and above the power of giving me that idea; and the result is that it is found to be God.

Finally, when God is said to be *unthinkable,* that applies to the thought that grasps Him adequately, and does not hold good of that inadequate thought which we possess and which suffices to let us know that He exists. It likewise does not matter though *the idea of the unity of all God's perfections is formed in the same way as 'Porphyrian' universals.* Though there is this important difference, that it designates a peculiar and positive perfection in God, while generic unity adds nothing real to the nature of the single individuals it unites.

THIRDLY, when I said that *we could know nothing with certainty unless we were first aware that God existed,* I announced in express terms that I referred only to the science apprehending such conclusions *as can recur in memory without attending further to the proofs which led me to make them.* Further, knowledge of first principles is not usually called science by dialecticians. But when we become aware that we are thinking beings, this is a primitive act of knowledge derived from no syllogistic reasoning. He who says, '*I think, hence I am, or exist,*' does not deduce existence from thought by a syllogism, but, by a simple act of mental vision, recognises it as if it were a thing that is known *per se.* This is evident from the fact that if it were syllogistically deduced, the major premise, *that everything that thinks is, or exists,* would have to be known previously; but yet that has rather been learned from the experience of the individual—that unless he exists he cannot think. For our mind is so constituted by nature that general propositions are formed out of the knowledge of particulars.

That *an atheist can know clearly that the three angles of a triangle are equal to two right angles,* I do not deny, I merely affirm that, on the other hand, such knowledge on his part cannot constitute true science, because no knowledge that can be rendered doubtful should be called science. Since he is, as supposed, an Atheist, he cannot be sure that he is not deceived in the things that seem most evident to him, as has been sufficiently shown; and though perchance the doubt does not occur to him, nevertheless it may come up, if he examine the matter, or if another suggests it; he can never be safe from it unless he first recognises the existence of a God.

And it does not matter though he think he has demonstrations proving that there is no God. Since they are by no means true, the errors in them can always be pointed out to him, and when this takes place he will be driven from his opinion.

This would certainly not be difficult to do, if to represent all his proofs he were to bring into play only that principle you here append, viz., *that what is infinite in every kind of perfection excludes every other entity whatsoever, etc.* For, in the first place, if he is asked whence comes his knowledge that that exclusion of all other entities is a characteristic of the infinite, there is nothing he can reasonably say in reply; for by the word *infinite* neither is he wont to understand that which excludes the existence of finite things, nor can he know anything of the characteristic of that which he deems to be nothing, and to have hence no characteristics at all, except what is contained merely in the meaning he has learned from others to attach to the word. Next, what could be the power of this imaginary infinite if it could never create anything? Finally, because we are aware of some power of thinking within us, we easily conceive that the power of thinking can reside in some other being, and that it is greater than in us. But though we think of it as increased to infinity, we do not on that account fear that the power we have should become less. And the same holds good of all the other attributes we ascribe to God, even that of His might, provided that we assume that no such power exists in us except as subject to the Divine will. Hence evidently He can be known as infinite without any prejudice to the existence of created things.

No difficulty is caused by the objection that *we have*

often found that others have been deceived in matters
which they believed they alone know clearly. For we
have never noticed that this has occurred, nor could
anyone find it to occur with these persons who have
sought to draw the clearness of their vision from the
intellect alone, but only with those who have made either
the senses or some erroneous preconception the source
from which they derived that evidence.

. . . .

SEVENTHLY, in the synopsis of my Meditations I
stated the reason why I have said nothing about the
immortality of the soul. That I have sufficiently proved
its distinctness from any body, I have shown above.
But I admit that I cannot refute your further contention, viz., that *the immortality of the soul does not
follow from its distinctness from the body, because that
does not prevent its being said that God in creating it
has given the soul a nature such that its period of
existence must terminate simultaneously with that of the
corporeal life.* For I do not presume so far as to
attempt to settle by the power of human reason any of
the questions that depend upon the free-will of God.
Natural knowledge shows that the mind is different
from the body, and that it is likewise a substance; but
that the human body, in so far as it differs from other
bodies, is constituted entirely by the configuration of
its parts and other similar accidents, and finally that the
death of the body depends wholly on some division or
change of figure. But we know no argument or example
such as to convince us that the death or the annihilation
of a substance such as the mind is, should follow from
so light a cause as is a change in figure, which is no
more than a mode, and indeed not a mode of mind, but
of body that is really distinct from mind. Nor indeed
is there any argument or example calculated to convince

us that any substance can perish. But this is sufficient to let us conclude that the mind, so far as it can be known by aid of a natural philosophy, is immortal.

But if the question, which asks whether human souls cease to exist at the same time as the bodies which God has united to them are destroyed, is one affecting the Divine power, it is for God alone to reply. And since He has revealed to us that this will not happen, there should be not even the slightest doubt remaining.

It remains for me to thank you for your courtesy and candour in deigning to bring to my notice not only the difficulties that have occurred to you, but also those that can be brought forward by Atheists and people of hostile intent. I see nothing in what you have brought forward of which I have not already in my Meditations given a solution and ruled out of court. (For those objections *about insects bred by the sun, about the natives of Canada, the people of Nineveh, the Turks, etc.,* cannot occur to those who follow the way I have pointed out, and abstract for a time from everything due to the senses, in order to pay heed to the dictates of the pure and uncorrupted reason, and consequently I thought that I had adequately barred them out.) But though this is so, I consider that these objections of yours will aid my purpose. For I scarce expect to have any readers who will care to attend so accurately to all that I have written as to bear in memory all that has gone before, when they have come to the end; and those who do not do so will easily fall into certain perplexities, which they will either find to be satisfactorily explained in this reply of mine, or which will occasion them to examine into the truth still further.

Further, in the matter of the counsel you give me about *propounding my arguments in geometrical fashion, in order that the reader may perceive them as it were with a single glance,* it is worth while setting forth here the extent to which I have followed this method and that to which I intend in future to follow it. Now there are two things that I distinguish in the geometrical mode of writing, viz., the order and the method of proof.

The order consists merely in putting forward those things first that should be known without the aid of what comes subsequently, and arranging all other matters so that their proof depends solely on what precedes them. I certainly tried to follow this order as accurately as possible in my Meditations; and it was through keeping to this that I treated of the distinction between the mind and the body, not in the second Meditation, but finally in the sixth, and deliberately and consciously omitted much, because it required an explanation of much else besides.

Further, the method of proof is two-fold, one being analytic, the other synthetic.

Analysis shows the true way by which a thing was methodically discovered and derived, as it were effect from cause, so that, if the reader care to follow it and give sufficient attention to everything, he understands the matter no less perfectly and makes it as much his own as if he had himself discovered it. But it contains nothing to incite belief in an inattentive or hostile reader; for if the very least thing brought forward escapes his notice, the necessity of the conclusions is lost; and on many matters which, nevertheless, should be specially noted, it often scarcely touches, because they are clear to anyone who gives sufficient attention to them.

Synthesis contrariwise employs an opposite procedure, one in which the search goes as it were from effect to cause (though often here the proof itself is from cause to effect to a greater extent than in the former case). It does indeed clearly demonstrate its conclusions, and it employs a long series of definitions, postulates, axioms, theorems and problems, so that if one of the conclusions that follow is denied, it may at once be shown to be contained in what has gone before. Thus the reader, however hostile and obstinate, is compelled to render his assent. Yet this method is not so satisfactory as the other and does not equally well content the eager learner, because it does not show the way in which the matter taught was discovered.

It was this synthesis alone that the ancient Geometers employed in their writings, not because they were wholly ignorant of the analytic method, but, in my opinion, because they set so high a value on it that they wished to keep it to themselves as an important secret.

But I have used in my Meditations only analysis, which is the best and truest method of teaching. On the other hand synthesis, doubtless the method you here ask me to use, though it very suitably finds a place after analysis in the domain of geometry, nevertheless cannot so conveniently be applied to these metaphysical matters we are discussing.

For there is this difference between the two cases, viz., that the primary notions that are the presuppositions of geometrical proofs harmonise with the use of our senses, and are readily granted by all. Hence, no difficulty is involved in this case, except in the proper deduction of the consequences. But this may be performed by people of all sorts, even by the inattentive, if only they remember what has gone before; and the minute subdivisions of propositions is designed for the purpose of rendering citation easy and thus making people recollect even against their will.

On the contrary, nothing in metaphysics causes more

trouble than the making the perception of its primary notions clear and distinct. For, though in their own nature they are as intelligible as, or even more intelligible than those the geometricians study, yet being contradicted by the many preconceptions of our senses to which we have since our earliest years been accustomed, they cannot be perfectly apprehended except by those who give strenuous attention and study to them, and withdraw their minds as far as possible from matters corporeal. Hence if they alone were brought forward it would be easy for anyone with a zeal for contradiction to deny them.

This is why my writing took the form of Meditations rather than that of Philosophical Disputations or the theorems and problems of a geometer; so that hence I might by this very fact testify that I had no dealings except with those who will not shrink from joining me in giving the matter attentive care and meditation. For from the very fact that anyone girds himself up for an attack upon the truth, he makes himself less capable of perceiving the truth itself, since he withdraws his mind from the consideration of those reasons that tend to convince him of it, in order to discover others that have the opposite effect.

But perhaps some one will here raise the objection, that, while indeed a man ought not to seek for hostile arguments when he knows that it is the truth that is set before him, yet, so long as this is in doubt, it is right that he should fully explore all the arguments on either side, in order to find out which are the stronger. According to this objection it is unfair of me to want to have the truth of my contentions admitted before they have been fully scrutinised, while prohibiting any consideration of those reasonings that oppose them.

This would certainly be a just criticism if any of the

matters in which I desire attention and absence of hostility in my reader were capable of withdrawing him from the consideration of any others in which there was the least hope of finding greater truth than in mine. But consider that in what I bring forward you find the most extreme doubt about all matters, and that there is nothing I more strongly urge than that every single thing should be most carefully examined and that nothing should be admitted but what has been rendered so clear and distinct to our scrutiny that we cannot withhold our assent from it. Consider too that, on the other hand, there is nothing else from which I wish to divert the minds of my readers, save beliefs which they have never properly examined and which are derived from no sound reasoning, but from the senses alone. Therefore I hardly think that anyone will believe that there is much risk in confining his attention to my statement of the case; the danger will be precisely that of turning his gaze away from preconceptions in order to behold new truths that in some measure conflict with them, and dissipate the darkness of the prejudices due to our senses.

Hence, in the first place, I rightly require singular attention on the part of my readers and have specially selected the style of writing which I thought would best secure it and which, I am convinced, will bring my readers more profit than they would acquire if I had used the synthetic method, one which would have made them appear to have learned more than they really had. But besides this I deem it quite fair to ignore wholly and to despise as of no account the criticisms of those who refuse to accompany me in my Meditations and cling to their preconceived opinions.

But I know how difficult it will be, even for one who does attend and seriously attempt to discover the

truth, to have before his mind the entire bulk of what
is contained in my Meditations, and at the same time
to have distinct knowledge of each part of the argument; and yet, in my opinion, one who is to reap the
full benefit from my work must know it both as a
whole and in detail.   Consequently I append here
something in the synthetic style that may I hope be
somewhat to my readers' profit.   I should, however,
like them kindly to notice that I have not cared to
include here so much as comes into my Meditations,
for that would have caused me to be much more prolix
than in the Meditations themselves, nor shall I explain
in such accurate detail that which I do include; this is
partly for brevity and partly to prevent anyone, believing that what is here written is sufficient, examining
without adequate care the actual Meditations, a work
from which, I am convinced, much more profit will be
derived.

FROM THE THIRD SET OF OBJECTIONS[1]

The objection

(In opposition to the Second Meditation, *Concerning
the nature of the Human Mind.*)

I am a thing that thinks; *quite correct.   From the
fact that I think, or have an image, whether sleeping
or waking, it is inferred that I am exercising thought;
for I think and I am exercising thought mean the same
thing.   From the fact that I am exercising thought it
follows that* I am, *since that which thinks is not nothing.
But, where it is added,* this is the mind, the spirit, the
understanding, the reason, *a doubt arises.   For it does*

---

[1] The objections of the "celebrated English philosopher"
Thomas Hobbes.

not seem to be good reasoning to say: I am exercising thought, *hence* I am thought; *or* I am using my intellect, *hence* I am intellect. *For in the same way I might say,* I am walking; *hence* I am the walking. *It is hence an assumption on the part of M. Descartes that that which understands is the same as the exercise of understanding which is an act of that which understands, or, at least, that that which understands is the same as the understanding, which is a power possessed by that which thinks.* Yet all Philosophers distinguish a subject from its faculties and activities, i.e., from its properties and essences; for the* entity *itself is one thing, its* essence *another.* Hence it is possible for a thing that thinks to be the subject of the mind, reason, or understanding, and hence to be something corporeal; and the opposite of this has been assumed, not proved. Yet this inference is the basis of the conclusion that M. Descartes seems to wish to establish.*

In the same place he says, I know that I exist; the question is, who am I—the being that I know? *It is certain that the knowledge of this being thus accurately determined does not depend on those things which I do not yet know to exist.*

It is quite certain that the knowledge of this proposition, I exist, *depends upon that other one,* I think, *as he has himself correctly shown us. But whence comes our knowledge of this proposition,* I think? *Certainly from that fact alone, that we can conceive no activity whatsoever apart from its subject, e.g., we cannot think of leaping apart from that which leaps, of knowing apart from a knower, or of thinking without a thinker.*

And hence it seems to follow that that which thinks is something corporeal; for, as it appears, the subjects of all activities can be conceived only after a corporeal fashion, or as in material guise, as M. Descartes himself afterwards shows, when he illustrates by means of wax, this wax was understood to be always the same thing, i.e. the identical matter underlying the many successive changes, though its colour, consistency, figure and other activities were altered. Moreover it is not by another thought that I infer that I think; for though anyone may think that he has thought (to think so is precisely the same as remembering), yet we cannot think that we are thinking, nor similarly know that we know. For this would entail the repetition of the question an infinite number of times; whence do you know, that you know, that you know, that you know?

Hence, since the knowledge of this proposition, I exist, *depends upon the knowledge of that other, I* think, *and the knowledge of it upon the fact that we cannot separate thought from a matter that thinks, the proper inference seems to be that that which thinks is material rather than immaterial.*

Descartes' Reply

Where I have said, *this is the mind, the spirit, the intellect, or the reason,* I understood by these names not merely faculties, but rather what is endowed with the faculty of thinking; and this sense the two former terms commonly, the latter frequently bear. But I used them in this sense so expressly and in so many places that I cannot see what occasion there was for any doubt about their meaning.

Further, there is here no parity between walking and thinking; for walking is usually held to refer only to that action itself, while thinking applies now to the action, now to the faculty of thinking, and again to that in which the faculty exists.

Again I do not assert that that which understands

and the activity of understanding are the same thing,
nor indeed do I mean that the thing that understands
and the understanding are the same, if the term understanding, be taken to refer to the faculty of understanding; they are identical only when the understanding means the thing itself that understands. I admit
also quite gladly that, in order to designate that thing
or substance, which I wished to strip of everything
that did not belong to it, I employed the most highly
abstract terms I could; just as, on the contrary this
Philosopher uses terms that are as concrete as possible,
e.g., *subject, matter, body,* to signify that which thinks,
fearing to let it be sundered from the body.

But I have no fear of anyone thinking that his
method of coupling diverse things together is better
adapted to the discovery of the truth than mine, that
gives the greatest possible distinctness to every single
thing. But, dropping the verbal controversy, let us
look to the facts in dispute.

A thing that thinks, he says, *may be something corporeal; and the opposite of this has been assumed; not
proved.* But really I did not assume the opposite,
neither did I use it as a basis for my argument; I left
it wholly undetermined until Meditation VI, in which
its proof is given.

Next he quite correctly says, that *we cannot conceive any activity apart from its subject,* e.g., thought
apart from that which thinks, since that which thinks
is not nothing. But, wholly without any reason, and in
opposition to the ordinary use of language and good
Logic, he adds, *hence it seems to follow that that which
thinks is something corporeal;* for *the subjects of all
activities are* indeed *understood as falling within the
sphere of substance* (or even, if you care, *as wearing*

the guise of matter, viz., metaphysical matter), but not on that account are they to be defined as bodies.

On the other hand both logicians and as a rule all men are wont to say that substances are of two kinds, spiritual and corporeal. And all that I proved, when I took wax as an example, was that its colour, hardness, and figure did not belong to the formal nature of the wax itself [i.e., that we can comprehend everything that exists necessarily in the wax, without thinking of these]. I did not there treat either of the formal nature of the mind, or even of the formal nature of body.

Again it is irrelevant to say, as this Philosopher here does, that one thought cannot be the subject of another thought. Who, except my antagonist himself, ever imagined that it could? But now, for a brief explanation of the matter—it is certain that no thought can exist apart from a thing that thinks; no activity, no accident can be without a substance in which to exist. Moreover, since we do not apprehend the substance itself immediately through itself, but by means only of the fact that it is the subject of certain activities, it is highly rational, and a requirement forced on us by custom, to give diverse names to those substances that we recognise to be the subjects of clearly diverse activities or accidents, and afterwards to inquire whether those diverse names refer to one and the same or to diverse things. But there are *certain* activities, which we call *corporeal,* e.g., magnitude, figure, motion, and all those that cannot be thought of apart from extension in space; and the substance in which they exist is called *body.* It cannot be pretended that the substance that is the subject of figure is different from that which is the subject of spatial motion, etc., since all these activities agree in presupposing extension. Further, there are other activities, which we call *thinking* activities,

e.g., understanding, willing, imagining, feeling, etc.,
which agree in falling under the description of thought,
perception, or consciousness. The substance in which
they reside we call a *thinking thing* or *the mind,* or
any other name we care, provided only we do not
confound it with corporeal substance, since thinking
activities have no affinity with corporeal activities, and
thought, which is the common nature in which the
former agree, is totally different from extension, the
common term for describing the latter.

But after we have formed two distinct concepts of
those two substances, it is easy, from what has been
said in the sixth Meditation, to determine whether they
are one and the same or distinct.

The objection

In reference to the third Meditation—concerning
God—some of these (thoughts of man) are, so to speak,
images of things, and to these alone is the title 'idea'
properly applied; examples are my thought of a man, or
of a Chimera, of Heavens, of an Angel, or [even] of
God.

*When I think of a man, I recognize an idea, or image,
with figure and colour as its constituents; and concerning this I can raise the question whether or not it is
the likeness of a man. So it is also when I think of the
heavens. When I think of the chimera, I recognize an
idea or image, being able at the same time to doubt
whether or not it is the likeness of an animal, which,
though it does not exist, may yet exist or has at some
other time existed.*

*But, when one thinks of an Angel, what is noticed
in the mind is now the image of a flame, now that of
a fair winged child, and this, I may be sure, has no*

likeness to an Angel, and hence is not the idea of an Angel. But believing that created beings exist that are the ministers of God, invisible and immaterial, we give the name of Angel to this object of belief, this supposed being, though the idea used in imagining an Angel is, nevertheless, constructed out of the ideas of visible things.

It is the same way with the most holy name of God; we have no image, no idea corresponding to it. Hence we are forbidden to worship God in the form of an image, lest we should think we could conceive Him who is inconceivable.

Hence it appears that we have no idea of God. But just as one born blind who has frequently been brought close to a fire and has felt himself growing warm, recognizes that there is something which made him warm, and, if he hears it called fire, concludes that fire exists, though he has no acquaintance with its shape or colour, and has no idea of fire nor image that he can discover in his mind; so a man recognizing that there must be some cause of his images and ideas, and another previous cause of this cause and so on continuously, is finally carried on to a conclusion, or to the supposition of some eternal cause, which, never having begun to be, can have no cause prior to it: and hence he necessarily concludes that something eternal exists. But nevertheless he has no idea that he can assert to be that of this eternal being, and he merely gives a name to the object of his faith or reasoning and calls it God.

Since now it is from this portion, viz., that there is an idea of God in our soul, that M. Descartes proceeds to prove the theorem that God (an all-powerful, all-wise Being, the creator of the world) exists, he should have explained this idea of God better, and he should

Descartes' Reply

have deduced from it not only God's existence, but also the creation of the world.

Here the meaning assigned to the term idea is merely that of images depicted in the corporeal imagination; and, that being agreed on, it is easy for my critic to prove that there is no proper idea of Angel or of God. But I have, everywhere, from time to time, and principally in this place, shown that I take the term idea to stand for whatever the mind directly perceives; and so when I will or when I fear, since at the same time I perceive that I will and fear, that very volition and apprehension are ranked among my ideas. I employed this term because it was the term currently used by Philosophers for the forms of perception of the Divine mind, though we can discover no imagery in God; besides I had no other more suitable term. But I think I have sufficiently well explained what the idea of God is for those who care to follow my meaning; those who prefer to wrest my words from the sense I give them, I can never satisfy. The objection that here follows, relative to the creation of the world, is plainly irrelevant [for I proved that God exists, before asking whether there is a world created by him, and from the mere fact that God, i.e., a supremely perfect being exists, it follows that if there be a world it must have been created by him].

The objection

For without doubt those ideas, which reveal substance to me, are something greater, and, so to speak, contain within them more objective reality than those which represent only modes or accidents. And again, that by means of which I apprehend a supreme God who is eternal, infinite, omniscient, all-powerful, and the creator of all else there is besides, assuredly possesses more objective reality than those ideas that reveal to us finite substances.

I have frequently remarked above that there is no idea either of God or of the soul; I now add that there is no idea of substance. For substance (the substance that is a material, subject to accidents and changes) is perceived and demonstrated by the reason alone, without yet being conceived by us, or furnishing us with any idea. If that is true, how can it be maintained that the ideas which reveal substance to me are anything greater or possess more objective reality than those revealing accidents to us? Further I pray M. Descartes to investigate the meaning of more reality. Does reality admit of more and less? Or, if he thinks that one thing can be more a thing than another, let him see how he is to explain it to our intelligence with the clearness called for in demonstration, and such as he himself has at other times employed.

Descartes' Reply

I have frequently remarked that I give the name idea to that with which reason makes us acquainted just as I also do to anything else that is in any way perceived by us. I have likewise explained how reality admits of more and less: viz., in the way in which substance is greater than mode; and if there be real qualities or incomplete substances, they are things to a greater extent than modes are, but less than complete substances. Finally, if there be an infinite and independent substance, it is more a thing than a substance that is finite and dependent. Now all this is quite self-evident [and so needs no further explanation].

FROM THE FOURTH SET OF OBJECTIONS[1]

The objection

The first thing that here occurs to me to be worthy of remark is that our distinguished author should have taken as the foundation of the whole of his philosophy the doctrine laid down [before him] by St. Augustine, a man of most penetrating intellect and of such note, not only in the sphere of theology, but in that of philosophy as well. In 'De Libera arbitrio,' Book II, chap. 3, Alipius, when disputing with Euodius, setting about a proof of the existence of God, says: Firstly, to start with the things that are most evident, I ask you whether you yourself exist, or are you apprehensive lest in [answering] this question you are in error, when in any case, if you did not exist you could never be in error? *Similar to this are the words of our author:* But perhaps there exists an all-powerful being, extremely cunning, who deceives me, who intentionally at all times deceives me. There is then no doubt that I exist, if he deceives me. *But let us proceed, and, to pursue something more relevant to our purpose, let us discover how, from this principle, we can demonstrate the fact that our mind is [distinct and] separate from our body.*

I am able to doubt whether I have a body, nay, whether any body exists at all; yet I have no right to doubt whether I am, or exist, so long as I doubt or think.

Hence I, who doubt and think, am not a body; otherwise in entertaining doubt concerning body, I should doubt about myself.

Nay, even though I obstinately maintain that no

---

[1] These are the objections of M. Arnauld.

*body at all exists, the position taken up is unshaken:
I am something, hence I am not a body.*

*This is really very acute, but someone could bring up
the objection which our author urges against himself;
the fact that I doubt about body or deny that body
exists, does not bring it about that no body exists.*
Hence perhaps it happens that these very things which
I suppose to be nothing, because they are unknown to
me, yet do not in truth differ from that self which I
do know. I know nothing about it, *he says,* I do not
dispute this matter; [I can judge only about things
that are known to me.] I know that I exist; I enquire
who I, the known self, am; it is quite certain that the
knowledge of this self thus precisely taken, does not
depend on those things of the existence of which I am
not yet acquainted.

*But he admits in consonance with the argument laid
down in the Method, that the proof has proceeded only
so far as to exclude from the nature of the human mind
whatsoever is corporeal,* not from the point of view
of the ultimate truth, but relatively only to his consciousness (the meaning being that nothing at all was
known to him to belong to his essential nature, beyond
the fact that he was a thinking being). *Hence it is
evident from this reply that the argument is exactly
where it was, and that therefore the problem which he
promises to solve remains entirely untouched. The
problem is:* how it follows, from the fact that one is
unaware that anything else [(except the fact of being
a thinking thing)] belongs to one's essence, that nothing else really belongs to one's essence. *But, not to
conceal my dullness, I have been unable to discover in
the whole of Meditation II where he has shown this.*

Concerning God

The first proof of the existence of God, that unfolded by our author in Meditation III, falls into two parts. The former is, that God exists, if the idea of Him exists in me; the second shows that I, in possessing this idea, can derive my existence only from God.

M. Descartes contends that existence per se should be taken not negatively but positively, *especially in so far as it refers to God. So that God* in a certain sense stands to Himself in the same way as an efficient cause does to its effect. *Now this seems to me to be a strong assertion and to be untrue.*

Hence, while in part I agree with M. Descartes, I partly differ from him. I admit that I cannot be self-derived except in a positive sense, but I deny that the same should be said of God. Nay, I think that it is a manifest contradiction that anything should be positively self-derived in the sense of proceeding from itself as a cause. Hence I come to the same conclusion as our author, but by quite another route, as I shall here set forth:—

In order to be self-derived, I should have to proceed from myself positively *and in the sense of coming from myself as a cause: hence I cannot be self-derived.*

To prove the major premiss of this syllogism, I rely on the grounds of my antagonist drawn from the doctrine that, since the various parts of time can all be dissevered from each other, from the fact that I exist it does not follow that I shall in future exist, unless some cause, as it were, re-creates me at every single moment.

In the matter of the minor, [*viz., that I cannot proceed from myself* positively *and as it were from a cause*] *I deem it to be so evident to the light of nature that its proof would be vain, a proving of the known by the less known. Indeed, our author seems to have acknowledged its truth, since he has not dared openly to deny it. Consider, I pray, those words in his reply to his theological opponent.*

I have not, *so run his words,* said that it is impossible for anything to be its own efficient cause: for, although that statement is manifestly true when the meaning of efficient cause is restricted to those causes that are prior to their effects or different from them, yet it does not seem necessary to confine the term to this meaning in the present investigation, for the light of nature does not require that the notion of an efficient cause should compel it to be prior to its effect.

This is excellent so far as the first part goes, but why has he omitted the second? Has he not omitted to add that the same light of nature does not require that the notion of an efficient cause should compel it to be different from its effect, only because the light of nature does not permit him to assert that?

Now surely, if every effect depends upon a cause and receives its existence from a cause, is it not clear that the same thing cannot depend upon itself, cannot receive its existence from itself?

Further, every cause is the cause of an effect, every effect the effect of a cause; hence there is a mutual relation between cause and effect. But a mutual relation can be possessed only by two things.

Again, it is merely absurd to conceive of a thing as receiving existence and yet possessing that very existence before the time at which we conceive that it received it; but that would be the result if we attributed the notions of cause and effect to the same thing in respect of itself. What is the notion of cause? The conferring of existence. What is the notion of effect?

The receiving of existence. Moreover, the notion of cause is prior in nature to that of effect.

But we cannot conceive a thing by means of the notion of cause as giving existence, unless we conceive it as possessing existence. Hence we should have to conceive that a thing possessed existence before conceiving it to receive existence; yet when anything receives, the receiving precedes the possessing.

This reasoning may be otherwise couched thus:— no one gives what he does not possess; hence no one can give himself existence unless he already possess it, but, if he already possess it, why should he give it to himself?

Finally, M. Descartes asserts that the light of nature lets us know that the distinction between creation and conservation is solely a distinction of the reason. *But this self-same light of nature lets us know that nothing can create itself, and that hence nothing can conserve itself.*

But to pass down from the general thesis to the particular one concerning God, it will now, in my opinion, be more evident that God can be self-derived not in the positive sense, *but only* negatively, *i.e., in the sense of* not proceeding from anything else.

For the idea of an infinite being contains within it that of infinite duration, i.e., a duration bounded by no limits, and hence indivisible, unchanging, and existing all at once; one in which it is only erroneously and by reason of the imperfection of our intellect that the conception of prior and posterior can be applied.

Whence it manifestly follows that the infinite Being cannot be thought to exist even for one moment without our conceiving at the same time that it always has and always will exist (a fact that our author himself else-

*where proves); hence it is idle to ask why it continues
in existence.*

*Nay, as Augustine frequently shows (an author whom
none since the time of the sacred writers have surpassed
in the worthiness and sublimity of what they say concerning God), in God there is no past or future, but
always present existence [which clearly shows that we
cannot without absurdity ask why God continues to
exist].*

*Further, God cannot be thought to be self-derived in
the positive sense, as if He originally brought Himself
into existence, for in that case He would have existed
before He existed. He is said to be self-derived merely
because, as our author frequently declares, as a fact
He maintains Himself in existence.*

Hence in opposition to what M. Descartes says: the
light of nature tells us that nothing exists about which
the question, why it exists, cannot be asked, whether
we enquire for its efficient cause, or, if it does not
possess one, demand why it does not have one, *I reply
that the answer to the question why God exists should
not be in terms of efficient causality, but merely 'because
He is God,' i.e., an infinite Being. And when we are
asked for the efficient cause of God, we must reply that
He needs no efficient cause. And if our interrogator
plies us with the question why no efficient cause is required, we must answer 'because He is an infinite Being,
and in such a case existence and essence are identical';
for only those things, the actual existence of which can
be distinguished from their essence, require an efficient
cause.*

*The only remaining scruple I have is an uncertainty
as to how a circular reasoning is to be avoided in saying:*
the only secure reason we have for believing that what

we clearly and distinctly perceive is true, is the fact that God exists.

But we can be sure that God exists, only because we clearly and evidently perceive that; therefore prior to being certain that God exists, we should be certain that whatever we clearly and evidently perceive is true.

I am confident that M. Descartes, whose piety is so well known to us, will weigh this with diligence and attention and will judge that he must take the greatest pains, lest, while meaning to maintain the cause of God against the attacks of the impious, he appears to have at all endangered that faith, which God's own authority has founded, and by the grace of which he hopes to obtain that eternal life, of which he has undertaken to convince the world.

Descartes' Reply

I shall not take up time here by thanking my distinguished critic for bringing to my aid the authority of St. Augustine, and for expounding my arguments in a way which betokened a fear that others might not deem them strong enough.

I come first of all to the passage where my demonstration commences of how, *from the fact that I knew that nothing belongs to my essence* (i.e., to the essence of the mind alone) *beyond the fact that I am a thinking being, it follows that in actual truth nothing else does belong to it.* That was, to be sure, the place where I proved that God exists, that God, to wit, who can accomplish whatever I clearly and distinctly know to be possible.

For although much exists in me of which I am not yet conscious (for example, in that passage I did, as a fact, assume that I was not yet aware that my mind had the power of moving the body, and that it was substantially united with it), yet since that which I do perceive is adequate to allow of my existing with it as my sole possession, I am certain that God could have created me without putting me in possession of those other attributes of which I am unaware. Hence it was that those additional attributes were judged not to belong to the essence of the mind.

For in my opinion nothing without which a thing can still exist is comprised in its essence, and although mind belongs to the essence of man, to be united to a human body is in the proper sense no part of the essence of mind.

But now I must explain how it is that, *from the mere fact that I apprehend one substance clearly and distinctly apart from another, I am sure that the one excludes the other.*

Really the notion of *substance* is just this—that which can exist by itself, without the aid of any other substance. No one who perceives two substances by means of two diverse concepts ever doubts that they are really distinct.

Consequently, if I had not been in search of a certitude greater than the vulgar, I should have been satisfied with showing in the Second Meditation that *Mind* was apprehended as a thing that subsists, although nothing belonging to the body be ascribed to it, and conversely that *Body* was understood to be something subsistent without anything being attributed to it that pertains to the mind. And I should have added nothing more in order to prove that there was a real distinction between mind and body: because commonly we judge that all things stand to each other in respect to their actual relations in the same way as they are related in our consciousness. But, since one of those hyperbolical doubts adduced in the First Meditation went so far as to prevent me from being sure of this very fact (viz., that things are in their true nature exactly as we perceive them to be), so long as I supposed that I had no knowledge of the author of my being, all that I have said about God and about truth in the Third, Fourth and Fifth Meditations serves to further the conclusion as to the real distinction between *mind* and *body,* which is finally completed in Meditation VI.

There is no conflict between my theory and the point M. Arnauld next brings up, *that it is no marvel if, in deducing my existence from the fact that I think, the idea I thus form of myself represents me merely as a thinking being.* For, similarly when I examine the nature of body I find nothing at all in it that savours of thought; and there is no better proof of the distinctness of two things than if, when we study each separately, we find nothing in the one that does not differ from what we find in the other.

Further, I fail to see how this argument *proves too much.* For, in order to prove that one thing is really distinct from another, nothing less can be said, than that the divine power is able to separate one from the other. I thought I took sufficient care to prevent anyone thence inferring that *man was* merely *a spirit that makes use of a body;* for in this very Sixth Meditation in which I have dealt with the distinction between mind and body, I have at the same time proved that mind was substantially united with body; and I employed arguments, the efficacy of which in establishing this proof I cannot remember to have seen in any other case surpassed. Likewise, just as one who said that a man's arm was a substance really distinct from the rest of his body, would not therefore deny that it belonged to the nature of the complete man, and as in saying that the arm belongs to the nature of the complete man no suspicion is raised that it cannot subsist by itself, so I think that I have neither proved too much in showing that mind can exist apart from body, nor yet too little in saying that it is substantially united to the body, because that substantial union does not prevent the formation of a clear and distinct concept of the mind alone as of a complete thing. Hence this differs greatly from the concept of a superficies or of a line, which cannot be apprehended as complete things unless, in addition to length and breadth, depth be ascribed to them.

Finally, the fact that *the power of thinking is asleep in infants and in maniacs*—though not indeed *extinct*, yet troubled—should not make us believe that it is conjoined with the corporeal organs in such a way as to be incapable of existing apart from them. The fact that our thought is often in our experience impeded by them, does not allow us to infer that it is produced by them; for this there is not even the slightest proof.

I do not, however, deny that the close conjunction between soul and body of which our senses constantly give us experience, is the cause of our not perceiving their real distinction without attentive reflection. But, in my judgment, those who frequently revolve in their thought what was said in the Second Meditation, will easily persuade themselves that mind is distinguished from body not by a mere fiction or intellectual abstraction, but is known as a distinct thing because it is really distinct.

I make no reply to M. Arnauld's additions about the immortality of the soul, because they are not in conflict with my doctrine. As for the matter of the souls of brutes, this is not the place to treat the subject, and I could not, without taking in the whole of Physics, say more about them than in the explanations given in the fifth part of the discourse on Method. Yet, not to pass over the matter altogether, I should point out that the chief thing to note appears to me to be that motion is impossible alike in our own bodies and in those of the brutes, unless all the organs or instruments are present, by means of which it can be effected in a machine. Hence in our very selves the mind [(or the soul)] by no means moves the external limbs immediately, but merely directs the subtle fluid styled the animal spirits, that passes from the heart through the brain towards the muscles, and determines this fluid to perform definite motions, these animal spirits being in their own nature capable of being utilized with equal facility for many distinct actions. But the greater part of our motions do not depend on the mind at all. Such are the beating of the heart, the digestion of our food, nutrition, respiration when we are asleep, and even walking, singing and similar acts when we are awake, if performed without the mind attending to them. When a man in falling thrusts out his hand to save his head he does that without his reason counselling him so to act, but merely because the sight of the impending fall penetrating to his brain, drives the animal spirits into the nerves in the manner necessary for this motion, and for producing it without the mind's desiring it, and as though it were the working of a machine. Now, when we experience this as a fact in ourselves, why should we marvel so greatly *if the light reflected from the body of a wolf into the eyes of a sheep* should be equally capable of exciting in it the motion of flight?

But if we wish by reasoning to determine whether any of the motions of brutes are similar to those which we accomplish with the aid of the mind, or whether they resemble those that depend alone upon the *influxus* of the animal spirits and the disposition of the organs, we must pay heed to the differences that prevail between the two classes: viz., those differences explained in the fifth part of the Discourse on Method, for I have been able to discover no others. Then it will be seen that all the actions of brutes resemble only those of ours that occur without the aid of the mind. Whence we are driven to conclude that we can recognize no principle of motion in them beyond the disposition of their organs and the continual discharge of the animal spirits that are produced by the beat of the heart as it rarefies the blood. At the same time we shall perceive that we have had no cause for ascribing anything more to them, beyond that, not distinguishing these two principles of motion, when previously we have noted that the principle depending solely on the animal spirits and organs exists in ourselves and in the brutes alike, we have inadvisedly believed that the other principle, that consisting wholly of mind and thought, also existed in them. And it is true that a persuasion held from our earliest years, though afterwards shown by argument to be false, is not easy and only by long and frequent attention to these arguments expelled from our belief.

Reply to the Second Part, Concerning God

Up to this point I have attempted to refute M. Arnauld's arguments and to withstand his attack; for the rest, as they are wont who combat with a stronger antagonist, I shall not oppose myself directly to his onslaught, but rather avoid the blow.

The second [objection] is, that God is self-originated *in a positive sense, the sense implying as it were derivation from a cause.* Here I had in mind merely that the reason why God requires no efficient cause in order to exist, is based on something positive, to wit, the very immensity of God, than which nothing can be more positive. M. Arnauld, however, shows that God is neither self-produced nor conserved by Himself by any positive activity belonging to an efficient cause; and this I likewise clearly affirm.

Let us now turn to the chief charge my distinguished critic brings against me. To me, indeed, there seems to be nothing worthy of censure in the passage mentioned, viz., where I said *that it is quite permissible for us to think that God in a certain sense stands to Himself in the same way as an efficient cause does to its effect.* For by this very statement I have denied that doctrine which M. Arnauld thinks *bold and untrue,* viz., that God is His own efficient cause. In saying that *in a certain sense God stood so to Himself,* I showed that I did not think the relation to be identical in both cases; and in introducing what I said with these words— *it is quite permissible for us to think,* I showed that the matter could only be explained by the imperfection of the human understanding. But in the rest of what I wrote I have confirmed this at every point; for at the very beginning, where I said that *nothing existed as to the efficient cause of which we might not inquire,* I added, *or if it does not possess an efficient cause, demand why that is awanting.* The words sufficiently show that I believed something did exist which does not require an efficient cause. Moreover, what else could that be than God? Shortly afterwards I said that *in God there is such a great and inexhaustible power, that He has needed no assistance in order to exist, and requires none for His preservation, and hence He is in a certain way the cause of His own existence.* Here the expression *cause of His own existence* can by no means be understood as efficient cause; it merely means

that the inexhaustible power of God is the cause or
reason why He needs no cause. It was because that
inexhaustible power, or immensity of His essence, is
as highly *positive* as is possible, that I said that the
reason or cause why God does not require a cause was
a positive one. This I could not have affirmed of any
finite thing however perfect in its own kind; if it
were alleged to be *self-derived,* this could be understood only *in a negative sense,* since no reason could
be derived from its positive nature on account of which
we could understand that it did not require an efficient
cause.

Therefore I can readily admit everything M. Arnauld
brings forward in order to prove that God is not His
own efficient cause, and that He does not conserve
Himself by any transeunt action, or any continual reproduction of Himself; and this is the sole conclusion
of his argument. But, as I hope, even he will not deny
that that immensity of power, on account of which
God needs no cause in order to exist, is in Him something *positive,* and that nothing *positive* of this type
could be conceived in any other thing, on account of
which it should require no cause in order to exist;
and this alone was what I meant to express in saying
that nothing could be understood to be *self-derived*
unless *in a negative sense,* except God alone. I had
no need to assume more than this, in order to resolve
the difficulty that had been brought forward.

But since my critic warns me with such seriousness
that *Theologians, almost without exception, must take
offence at the doctrine that God is self-originated in a
positive sense, and proceeds, as it were, from a cause,*
I shall explain in more detail why this fashion of speech
is in this question exceedingly useful, and even neces-

sary, and why it seems to me to be quite free from any suspicion of being likely to cause offence.

I am aware that the Theologians of the Latin church do not employ the word 'cause' in matters of divinity, where they treat of the procession of persons in the Holy Trinity, and that where the Greeks used αιτιον and αρχη indifferently, they have preferred to employ the word *principium* alone taken in its most general sense, lest from the usage anyone might infer that the Son was not so great as the Father. But where no such danger of error can come in, and the question relates to God not as a trinity but as a unity, I see no reason why the word *cause* should be so much shunned, especially when we have come to the point when it seems very useful and almost necessary to employ the term.

No term can have a higher utility than to prove the existence of God; and none can be more necessary than this if, without it, God's existence cannot be clearly demonstrated.

But I think that it is manifest to all, that to consider the efficient cause is the primary and principal, not to say the only means of proving the existence of God. We shall not be able to pursue this proof with accuracy, if we do not grant our mind the liberty of asking for an efficient cause in every case, even in that of God; for with what right should we exclude God, before we have proved that He exists? Hence in every single case we must inquire whether it is *derived from itself or from something else;* and indeed by this means the existence of God may be inferred, although it be not expressly explained what is the meaning of anything being *self-derived.* For those who follow the guidance of the light of nature alone, spontaneously form here a concept common to efficient and formal cause alike.

Hence, when a thing is *derived from something else* it is derived from that as from an efficient cause; but what is *self-derived* comes as it were from a formal cause; it results from having an essential nature which renders it independent of an efficient cause. On this account I did not explain that matter in my Meditations, assuming that it was self-evident.

But when those who are accustomed to judge in accordance with the notion that nothing can be its own efficient cause, and are familiar with the accurate distinction between formal and efficient cause, see the question raised whether anything is self-derived, it easily follows that, taking that to apply only to the efficient cause properly so styled, they think that the expression *self-derived* should not be held to mean derived from itself *as from a cause,* but merely in a negative sense and as *not having a cause;* and so consequently it results that the existence of something is implied, into the cause of the existence of which we ought not to inquire. But if this interpretation of *self-derived* were admitted, there would be no reason by which to prove God's existence from His effects, as was shown correctly by the author of the first Objections; hence we must on no account sanction it.

But in order to reply expressly to this, let me say that I think we must show that, intermediate between *efficient cause,* in the proper sense, and *no cause,* there is something else, viz., *the positive essence of a thing,* to which the concept of efficient cause can be extended in the way in which in Geometry we are wont to extend the concept of a circular line, that is as long as possible, to that of a straight line; or the concept of a rectilinear polygon with an indefinite number of sides to that of a circle. I see no better way of explaining this than in saying, as I did, *that the meaning of efficient cause was in the present investigation not to be confined to those causes which are prior in time to their effects, or different from them; in the first place because the question (whether a thing can be its own efficient cause) would be unmeaning, since no one is unaware that the same thing cannot be prior to or different from itself; secondly because the former of these two conditions can be omitted from the concept without impairing the integrity of the notion of efficient cause.*

For the fact that the cause need not be prior in time is evident from its not having the character of a cause except while it produces its effect, as I have said.

But from the fact that the second condition cannot also be annulled, we may only infer that it is not an efficient cause in the proper sense of the term, which I admit. We cannot, however, conclude that it is in no sense a positive cause, which may be held to be analogous to an efficient cause; and this is all that my argument requires. For by the very light of nature by which I perceive that I should have given myself all the perfections of which I have any idea, if I had indeed given myself existence, I am aware also that nothing can give itself existence in that way which is implied by the meaning to which we restrict the term efficient cause, viz., in a way such that the same thing, in so far as it gives itself being, is different from itself in so far as it receives being; for to be the same thing and not the same thing, i.e., a different thing, is a contradiction.

Thus it comes that when the question is raised whether anything can give itself existence, this must be understood merely to mean whether anything has a nature or essence such that it does not need to have any efficient cause in order to exist.

I have pursued this topic at somewhat greater length

than the subject demanded, in order to prove that it is a matter of great anxiety to me to prevent anything from appearing in my writings capable of giving just offence to theologians.

Finally, to prove that I have not argued in a circle in saying, *that the only secure reason we have for believing that what we clearly and distinctly perceive is true, is the fact that God exists; but that clearly we can be sure that God exists only because we perceive that,* I may cite the explanations that I have already given at sufficient length in my reply to the second set of Objections, numbers 3 and 4. There I distinguished those matters that in actual truth we clearly perceive from those we remember to have formerly perceived. For first, we are sure that God exists because we have attended to the proofs that established this fact; but afterwards it is enough for us to remember that we have perceived something clearly, in order to be sure that it is true; but this would not suffice, unless we knew that God existed and that he did not deceive us.

The fact *that nothing can exist in the mind, in so far as it is a thinking thing, of which it is not conscious,* seems to me self-evident, because we conceive nothing to exist in it, viewed in this light, that is not thought, and something dependent on thought; for otherwise it would not belong to the mind, in so far as it is a thinking thing. But there can exist in us no thought of which, at the very moment that it is present in us, we are not conscious. Wherefore I have no doubt that the mind begins to think at the same time as it is infused into the body of an infant, and is at the same time conscious of its own thought, though afterwards it does not remember that, because the specific forms of these thoughts do not live in the memory.

But it has to be noted that, while indeed we are

always in actuality conscious of acts or operations of the mind, that is not the case with the faculties or powers of mind, except potentially. So that when we dispose ourselves to the exercise of any faculty, if the faculty reside in us, we are immediately actually conscious of it; and hence we can deny that it exists in the mind, if we can form no consciousness of it.

Letter from M. Descartes to M. Clerselier

To Serve as a Reply to a Solution of the Principal Objections Taken by M. Gassendi to the Preceding Replies.

Your friends mark six objections to Meditation II. The first is that in the statement, *I think, hence I exist,* the author of these criticisms will have it that I imply the assumption of this major premiss, *he who thinks, exists,* and that I have thus already espoused a prejudice. Here he once more mishandles the word *prejudice:* for though we may apply this term to that proposition when it is brought forward without scrutiny, and we believe it merely because we remember we have made this same judgment previously, we cannot maintain on every occasion that it is a prejudice, i.e., when we subject it to examination, the cause being that it appears to be so evident to the understanding that we should fail to disbelieve it even on the first occasion in our life on which it occurred to us, on which occasion it would not be a prejudice. But the greater error here is our critic's assumption that the knowledge of particular truths is always deduced from universal propositions in consonance with the order of the sequence observed in the syllogism of dialectic. This shows that he is but little acquainted with the method by which truth should be investigated. For it is cer-

tain that in order to discover the truth we should always
start with particular notions, in order to arrive at
general conceptions subsequently, though we may also
in the reverse way, after having discovered the universals, deduce other particulars from them. Thus in
teaching a child the elements of geometry we shall
certainly not make him understand the general truth
that *'when equals are taken from equals the remainders
are equal,'* or that *'the whole is greater than its parts,'*
unless by showing him examples in particular cases.
For want of guarding against this error our author has
been led astray into the many fallacious reasonings
which have gone to swell his book. He has merely
constructed false major premises according to his
whim, as though I had deduced from these the truths
I have explained.

FROM THE FIFTH SET OF OBJECTIONS[1]

Letter from P. Gassendi to M. Descartes

SIR:

*Our friend Mersenne did me a great kindness in
communicating to me your magnificent work—your
Meditations on First Philosophy. The excellence of
your arguments, the perspicuity of your intellect, and
the brilliance of your expression have caused me extraordinary delight. It gives me great pleasure to com-
pliment you on the sublimity and felicity with which
your mind assails the task of extending the bound-
aries of the sciences and bringing to light those matters
that preceding ages have found most difficult to drag
from their obscurity. Nay, I cannot without shame-*

---

[1] These are the objections of P. Gassendi, theologian and
Epicurean philosopher, who was styled by Gibbon "the best
philosopher among men of letters, and the best man of letters
among philosophers."

*facedness expose my difficulties to your gaze, sure as
I am that there is none of them that has not often, sug-
gested itself to you in your reflections, and which you
have not with full consciousness dismissed as of no
account, or determined to keep out of sight. Consequently, though I bring forward certain hypotheses, I
bring them forward merely as hypotheses, and they are
hypotheses that affect not the truths themselves of
which you have undertaken the proof, but the method
and the cogency of your proof. I unaffectedly acknowledge the existence of Almighty God and the immortality of our souls; my doubts concern merely the
validity of the reasoning by which you prove those
matters, as well as other things involved in the scheme
of Metaphysical science.*

RELATIVE TO MEDITATION I

*Of the things which may be brought within the sphere
of the doubtful*

*In the matter of the first Meditation, there is really
little for me to linger over; I agree with your plan
of freeing your mind from every prejudice. On one
point only I am not clear; that is, why you should
not have preferred to indicate simply and with few
words that what you previously knew was uncertain,
in order subsequently to choose what might be found
to be true, rather than by regarding everything as
false, not so much to dismiss an old prejudice, as to
take up with a new one. Say what you will, no one
will be convinced that you have convinced yourself that
none of the things you have learned are true, and that
your senses, or a dream, or God, or an evil spirit have
imposed on you. Would it not have been better and
more consonant with philosophic candour and the love*

of the truth to state the actual facts in a straightforward and simple manner, rather than to incur the possible objection of having recourse to an artifice, of eagerness for verbal trickery and seeking evasions? Yet, since you have been pleased to take this way, I shall make no further criticism on it.

RELATIVE TO MEDITATION II

Of the Nature of the Human Mind; and that it is more easily known than the body

When it comes to the second Meditation, I see that you still persist in keeping up the game of pretence, and fail utterly to notice that you, the author of the pretence, exist; *which thus establishes the* conclusion that this proposition:—I am, I exist, is true each time that you pronounce it, or that you mentally conceive it. *But I don't see that you needed all this mechanism, when you had other grounds for being sure, and it was true, that you existed. You might have inferred that from any other activity, since our natural light informs us that whatever acts also exists.*

Your conclusion is: I am, to speak accurately, a Thing which thinks, that is to say, a mind or a soul, or an understanding, or a reason. *Here I confess that I have been suffering from a deception. For I believed that I was addressing the human soul, or that internal principle, by which a man lives, feels, moves from place to place and understands, and after all I was only speaking to a mind, which has divested itself not only of the body but of the soul itself. Have you, my worthy sir, in attaining to this result, followed the example of those ancients, who, though they thought that the soul was diffused throughout the whole body, believed that its principal part—the dominating part—*

was located in a determinate region of the body, e.g., in the brain, or in the heart? Not that they judged that the soul was not also to be found there, but that they believed that the mind was, as it were, added to the soul existing there, was linked to it, and along with it informed that region. I ought really to have remembered that from the discussion in your Discourse on Method. But this will not gain the adhesion of those who cannot comprehend how you can think during a lethargic sleep, or while in the womb. Besides, I have a difficulty here as to whether you think that you have been infused into the body or one of its parts during the uterine stage of existence or at birth. But I should be loth to be troublesome with my enquiries, or to reflect whether you remember what your thoughts were when in the womb, or in the days, months, and years succeeding your birth; or, if you replied that you had forgotten, to ask why this was so. Yet I suggest that you should remember how obscure, how meagre, how nearly non-existent your thought must have been during those periods of life.

Proceeding, you maintain that you are not the complex of members which we call the human body. *But that must be admitted because you are considering yourself solely as a thing which thinks, as a part of the concrete human whole, distinct from this exterior and more solid part.* 'I am not,' *you say,* 'a subtle air distributed through these members, I am not a wind, a fire, a vapour, nor a breath, nor anything which I can construct in imagination. For I have assumed that all these were nothing; and let that supposition be unchanged.' *But halt here, O Mind, and let those suppositions or rather those fictions take themselves off. You say,* 'I am not air or anything of such a nature.' *But, if the total soul be something of the kind, where-*

fore may not you who are thought to be the noblest part of the soul, be deemed to be, as it were, the flower, or the subtlest, purest, and most active part of it. You say, 'perhaps those same things which I supposed were non-existent, are real things and are not different from the self which I know? I do not know about this, I shall not dispute about it now.' *But if you do not know, if you do not dispute the matter, why do you assume that you are none of these things?* 'I know,' *you say,* 'that I exist; but the knowledge of my existence taken in its precise significance cannot depend on that which I do not know.' *Granted, but remember that you have not proved that you are not air, or a vapour, or many other things.*

RELATIVE TO MEDITATION III

Of God: That He exists

In your Third Meditation, from the fact that your clear and distinct knowledge of the proposition, I am a thing which thinks, *was recognized by you to be the cause of your certainty of its truth, you infer that you are able to set up this general Rule:* that all things which I perceive very clearly and very distinctly are true. *But though amid the obscurity that surrounds us, there may very well be no better Rule obtainable, yet when we see that many minds of the first rank, which seem to have perceived many things so clearly and distinctly, have judged that the truth of things is hidden either in God or in a well, may it not be open to us to suspect that the Rule is perhaps fallacious? And really, since you are not ignorant of the argument of the Sceptics, tell me what else can we infer to be true as being clearly and distinctly perceived, except that that which appears to anyone does appear? Thus it is true that the taste of a melon appears to me to be of this precise kind. But how shall I persuade myself that therefore it is true that such a savour exists in the melon? When as a boy and in enjoyment of good health, I thought otherwise, indeed, perceiving clearly and distinctly that the melon had another taste. Likewise, I see that many men think otherwise also, as well as many animals that are well equipped in respect of the sense of taste and are quite healthy. Does then one truth conflict with another? Or is it rather the case that it is not because a thing is clearly and distinctly perceived that it is of itself true, but that that only is true which is clearly and distinctly perceived to be so.*

Next, though every highest perfection is wont to be ascribed to God, all such seem to be derived from the things which we customarily admire in ourselves, e.g., length of existence, power, knowledge, kindness, blessedness, etc.; we amplify these as much as possible, and then pronounce God to be everlasting, all-powerful, all-knowing, most excellent, most blessed, etc., but the idea which represents all these attributes does not contain more objective reality on that account than the finite things taken together have, out of the ideas of which that idea is compounded, afterwards being magnified in the aforesaid way. For neither does he who says eternal, thereby embrace in his mind the total extent of the duration of that which has never begun to be and never will cease to exist; nor does he who says omnipotent envisage the whole multitude of possible effects; and so in the case of the others.

Lastly, can anyone affirm that he possesses an idea of God which is true, or which represents God as He is? How slight a thing would God be, unless He were other and had other attributes than this feeble idea

*of ours contains! Must we not believe that man rela-
tively to God has a smaller proportion of perfection
than that which the tiniest creature, a tick, burrowing
in its skin, possesses relatively to an elephant? Hence,
if the man who from observation of the perfections of
the tick should construct in his mind an idea which
he maintained was that of an elephant, would be held
to be very silly, how can he be satisfied with himself,
who out of human perfections that he beholds shapes
an idea which is, he contends, that of God, and resembles Him? Tell me also how we recognise in God
those perfections which in ourselves we find to be so
tiny? And when we have detected them, what sort
of essence must we therefore imagine is that of God?
God is most certainly infinitely beyond the widest grasp,
and when our mind addresses itself to the contemplation
of God, it not only gets befogged but comes to a stand-
still. Hence it follows both that we have no reason to
assert that we possess any cognate idea which represents God, and it is enough if, on the analogy of our
human qualities, we derive and construct an idea of
some sort or other for our use—an idea which does not
transcend human comprehension, and contains no reality
which we do not perceive in other things or by means
of other things.*

Next you run over the list of the ideas you possess,
and besides the idea of yourself you enumerate the ideas
of God, of corporeal and inanimate things, of angels,
animals and men; this is in order that, since you say
there is no difficulty about the idea of yourself, you may
infer that the ideas of men, of animals and of angels
are composed of those which you have of yourself and
of God, and that the ideas of corporeal things might
have proceeded from you also. *But here it occurs to
me to wonder how you can be said to have an idea of*

yourself (and one so fertile as to furnish you with such a supply of other ideas) and how it can be maintained that the matter presents no difficulties; when, nevertheless, you have really either no idea of yourself, or one which is very confused and imperfect, as we have already observed in passing judgment on the previous Meditation. In it you even inferred that nothing could be more easily and more clearly perceived by you than yourself. What if it be the case that, as you do not and cannot possess an idea of yourself, it may be said that anything else is more capable of being easily and clearly perceived by you than yourself?

In my reflections as to the reason why it is the case that neither does sight see itself, nor the understanding understand itself, the thought presents itself to me that nothing acts on itself. Thus neither does the hand (or the tip of the finger) strike itself nor does the foot kick itself. But since in other cases, in order for us to acquire knowledge of a thing, that thing must act on the faculty that discerns it and must convey into it the semblance of itself, or inform it with its sensible appearance; it is quite clear that the faculty itself, since it is not outside itself, cannot convey a similar semblance of itself into itself, and cannot consequently acquire knowledge of itself, or, what is the same thing, perceive itself. And why, do you think, does the eye, though incapable of seeing itself in itself, yet see itself in the mirror? Why, because there is a space between the eye and the mirror, and the eye so acts on the mirror, conveying thither its sensible appearance, that the mirror re-acts on it again, conveying back to the eye that sensible appearance's own appearance. Give me then a mirror in which you yourself may in similar fashion act; I promise you that the result will be that this will reflect back your semblance into your-

*self, and that you then will at length perceive yourself,
not indeed by a direct, but a reflected cognition. But,
if you do not give this, there is no hope of your knowing
yourself.*

You say that those characteristics which you understand to exist in God are of such a nature as to be
incapable of proceeding from you alone: *your intention
in so doing is* to show that they must proceed from
God. *But, firstly, nothing is more true than that they
have not proceeded from you alone, so that you have
had no knowledge of them derived from yourself and
merely by means of your own efforts; for they have
proceeded and are derived from objects, from parents,
from masters, from teachers, and from the society in
which you have moved. But you will say: 'I am mind
alone: I admit nothing outside of myself, not even
the ears by which I hear nor the people who converse
with me.' You may assert this: but would you assert
it, unless you heard us with your ears, and there were
men from whom you learned words. Let us talk in
earnest, and tell me sincerely: do you not derive those
word-sounds which you utter in speaking of God, from
the society in which you have lived? And since the
sounds you use are due to intercourse with other men,
is it not from the same source that you derive the
notions underlying and designated by those sounds?
Hence though not due to you alone, they do not seem
on that account to proceed from God, but to come from
some other quarter. Further, what is there in those
things which, on the opportunity first being furnished
by the objects, you could not henceforth derive from
yourself? Do you, for that reason, apprehend something which is beyond human grasp? It is true that
if you comprehended the nature of God there would
be reason for your thinking that it was from God you*

derived this knowledge. But all those terms which you apply to God are merely certain perfections observed to exist in human beings and other things, which the human mind is able to understand, collect and amplify, as has already been said several times.

You next ask, whether, possessing now as you do the idea of a being more perfect than yourself, you yourself could exist, if no such being existed? Your reply is: 'From whom then could I derive my existence? Perhaps from myself or from my parents, or from some other source less perfect than God?' Then you go on to prove that you do not derive your existence from yourself. But this is not at all necessary. You also state the reason why you have not always existed. But that also is superfluous, except in so far as you wish at the same time to infer that you depend upon a cause which not only produces you, but also conserves you. Thus from the fact that your lifetime falls into many parts, you infer that you must be created in each one of them, on account of the mutual independence that exists among them. But consider if this can be so understood. There are indeed certain effects which, in order to continue in existence and never at any moment to fail, require the continuous and efficient presence of the cause which started them. An example of such an effect is the light of the sun (though effects of this kind are not so much actually identical, but rather equivalent, as in the case of a river its water is said to be). But there are other things which we see continue, not merely when the cause which they acknowledge is no longer active, but, if you care, even when it is destroyed and reduced to nothing. Of such a sort are things which are procreated or manufactured, so many in number as to make it distasteful to recount them; but it suffices that you are one of these, whatsoever the cause of

your existence turn out to be. But, *you maintain,* the
different parts of the time in which you exist do not
depend on one another. *Here we may object and ask,
what thing there is of which we can think, the parts
of which are more inseparable from one another?
What thing has parts, the order and connection of which
is more inviolable? Is there anything in which there
is less power of detaching the prior from the posterior
of its parts, in which they cohere more closely and
depend more on one another? But not to press this
point, I ask what difference this dependence or independence of the parts of time, which are external, successive and non-active, makes to your production or
reproduction? Certainly nothing more than the flow
or passage by of the particles of water makes to the
production and reproduction of a rock past which the
river flows.*

You proceed: And one certainly ought not to find it
strange that God, in creating me, placed this idea
within me, to serve as the mark of the workman imprinted on his work. It is likewise not essential that
this mark should be something different from the work
itself. For, from the sole fact that God created me,
it is most probable that in some way He has placed
His image and similitude upon me, and that I perceive this similitude (in which the idea of God is contained) by means of the same faculty by which I
perceive myself: that is to say, when I reflect on myself,
I not only know that I am something incomplete and
dependent on another, something also which incessantly
aspires after what is greater and better than myself;
but I also know that He on whom I depend possesses
in Himself all the great things to which I aspire, and
that not indefinitely or potentially alone, but really,
actually, and infinitely, and that thus He is God. *There*

*is indeed much appearance of truth in all this, and my
objection is not that it is not true. But, I ask you,
where do you get your proof? Passing by what has
been already said let us ask:* If the idea of God exists
in you like the mark of the workman imprinted on his
work, *what is the mode in which it is impressed? What
is the form of that mark? How do you detect it?
If it is not other than the work or thing itself, are you
then an idea? Are you yourself nothing else than a
mode of thought? Are you both the mark impressed
and the subject on which it is impressed?* You say
that it is to be believed that you have been fashioned
after the image and similitude of God. *To religious
faith this is indeed credible, but how can it be understood by the natural reason, unless you make God to
have a human form? And in what can this similitude
to this Eternal Being consist? Can you, who are dust
and ashes, presume to be similar to Him, who is of an
incorporeal, boundless, entirely perfect, most glorious
and, what is the principal matter, an entirely invisible
and incomprehensible nature? Have you known that
face to face, so as to be able, by comparing yourself
with it, to affirm that you resemble it?* You say that
it is to be believed owing to the fact that He created
you. *On the contrary that fact makes it incredible;
inasmuch as the work does not resemble the workman,
unless when it is generated by him by a communication
of his nature.* But you have not been begotten by
God in this way; nor are you His offspring or a
participator in His nature. You have merely been
created by Him, i.e., made by Him according to an idea;
and hence you cannot say that you resemble Him more
than the house resembles the workman who builds its
walls. *And this is true even though we grant, what you
have not yet proved, your creation by God.* You say

that you perceive a likeness, while at the same time
you understand that you are a thing which is incomplete,
dependent and aspiring towards what is better. *But
is not this rather a proof of God's dissimilitude, since
He on the contrary is most complete, most independent
and entirely self-sufficient, being greatest and best of
all? I pass by the fact that when you know yourself
to be dependent, you do not therefore immediately
understand that that on which you depend is other
than your parents; while if you do understand it to
be something else, no reason offers why you should
think that you resemble it. I pass by the fact also that
it is strange that the rest of mankind or of minds do
not understand the same thing as you do; and especially
since there is no reason why we should refuse to think
that God has impressed the idea of Himself on them as
on you. Assuredly this one thing especially proves that
there is no such idea which has been impressed on us by
God; since if there had been, it would have been imprinted on all and, likewise, as one and the same, and
all men would conceive God by means of a similar form
and semblance, would ascribe the same qualities to him,
and think the same thing about Him. And the opposite
is most notorious. These discussions, however, have
now taken up too much time.*

RELATIVE TO MEDITATION IV

Of the True and the False

You pronounce the opinion that you ought not to be
astonished if certain things are done by God, the reason
of which you do not understand. *That is indeed quite
correct; but still it is surprising that you possess a
true idea which represents God as all-knowing, all-
powerful and wholly good, while you nevertheless see*

*!hat certain of his works are not absolutely perfect and
complete. So that since He at least might have made
them more perfect, but yet did not do so, that seems to
argue that He either did not know how, or could not,
or did not wish to do so. At least it would be an imperfection in Him, if, possessing both the knowledge
and the power to do so, He had refused, and had
preferred imperfection to perfection.*

*The solution you next offer is, that the creature,
recognised as imperfect, should be considered not as
a whole, but rather as a part of the universe, from
which point of view it will be perfect. Your distinction
is certainly to be commended, but at the present point
we are not treating of the imperfection of a part in so
far as it is a part and is compared with the integrity
of the whole, but in so far as it is something complete
in itself and performs a special function. And when
you relate this again to the universe the difficulty always
remains, whether in truth the universe would have been
more perfect, if all its parts had been perfect, than as
the case actually holds, when many of its parts are
imperfect. Thus that State will be more perfect in
which all the citizens are good, than another in which
many or some are bad.*

*Whence, also, when a little later you say: that the
perfection of the universe is in some sense greater, in
that certain of its parts are not exempt from error,
than if they all had been alike, it is exactly as if you
were to say that the perfection of a state is greater in
that some of its citizens are evil than in the case when
they are all good. This lets us see that just as it
ought evidently to be the desire of a good prince that
all his subjects should be good, so it seems it should
have been the resolution of the Author of the universe
to create and keep all its parts free from defect. And*

*though you are able to allege that the perfection of
those parts which are free from defect, appears greater
when contrasted with those which are not exempt from
it, that nevertheless is merely accidental; just as the
virtue of good men, if more striking owing to the con-
trast between the good and the evil, is so only by accident. Consequently, just as we should not want any of
the citizens to be evil, in order that the good might
thereby become more distinguished, so, it seems, it
ought never to have come to pass that any part of the
universe should be subject to error, in order that the
parts that were free from it might thus be rendered
more conspicuous.*

You add: that neither must you complain that God
concurs with you in the act of erring; because all these
acts are true and good in so far as they depend upon
God, and in a certain sense more perfection accrues
to you from the fact that you can form such acts than
if you could not do so; while the privation in which
alone the formal reason of falsity or error consists,
does not require any concurrence on the part of God,
since it is not a real thing nor is related to Him. *But
subtle though that distinction be, it is nevertheless not
quite satisfactory. If indeed God does not concur in
the privation which is present in the act and is its falsity
and error, He yet concurs in the act; and unless He
concurred with it there would be no privation. Besides,
He Himself is the Author of that power which is deceived or falls into error, and consequently is the source
of a power which, so to speak, lacks power. Thus the
defect in the act is, it seems, to be referred not so
much to that power which lacks power as to its Author
who created it with this lack of power and, though
he was able to do so, declined to make it effective,
or more effective than it is. It is certainly counted no*

fault in a workman if he does not take the trouble of making a very large key to open a little casket, but if, after making it so small, he shapes it so that it fails to open the box, or does so with difficulty. Thus also, though God is indeed not to be blamed for giving to a mannikin a faculty of judging not so great as he thought would be necessary for either all or most or the greatest of creatures, it is still strange why he has assigned to us a faculty which is so uncertain, so confused, and so unequal to the task of deciding those few things on which He has willed that man should pass judgment.

Finally the form of error does not seem to consist in the incorrect use of the free will, as you maintain, so much as in the dissonance between the judgment and the thing whereof we judge; it seems to arise indeed from the fact that the understanding apprehends that thing otherwise than as it is. Whence it seems to be not so much the blame of the free will, which judges wrong, as of the understanding which does not give the correct reason. Thus the dependence of the power of choice upon the understanding seems to be such that, if the intellect indeed perceives something clearly or seems to do so, the will passes a judgment which is agreed on and determinate, whether that be really true, or whether it be thought to be true; if, on the other hand the perception on the part of the understanding be obscure, then our will passes a judgment which is doubtful and hesitating, though taken for the time to be more true than its opposite, and this whether the matter is really true or false. The result is that it is not so much in our power to guard against error, as to refrain from persisting in error, and that the appropriate exercise of judgment is not so much the reinforcing of the strength of the will, as the applica-

*tion of the understanding to the discovery of clearer
knowledge than that which our judgment is always
likely to follow.*

RELATIVE TO MEDITATION V

Of the essence of material things; and, again, of God, that He exists

*In the Fifth Meditation you first say that you distinctly imagine quantity, i.e., extension in length,
breadth and depth; likewise number, figure, situation,
motion and duration. Out of all these, the ideas of
which you say you possess, you select figure and, from
among the figures, the triangle, of which you write as
follows:* although there may nowhere in the world be
such a figure outside my thought, or ever have been,
there is nevertheless in this figure a determinate nature,
which I have not invented, and which does not depend
upon my mind, as appears from the fact that divers
properties can be demonstrated of that triangle, viz.,
that its three angles are equal to two right angles,
that the greatest side is subtended by the greatest
angle, and the like, which now, whether I wish it or
do not wish it, I recognise very clearly, even though I
have never thought of them at all before when I
imagined a triangle, and which therefore have not been
invented by me. *So much only do you have respecting
the essence of material things; for the few remarks
you add refer to the same matter. I have, indeed, no
desire to raise difficulties here; I suggest only that it
seems to be a serious matter to set up some immutable
and eternal nature in addition to God the all-powerful.*

*You declare finally that the certainty and truth of
all knowledge so depends upon our apprehension of
the true God alone, that, if we do not possess this, we
can have no true certainty or knowledge.*

In reply to this, my good Sir, since I admit that you are speaking seriously, there is nothing to say, but that it seems that you will have difficulty in getting anyone to believe that you were less certain of those geometrical proofs before the time when you established by reasoning the above conclusion about God, than after you had done so. For really those demonstrations seem to have an evidence and certainty of such a kind as by themselves to extort our assent to them, and when once recognised they do not allow the mind to have any further doubt. So true is this that the mind will as likely as not bid that evil Genius go to perdition; just as you might have done when you (although the existence of God was not yet known) asserted with much emphasis that you could not be imposed on about that proposition and inference: I think, hence I exist. Nay, even, however true it be, as nothing can be truer, that God exists, that He is the Author of everything, and that He is not a deceiver, since, nevertheless, these facts seem to be less evident than those geometrical proofs (of which the only proof required is that many controvert God's existence, His creation of the world, and many other truths), while no one denies the demonstrations of Geometry, is there anyone whom you can persuade that the evidence and certainty of the latter[1] is communicated to them from the former? Likewise who fancies that Diagoras, Theodorus, or any similar atheist, cannot be rendered certain of the truth of those mathematical demonstrations? Again, how often among believers do you come across one who, if asked why he is sure that in a (right angled) triangle the square on its base is equal to the square on its sides, will reply: because I know that God exists, and that God cannot

---

[1] I. E., the theorems of Geometry.

deceive, and that He is the cause of this fact as likewise as of all others.' Will he not rather reply: 'because I know it, and it has been shown to me by an indubitable demonstration'? How much the more likely is this to be the reply of Pythagoras, Plato, Archimedes, Euclid, and other mathematicians, none of whom seems to bring up the thought of God in order to be quite certain of his demonstrations! Yet, because you do not pledge your word for others, but only for yourself, and your attitude is also pious, there is really no reason for my objecting to it.

Relative to Meditation VI

Of the existence of Material Things, and of the real distinction between the Soul and the Body of Man

Finally you say: And although possibly (or rather certainly, as I shall say in a moment) I possess a body with which I am very intimately conjoined, yet because on the one side I have a clear and distinct idea of myself, inasmuch as I am only a thinking and not an extended thing, and on the other I possess a distinct idea of body, inasmuch as it is only an extended and not a thinking thing; it is certain that I am really distinct from my body, and can exist without it.

So this was your objective, was it? Hence, since the whole of the difficulty hinges on this, we must halt awhile, in order to see how you manage to make this position good. The principal matter here in question is the distinction between you and body. But what body do you here mean? Plainly this solid body composed of members, the body to which, without doubt, the following words refer: I possess a body connected with myself and it is certain that I am distinct from my body, *etc.*

But how, O Mind, is there no difficulty about this body?

But, not to urge this, my question is rather: are you not an extended thing, or are you not diffused throughout the body? I cannot tell what you will reply; for, though from the outset I recognised that you existed only in the brain, I formed that belief rather by conjecture than by directly following your opinion. I derived by conjecture from the statement which ensues, in which you assert, that you are not affected by all parts of the body, but only by the brain, or even by one of its smallest parts. *But I was not quite certain whether you were found therefore only in the brain or in a part of it, since you might be found in the whole body, but be acted on at only one part. Thus it would be according to the popular belief, which takes the soul to be diffused throughout the entire body, while yet it is in the eye alone that it has vision.*

Similarly the following words moved one to doubt: 'and although the whole mind seems to be united to the whole body,' etc. *You indeed do not there assert that you are united with the whole of the body, but you do not deny it. Howsoever it be, with your leave let me consider you firstly as diffused throughout the whole body. Whether you are the same as the soul, or something diverse from it, I ask you, O unextended thing, what you are that are spread from head to heel, or that are coextensive with the body, that have a like number of parts corresponding to its parts? Will you say that you are therefore unextended, because you are a whole in a whole, and are wholly in every part? I pray you tell me, if you maintain this, how you conceive it. Can a single thing thus be at the same time*

*wholly in several parts? Faith assures us of this in
the case of the sacred mystery (of the Eucharist).
But the question here is relative to you, a natural object,
and is indeed one relative to our natural light. Can
we grasp how there can be a plurality of places without there being a plurality of objects located in them?
Is not a hundred more than one? Likewise, if a thing
is wholly in one place, can it be in others, unless it is
itself outside itself, as place is outside place? Say
what you will, it will at least be obscure and uncertain whether you are wholly in any part and not rather
in the various parts of the body by means of your
several parts. And since it is much more evident that
nothing can exist as a whole in different places, it will
turn out to be still more clear that you are not wholly
in the single parts of your body but merely in the whole
as a whole, and that you are so by means of your
parts diffused through the whole and consequently that
you have extension.*

*Secondly let us suppose that you are in the brain
alone, or merely in some minute part of it. You perceive that the same thing is clearly an objection, since
however small that part be, it is nevertheless extended,
and you are coextensive with it, and consequently are
extended and have particular parts corresponding to
its particular parts. Will you say that you take that
part of the brain to be a point? That is surely incredible, but suppose it is a point. If it is indeed
something Physical, the same difficulty remains, because
such a point is extended and is certainly not devoid of
parts. If it is a Mathematical point you know that
it is given only by the imagination. But let it be given
or let rather us feign that in the brain there is given
a Mathematical point, to which you are united, and in
which you exist. Now, see how useless a fiction this*

will turn out to be. For, if it is to be assumed, we must feign it to exist in such a way that you are at the meeting place of the nerves by which all the regions informed by the soul transmit to the brain the ideas or semblances of the things perceived by the senses. But firstly, the nerves do not all meet at one point, whether for the reason that, as the brain is continued into the spinal marrow, many nerves all over the back pass into that, or because those which extend to the middle of the head are not found to terminate in the same part of the brain. But let us assume that they all do meet; none the less they cannot all unite in a mathematical point, since they are bodies, not mathematical lines, and so able to meet in a mathematical point. And supposing we grant that they do so unite, it will be impossible for the spirits[1] which pass through these to pass out of the nerves or to enter them, as being bodies; since body cannot be in or pass through what is not a place, as the mathematical point is. But though we should allow that the animal spirits do exist in or pass through what is not a place, nevertheless you, existing as you do in a point, in which there are neither right hand parts nor left hand, neither higher nor lower, nor anything similar, cannot judge as to whence they come nor what they report.

Moreover I say the same thing of those spirits which you must transmit in order to have feeling or to report tidings, and in order to move. I omit that we cannot grasp how you impress a motion upon them, you who are yourself in a point, unless you are really a body, or unless you have a body by which you are in contact

---

[1] The 'animal spirits' correspond to the 'nervous impulses' of modern psychology. Descartes and his contemporaries believed that an actual substance passed along the nerve when it was stimulated.

*with them and at the same time propel them. For,
if you say that they are moved by themselves, and that
you only direct their motion, remember that you somewhere else denied that the body is moved by itself; so
that we must thence infer that you are the cause of that
movement. Next, explain to us how such a direction
can take place without some effort and so some motion
on your part? How can there be effort directed towards anything, and motion on its part, without mutual
contact of what moves and what is moved? How can
there be contact apart from body, when (as is so clear
to the natural light)*

'Apart from body, naught touches or is touched?'

*In connection with this, you interpose several things
tending to the same conclusion, on all of which we
need not insist. One thing I note, and that is that you
say* that nature teaches you by the sensation of pain,
hunger, thirst, etc., that you are not lodged in the
body as a sailor in a ship, but that you are very
closely united with it and, so to speak, intermingled
with it so as to compose one whole along with it.
For if that were not the case, *you say,* "when my
body is hurt, I who am merely a thinking thing would
not feel pain, but should perceive the wound with the
mere understanding, just as the sailor perceives by
sight when something is damaged in his vessel, and
when my body has need of food or drink, I should
clearly understand this fact, and not have the confused
feelings of hunger and thirst. For all these sensations
of hunger, thirst, pain, etc., are in truth none other
than certain confused modes of thought which are
produced by the union and apparent intermingling of
mind and body."

This is indeed quite right; but it still remains to be

explained, how that union and apparent intermingling, *or* confusion, *can be found in you, if you are incorporeal, unextended and indivisible. For if you are not greater than a point, how can you be united with the entire body, which is of such great magnitude? How, at least, can you be united with the brain, or some minute part in it, which (as has been said) must yet have some magnitude or extension, however small it be? If you are wholly without parts, how can you mix or appear to mix with its minute subdivisions? For there is no mixture unless each of the things to be mixed has parts that can mix with one another. Further, if you are discrete, how could you be involved with and form one thing along with matter itself? Again since conjunction or union exists between certain parts, ought there not to be a relation of similarity between parts of this sort? But what must the union of the corporeal with the incorporeal be thought to be? Do we conceive how stone and air are fused together, as in pumice stone, so as to become a fusion of uniform character? Yet the similarity between stone and air which itself is also a body, is greater than that between body and soul, or a wholly incorporeal mind. Further, ought not that union to take place by means of the closest contact? But how, as I said before, can that take place, apart from body? How will that which is corporeal seize upon that which is incorporeal, so to hold it conjoined with itself, or how will the incorporeal grasp the corporeal, so as reciprocally to keep it bound to itself, if in it, the incorporeal, there is nothing which it can use to grasp the other, or by which it can be grasped.*

Hence, since you admit that you feel pain, I ask you how you think that you, if you are incorporeal and unextended, are capable of experiencing the sensation of pain. Thus the affection pain can only be understood as arising from some pulling asunder of bodily parts when something interferes and annuls their continuity. For example a state of pain is an unnatural state, but how can that be in an unnatural state or be affected contrary to nature, which by nature is of one sort, simple, indivisible and immutable? Again since pain is either alteration, or cannot occur without it, how can that be altered, which, being more devoid of parts than a point, cannot be altered nor can cease to be just as it is, unless it turns into nothing? I add also: since pain comes from the foot, the arm, and from other regions at the same time, ought there not to be in you various parts, in which you receive it in various ways, in order not to be confused and to regard it as being the pain of merely one part. But, in a word, the general difficulty always remains, viz., how the corporeal can have anything in common with the incorporeal, or what relationship may be established between the one and the other.

These, my good Sir, are the observations that occurred to me in connection with your Meditations. I repeat that you ought not to give yourself any thought about them, since my judgment is not of such moment as to deserve to have any weight with you. For as, when some food is pleasant to my palate, I do not defend my taste, which I see is offensive to others, as being more perfect than anyone else's; so, when my mind welcomes an opinion which does not please others, I am far from holding that I have hit upon the truer theory. I think that the truth is rather this—that each enjoys his own sensation; and I hold that it is almost as unjust to wish everyone to have the same belief, as to want all people to be alike in the sense of taste: I say so, in order that you may hold yourself free to dismiss everything that I have said as not worth a

straw, and to omit it altogether. It will be enough
if you acknowledge my strong affection for you, and do
not esteem as nought my admiration for your personal
worth. Perhaps some matter has been advanced some-
what inconsiderately, as is only too likely to happen
when one is expressing dissent. Any such passage
which may occur I wholly disavow and sacrifice; pray
blot it out, and be assured, that I have desired nothing
more than to deserve well of you and to keep my friend-
ship with you quite intact.

With kind regards.

Paris, 16th May, 1641.

THE AUTHOR'S REPLY TO THE FIFTH SET OF OBJECTIONS

SIR:

The essay in which you criticize my meditations is
exceedingly well-written and carefully executed, and
to me it appears that it will do much to set them in
a clear light. Consequently I consider that I am greatly
beholden to you for writing it, as well as to the Rev.
Father Mersenne for inciting you to do so. Our friend,
who is such an eager enquirer into all things, and who
more especially promotes unweariedly everything that
tends to the glory of God, knows that the best way of
determining whether my arguments are to be treated as
accurate demonstrations, is that some men of out-
standing eminence in scholarship and ability, should
subject them to a rigorous criticism, so as finally to
make trial of my powers of giving a satisfactory answer
to their objections. This is why he has challenged so
many to attempt the task, and has prevailed upon some
to do so, among whom I am glad to see you. For,
though in order to refute my opinions you have not so
much employed philosophical reasoning as made use of

certain oratorical devices so as to elude my argument, this is in itself a matter of gratification to me, since I shall for this reason infer that it will not be easy to bring up in opposition to me arguments which differ from those which you have read in the preceding criticisms urged by other people. Further, if such had existed, they would not have escaped your penetration and industry, and I hold that here your only purpose has been to bring to my notice those conceptions which might be used to avoid the force of my arguments by those whose minds are so immersed in matters of sense as to shrink from all metaphysical reflections, and that you thus gave me an opportunity for meeting these. Wherefore here I shall reply to you not as a keen-eyed philosopher, but as to one of these fleshly individuals whom you impersonate.

Of the Objections Urged Against the First Meditation

You say that *you approve of my determination to rid my mind of prejudices,* especially since no one can pretend that there is any fault to find with this; but you would prefer me to proceed *simply and with few words,* i.e., to carry out my resolve only in a perfunctory manner. This is forsooth to assume that it is very easy for all to free themselves from the errors in which, since infancy, they have been steeped, and that too much care may be employed in carrying this out, a contention which no one maintains. I suppose you wished to show that many men, though verbally admitting that prejudices should be avoided, nevertheless completely fail to avoid them, because they expend no toil and pains upon the attempt, and never think that anything which they have once admitted to be true should be regarded as a prejudice. You certainly play the rôle of such people excellently here, and omit none of their possible arguments, but there is nothing in this action which seems to suggest the Philosopher. Likewise a Philosopher would not have said *that I, in considering everything doubtful as false, did not so much dismiss an old prejudice as take up with a new one.* For he knows that falsities are often assumed instead of truths for the purpose of throwing light on the truth: for exmaple, Astronomers imagine the existence of the equator, the zodiac, and other circles in the heaven, while Geometricians attach new lines to given figures, and Philosophers frequently act in similar fashion. But the man who describes this as *having recourse to an artifice, eagerness for verbal trickery, and seeking evasions,* and declares *that it is unworthy of philosophical candour and the love of truth,* manifests that he at least has no desire to make use of philosophical candour or to employ any argument other than rhetorical humbug.

Concerning the Objections Brought Against the Second Meditation

Here you proceed to employ rhetorical wiles in place of reasoning; for you pretend that I speak in jest when I am quite serious, and takes as serious, and as uttered and asserted as true, what I propounded only as a question and as arising out of common opinion for the purpose of enquiring further into it.

What grounds have you for saying *that there was no need of such an elaborate mechanism in order to prove that I exist?* Really these very words of yours give me the best grounds for believing that my labours have not yet been sufficiently great, since I have as yet failed to make you understand the matter rightly.

When you say that *I could have inferred the same
conclusion from any of my other actions,* you wander
far from the truth, because there is none of my activities
of which I am wholly certain (in the sense of having
metaphysical certitude, which alone is here involved),
save thinking alone. For example, you have no right
to make the inference: *I walk, hence I exist,* except
in so far as our awareness of walking is a thought; it
is of this alone that the inference holds good, not of
the motion of the body, which sometimes does not exist,
as in dreams, when nevertheless I appear to walk.
Hence from the fact that I think that I walk I can very
well infer the existence of the mind which so thinks,
but not that of the body which walks. So it is also
in all other cases.

Next, with a not infelicitous comedy, you proceed to
question me, no longer as a complete man, but as a
soul in separation from the body; and in so doing you
seem to remind me that these objections proceed not
from the mind of an acute philosopher but from the
flesh alone. I ask you therefore, O flesh, or whatever
the name be by which you prefer to be known, have
you so little intercourse with the mind, that you have
not been able to note when I corrected that popular
notion, by which it is imagined that that which thinks
is like wind or some similar body? I corrected it then,
surely, when I showed that it could be supposed that no
wind or other body existed, and that nevertheless everything by means of which I recognise myself as a thinking being remains. Hence your subsequent questions
as to *why I cannot therefore be still a wind, and why
I cannot occupy space, and why I cannot be subject
to many motions, etc.,* are so devoid of sense as to
require no reply.

You have a difficulty, however, you say, *as to whether*

I think that the soul always thinks. But why should it not always think, when it is a thinking substance? Why is it strange that we do not remember the thoughts it has had when in the womb or in a stupor, when we do not even remember the most of those we know we have had when grown up, in good health, and awake? For the recollection of the thoughts which the mind has had during the period of its union with the body, it is necessary for certain traces of them to be impressed on the brain; and turning and applying itself to these the mind remembers. Is it remarkable if the brain of an infant or of one in a stupor is unfit to receive these residual impressions?

Concerning the Objections to the Third Meditation

Splendid! Here at length you do bring up an argument against me, a feat which, so far as I can make out, you have hitherto failed to accomplish. In order to prove *that it is not a sure rule that what we very clearly and distinctly perceive is true,* you allege that to great intellects, which it appears ought to have had the most numerous clear and distinct perceptions, it has seemed nevertheless that the truth of things was hidden either in God or at the bottom of a well. Here I admit that your argument as drawn from authority is quite right. But, O flesh, you should have remembered that you here were addressing a mind so far withdrawn from corporeal things that it does not even know that anyone has existed before it, and hence cannot be influenced by the authority of others. Your passage referring to the sceptics is a good enough commonplace, but proves nothing, as neither does your point about people facing death on behalf of false opinions, because it can never be proved that they clearly and distinctly perceive what they pertinaciously affirm. I do not question what you next say, viz., that it is not so much a question of taking pains to establish the truth of the rule, as of finding a method for deciding whether we err or not when we think that we perceive something clearly. But I contend that this has been carefully attended to in its proper place where I first laid aside all prejudices, and afterwards enumerated all the chief ideas, distinguishing the clear from the obscure and confused.

When you say that the idea of God possesses reality only *owing to the fact that we have heard certain attributes predicated of Him,* I should like you to tell us whence men at the beginning, the men from whom we have learned them, drew this very idea of God. If it was from themselves, why may we not derive this same idea from ourselves? If from a revelation by God, this proves that God exists.

Moreover in your next statement, *that he who says that anything is infinite attributes to a thing which he does not comprehend a name which he does not understand,* you fail to distinguish an exercise of intellect conformable to the scale of our understanding, such as each one of us experiences himself to employ in thinking about the infinite, with a concept adequate to the things, such as no one possesses not only in the matter of the infinite but perhaps not even in connection with any thing else, however small. Neither is it true that the infinite is apprehended by a negation of boundary or limitation, since on the contrary all limitation contains a negation of the infinite.

Further it is not the case that *the idea which represents all those perfections which we ascribe to God contains no more objective reality than finite things have.* You yourself confess that these perfections are amplified by our understanding in order to be ascribed to God. Do you, then, not think that the things which are so augmented are not greater than those that have not been so dealt with? Again, what can account for the power of amplifying all created perfections, i.e., of conceiving something greater or more ample than they, unless the fact that the idea of something greater, viz., of God, exists in us? Finally, neither is it true that *God will mean something very little, unless He be greater than as conceived by us;* for He is conceived as infinite and nothing can be greater than the infinite. You, however, confuse intellectual activity with imagination, and feign that we imagine God after the fashion of some huge man, in the same way as if one who had never seen an elephant were to imagine that it was like a very huge insect, e.g., a tick; which, I agree with you, would be excessively foolish.

No point that you raise here in disputing about ideas requires any reply, since you restrict the term idea solely to the images depicted in the fancy, while I extend it to whatever is thought.

But by the way I should like to ask what the argument is by which you prove *that nothing acts on itself.* It is, forsooth, not your wont to employ argument. But here you have used as an illustration the finger which does not strike itself and the eye which does not see itself in itself but in a mirror, to prove your case. To this we have an easy reply; it is not the eye which sees the mirror rather than itself, but the mind which alone recognizes both mirror, and eye, and itself as well. Likewise other examples can be given in the domain of corporeal things, e.g., when a top draws itself round in a circle, is not that rotation an action which it exerts on itself?

When you deny *that we continually require the activity of the primal cause in order that we may continue to exist,* you dispute a matter which all Metaphysicians affirm to be manifest, but one about which the unlearned often do not reflect, attending as they do only to causes *of coming* into being, but not to those *of being.* Thus an architect is the cause of a house and a father of his son *in respect of coming into being* merely, and for this reason, when it is an absolute production, an effect can remain in existence without any cause of this kind; but the sun is the cause of the light proceeding from it, and God is the cause of created things, not only *in respect of their coming into existence,* but also *in respect of their continuing to exist,* and must always expend His activity on the effect in the same way in order to make it stay the same thing.

This can be plainly demonstrated from what I explained about the independence of the parts of time, which you in vain attempt to elude by propounding *the necessary character of the connection between the parts of time* considered in the abstract. Here it is not a question of abstract time, but of the time or duration of something which endures; and you will not deny that the single moments of this time can be separated from their neighbours, i.e., that a thing which endures through individual moments may cease to exist.

When you allege *that we possess a power which suffices to guarantee our preservation, unless some destructive cause supervene,* you do not notice that you ascribe to the creature a perfection of the Creator, if the creature is to be able to continue in existence in independence of anything else; while you assign to the Creator the imperfection of a creature, because He must aim at non-existence by means of a positive act, whenever he wishes to cause a cessation of our existence.

When you ask *whence I get my proof that the idea of God is, as it were, the mark of a workman imprinted on his work, and what is the mode in which it is impressed, what is the form of that mark,* it is very much as if I, coming across a picture which showed a technique that pointed to Apelles alone as the painter, were to say that that inimitable technique was, so to speak, a mark impressed by Apelles on all his pictures in order to distinguish them from others, but you replied with the questions: 'what is the form of that mark?' and 'what is its mode of impression?' Such an enquiry would seem to merit laughter rather than any reply.

What answer do you deserve when you go on to say: *if it is not other than the work or thing itself, you yourself then are an idea, you are nothing but a mode of thought, you are yourself both the mark impressed and the subject on which it is impressed?* Would it not be an equally clever thing to urge, when I said that the technique of Apelles was that by which his pictures were distinguished from others, that it was nothing other than the pictures themselves: that therefore those pictures were nothing but the technique, and did not consist of matter at all, and that hence they were merely a mode of painting, etc.?

When, in order to disprove *that we are made after the image of God,* you state its consequence, that *God will therefore have a human form,* and go on to recount all the particulars in which human nature differs from the divine, is there anything cleverer in this than if, in order to show that certain pictures by Apelles were not made after the likeness of Alexander, you were to allege that this implied that Alexander was like a picture, whereas pictures were composed of wood and paint, not bones and flesh as Alexander is? Now the nature of an image is not such that it is identical with that of which it is an image in all particulars, but only that it copies it in certain respects; and it is clear that

that perfect power of thought which we understand to be in God, is represented by that less perfect faculty which we possess.

Finally when you say how strange it is *that other men do not think about God in the same way as I do, when He has impressed the idea of Himself on them exactly as on me,* it is precisely as if you were to marvel that since all are acquainted with the idea of a triangle, they do not all perceive an equal number of truths about it, and some probably reason about this very figure incorrectly.

Concerning the Objections to the Fourth Meditation

I have sufficiently explained our idea of *nothing,* and the way in which we participate in *non-existence,* by calling it a negative idea and saying that it means merely that we are not the supreme Being, and that we lack many things. But you are always discovering imaginary difficulties.

When you say *that I see that certain of God's works are not absolutely perfect and complete* you openly invent something which I have neither stated there nor thought; all that I said being that if certain things were considered not in the light of being but part of the world, as they really are, but as complete wholes, then they might seem to be imperfect.

Here you are everywhere guilty of a false assumption in taking as a positive imperfection *the fact that we are liable to err,* since this is really (except with respect to God) the negation of a greater perfection. Again the comparison between the citizens of a State and the parts of the universe is not strictly accurate; for a bad disposition on the part of citizens is, relatively to the State, something positive, but this does not apply to a man's being liable to err, or not possessing all perfections, when that is taken relatively to the good of the universe. A better comparison could be drawn between the man who would like to have the whole of the human body covered with eyes, in order that it might appear more beautiful, because no bodily part is more beautiful than the eye, and him who thinks that no existing creatures ought to be liable to err, i.e., should not be wholly perfect.

It is plainly a false supposition on your part *that God has assigned to some a function which is base, and has allotted imperfections to us,* and so forth. Plainly likewise it is false *that God has assigned to man a faculty of judgment which is so uncertain, so confused, and so unequal to the task of deciding those few things on which He has willed that man should pass judgment.*

You desire me here *briefly to state to what the will may extend, which escapes the understanding.* Precisely to everything in which we happen to err. Thus when you judge that the mind is a certain attenuated body, you are indeed able to understand that the mind is itself, i.e., a thinking thing, and likewise that an attenuated body is an extended thing; but assuredly you do not understand that the thing which thinks and the extended things are one and the same thing, you only wish to believe it because you have already believed it and do not willingly change your mind. Thus when you judge that an apple which has been poisoned will suit you as food, you indeed understand that its odour, colour, and similar qualities are pleasant, but not that the apple is therefore good for you as food; it is because you wish to believe it that you pass that judgment. So while I confess that there is nothing that we wish about which we do not understand something, I deny that what we understand equals what we will; for we may wish many things about the same matter of which

we understand very little. Moreover when we judge
wrongly, we do not therefore will wrongly, but perchance something wrong; neither do we understand
anything wrongly, we are only said to understand
awrong when we judge that we understand something
better than we really understand it.

You next deny certain truths about the indeter-
minateness of the will; and although they are in themselves quite evident, I refuse to undertake to prove
them before your eyes. For these matters are such that
anyone ought to experience them in himself, rather than
be convinced of them by ratiocination; but you, O flesh,
appear not to pay heed to what the mind transacts
within itself. Refuse then to be free, if freedom does
not please you; I at least shall rejoice in my liberty,
since I experience it in myself, and you have assailed
it not with proof but with bare negations merely.
Perchance I shall receive more credence from others,
because I affirm that which I have experienced and
anyone may experience in himself, than you who make
your denial merely because you chance not to have
experienced it.

Yet it can be shown conclusively from your words
that you yourself have had that experience. For in
denying *that we can guard against error,* because you
will not have it that the will can be borne towards
anything to which it is not determined by the understanding, you at the same time allow that *we can refrain
from persisting in error.* But to do so is wholly impossible unless the will has the power of directing itself
towards one side or the other apart from any determination by the understanding, the fact which you denied.
For, if the understanding has once determined the
will to propound some false judgment, I ask you: when
first it (the will) begins to take heed lest it continue

in error, what is it that determines it to do so? If that determination is due to itself then it can be moved in a certain direction without impulsion by the understanding, which you denied, and about which alone the dispute has been raised. If, on the other hand, it is the understanding which is responsible, it is not the will itself which takes heed; and what happens is merely that, just as it was formerly impelled towards the falsity which the understanding set before it, so now it accidentally happens to be directed towards the truth, because the understanding has set the truth before it. But besides this I should like to know what conception you have of the nature of falsity, and how you think that it can be an object of the understanding. I, who by falsity understand only the privation of truth, am convinced that it is an absolute contradiction that the understanding should apprehend the false under the guise of the truth; but this would be a necessary consequence if understanding could determine the will to embrace the false.

Concerning the Objections to the Fifth Meditation

You say *that it seems to you to be a serious matter to set up some immutable and eternal being in addition to God;* and you would be quite right if it were a question of existence, or merely if I had set up something with an immutability not dependent on God. But in the same way as the poets feign that, while the fates were indeed established by Jove, yet once established, he was restricted in his action by his maintenance of them; similarly I do not think that the essence of things and those mathematical truths which may be known about them, are independent of God; yet I think that because God so wished it and brought it to pass, they *are* immutable and eternal. Now whether you think

this to have serious consequences or the reverse, to me
it is sufficient if it is true.

Against these criticisms in which you point to
Diogenes, Theodorus, Pythagoras and others, and adduce the case of the Sceptics, who had doubts about
these very geometrical demonstrations, I affirm that
they would not have done so, if, as they might have
done, they had known God. Further, one thing is not
proved to be better known than another, because it
appears to be true to more people, but only because
to those who know both, as they may, it appears to be
prior in knowledge, and more evident and certain.

Concerning the Objections to the Sixth Meditation

Finally it is worthy of you alone, O flesh, to think
*that the idea of God, of an Angel, and of the human
mind, are corporeal, or after the fashion of the corporeal, derived forsooth from the human form, and from
other very subtle, simple, and imperceptible objects,
such as air or aether.* For whosover thus represents
God or the mind to himself, tries to imagine a thing
which is not imageable, and constructs nothing but a
corporeal idea to which he falsely assigns the name
God or mind. For, in the true idea of mind, nothing
is contained but thought and its attributes, of which
none is corporeal.

I shall not here delay to notice your tedious and
frequent repetitions of such statements as, e.g., *that
I have failed to prove certain matters,* which nevertheless I have demonstrated; *that I have treated only of
the solid body,* though I have dealt with every kind
of matter, even of the subtlest; etc. What opposition
other than a plain denial is merited by affirmations of
this kind, which are not supported by reason? Yet
incidentally I should like to discover what argument

you use to prove that I have treated of solid matter rather than of that which is subtle. Have I not said: '*I possess (a body) united with myself, and it is certain that I am distinct from my body?*' And I cannot see why these words are not equally applicable to an impalpable and to a solid body; nor do I think that anyone but you could fail to see this. Apart from this, in the second Meditation I made it evident that mind could be understood as an existing substance, though we did not understand anything to exist that was wind, or fire, or vapour, or breath, or anything else of a bodily nature, however impalpable and refined. I said, however, that at that point I did not discuss whether it was in truth distinct from every kind of body; but in the present passage I did discuss the matter and proved my assertion. But you show that you have wholly failed to comprehend the controversy by your confusion of the issue as to what may be known of the soul with the question as to that which the soul really is.

In adding that *the mind is not extended,* my intention was not thereby to explain what mind is, but merely to proclaim that those people are wrong who think that it is extended. In the same way if any people affirmed *that Bucephalus was Music* it would not be idle of others to deny the statement. In good truth your subsequent attempts to prove that mind is extended because it makes use of a body which is extended, seem to employ no better reason than if you were to argue that because Bucephalus neighs and whinnies, and so utters sounds that are comparable with Music, it followed that Bucephalus is Music. For, though mind is united with the whole body, it does not follow that it itself is extended throughout the body, because it is not part of its notion to be extended, but merely to think. Neither does it apprehend extension by means of an extended semblance existing in it, although it images it by applying itself to a corporeal semblance which is extended, as has already been said. Finally there is no necessity for it itself to be a body although it has the power of moving body.

What you say at this point *relatively to the union of mind and body* is similar to what precedes. At no place do you bring an objection to my arguments; you only set forth the doubts which you think follow from my conclusions, though they arise merely from your wishing to subject to the scrutiny of the imagination matters which, by their own nature, do not fall under it. Thus when you wish to compare the union of mind and body with the mixture of two bodies, it is enough for me to reply that no such comparison ought to be set up, because the two things are wholly diverse, and we must not imagine that there are parts in mind because it is aware of parts in body. Whence do you derive the conclusion that everything which mind knows must exist in mind? If that were so, then, when it was aware of the magnitude of the earth, it would be obliged to have that object within it, and consequently would not only be extended but greater in extent than the whole world.

Up to this point we have had a discussion between mind and flesh, and, as was but natural, in many things they disagreed. But now, at the end, I catch sight of the real Gassendi, and have grounds for suspecting that he is a man of great philosophical eminence. I salute him as a man noted for his intellectual candour and integrity of life, and shall endeavour, by employing all the courtesies which I can muster, to merit his friendship at all times. I therefore ask him not to take it amiss if, in replying to his objections I have used a Philosophical freedom, since their entire contents caused me very great pleasure. Among other things I rejoiced that such a long and carefully composed dissertation contained nothing in opposition to my reasoning, nothing opposed even to my conclusions, to which I was not able very easily to reply.

FROM THE SIXTH SET OF OBJECTIONS[1]

The objection

The difficulty arises from the indifference of the judgment or liberty which you refuse to allow to the perfection of choice, but ascribe to an imperfect will alone, thus removing the indifference as often as the mind clearly perceives what ought to be believed or performed or left undone. But do you not see that by positing this you destroy the liberty of God, from Whom you remove that indifference as to whether He will create this world rather than another or any world at all? Though yet it belongs to the faith to believe that God has from eternity been indifferent as to whether He would create one, or many, worlds, or no world. But who doubts that God has at all times had the clearest vision of all things that were to be done or left undone? Therefore the clearest vision and perception of things does not annul the indifference of choice; and if it cannot harmonize with human liberty, neither will it be compatible with the divine, since the essences of things are, like numbers, indivisible and unchanging. Wherefore indifference is included no less in the divine than in human freedom of choice.

How can the truths of Geometry or Metaphysics such as you mention be immutable and eternal, and yet not be independent of God? What is the species of causality by which they are related to Him or dependent on

---

1 Urged by divers theologians and philosophers.

Him? What possible action of God's could annul the nature of the triangle? And how could He from all eternity bring it to pass that it was untrue that twice four was eight? or that a triangle had not three angles? Hence either these truths depend upon the understanding alone while it thinks them, or upon existing things, or they are independent, since God evidently could not have brought it to pass that any of these essences or verities was not from all eternity.

Descartes' Reply

As to the freedom of the will, a very different account must be given of it as it exists in God and as it exists in us. For it is self-contradictory that the will of God should not have been from eternity indifferent to all that has come to pass or that ever will occur, because we can form no conception of anything good or true, of anything to be believed or to be performed or to be omitted, the idea of which existed in the divine understanding before God's will determined Him so to act as to bring it to pass. Nor do I here speak of priority of time; I mean that it was not even prior in order, or in nature, or in reasoned relation, as they say [in the schools], so that that idea of good impelled God to choose one thing rather than another. Thus, to illustrate, God did not will to create the world in time because he saw that it would be better thus than if he created it from all eternity; nor did he will the three angles of a triangle to be equal to two right angles because he knew that they could not be otherwise. On the contrary, because he worked to create the world in time it is for that reason better than if he had created it from all eternity; and it is because he willed the three angles of a triangle to be necessarily equal to two right angles that this is true and cannot be otherwise;

and so in other cases. And though it may be said that it is the merit of the saints which is the cause of their obtaining eternal life, this causes no difficulty; for their merits are not causes of their obtaining this in the sense that they determine God to will anything; they are merely the cause of an effect of which God wished them from all eternity to be the cause. Thus that supreme indifference in God is the supreme proof of his omnipotence. But as to man, since he finds the nature of all goodness and truth already determined by God, and his will cannot bear upon anything else, it is evident that he embraces the true and the good the more willingly and hence the more freely in proportion as he sees the true and the good the more clearly, and that he is never indifferent save when he does not know what is the more true or the better, or at least when he does not see clearly enough to prevent him from doubting about it. Thus the indifference which attaches to human liberty is very different from that which belongs to the divine. Neither does it here matter that the essences of things are said to be indivisible: for firstly no essence can belong in a univocal sense both to God and His creature; and finally indifference does not belong to the essence of human liberty, since we are free not only when our ignorance of the right renders us indifferent, but also, and chiefly, when a clear perception impels us to prosecute some definite course.

To one who pays attention to God's immensity, it is clear that nothing at all can exist which does not depend on Him. This is true not only of everything that subsists, but of all order, of every law, and of every reason of truth and goodness; for otherwise God, as has been said just before, would not have been wholly indifferent to the creation of what he has created. For

if any reason for what is good had preceded His pre-
ordination, it would have determined Him towards that
which it was best to bring about; but on the contrary
because He determined Himself towards those things
which ought to be accomplished, for that reason, as it
stands in Genesis, *they are very good;* that is to say,
the reason for their goodness is the fact that He wished
to create them so.   Nor is it worth while asking in
what class of cause fall that goodness or those other
truths, mathematical as well as metaphysical, which
depend upon God; for since those who enumerated the
classes of cause did not pay sufficient attention to
causality of this type, it would have been by no means
strange if they had given it no name.   Nevertheless
they did give it a name; for it can be styled efficient
causality in the same sense as the king is the efficient
cause of the laws, although a law is not a thing which
exists physically, but is merely as they say [in the
Schools] a moral entity.   Again it is useless to inquire
how God could from all eternity bring it about that it
should be untrue that twice four is eight, etc.; for I
admit that that cannot be understood by us.   Yet since
on the other hand I correctly understand that nothing
in any category of causation can exist which does not
depend upon God, and that it would have been easy for
Him so to appoint that we human beings should not
understand how these very things could be otherwise
than they are, it would be irrational to doubt concerning that which we correctly understand, because of that
which we do not understand and perceive no need to
understand.   Hence neither should we think *that eternal
truths depend upon the human understanding or on other
existing things;* they must depend on God alone, who, as
the supreme legislator, ordained them from all eternity.

THE PRINCIPLES OF PHILOSOPHY

FIRST PART

OF THE PRINCIPLES OF HUMAN KNOWLEDGE

PRINCIPLE XXIV

That in passing from the knowledge that God exists, to the knowledge of his creatures, we must recollect that our understanding is finite, and the power of God infinite.

Being thus aware that God alone is the true cause of all that is or can be, we shall doubtless follow the best method of philosophising, if, from the knowledge which we possess of His nature, we pass to an explanation of the things which He has created, and if we try from the notions which exist naturally in our minds to deduce it, for in this way we shall obtain a perfect science, that is, a knowledge of the effects through their causes. But in order that we may undertake this task with most security from error, we must recollect that God, the creator of all things, is infinite and that we are altogether finite.

PRINCIPLE XXV

And that we must believe all that God has revealed, even though it is above the range of our capacities.

Thus if God reveals to us or to others certain things concerning Himself which surpass the range of our natural power of intelligence, such as the mysteries of

the incarnation and the Trinity, we shall have no difficulty in believing them, although we may not clearly
understand them.   For we should not think it strange
that in the immensity of His nature, as also in the objects of His creation, there are many things beyond
the range of our comprehension.

Principle XXVI

*That we must not try to dispute about the infinite,
but just consider that all that in which we find no limits
is indefinite, such as the extension of the world, the
divisibility of its parts, the number of the stars, etc.*

We will thus never hamper ourselves with disputes
about the infinite, since it would be absurd that we who
are finite should undertake to decide anything regarding
it, and by this means in trying to comprehend it, so to
speak regard it as finite.   That is why we do not care
to reply to those who demand whether the half of an
infinite line is infinite, and whether an infinite number
is even or odd and so on, because it is only those who
imagine their mind to be infinite who appear to find it
necessary to investigate such questions.   And for our
part, while we regard things in which, in a certain
sense, we observe no limits, we shall not for all that
state that they are infinite, but merely hold them to be
indefinite.   Thus because we cannot imagine an extension so great that we cannot at the same time
conceive that there may be one yet greater, we shall
say that the magnitude of possible things is indefinite.
And because we cannot divide a body into parts which
are so small that each part cannot be divided into others
yet smaller, we shall consider that the quantity may
be divided into parts whose number is indefinite.   And

because we cannot imagine so many stars that it is impossible for God to create more, we shall suppose the number to be indefinite, and so in other cases.

Principle XXVII

What is the difference between the indefinite and the infinite?

And we shall name these things indefinite rather than infinite in order to reserve to God alone the name of infinite, first of all because in Him alone we observe no limitation whatever, and because we are quite certain that He can have none, and in the second place in regard to other things, because we do not in the same way positively understand them to be in every part unlimited, but merely negatively admit that their limits, if they exist, cannot be discovered by us.

Principle XXVIII

That we must not inquire into the final, but only into the efficient causes of created things.

Finally we shall not seek for the reason of natural things from the end which God or nature has set before him in their creation; for we should not take so much upon ourselves as to believe that God could take us into His counsels. But regarding Him as the efficient cause of all things, we shall merely try to discover by the light of nature that He has placed in us, applied to those attributes of which He has been willing we should have some knowledge, what must be concluded regarding the effects that we perceive by the senses; but we must keep in mind what has been said, that we must trust to this natural light only so long as nothing contrary to it is revealed by God Himself.

Principle XXIX

That God is not the cause of our errors.

The first of God's attributes which falls to be considered here is that He is absolutely true and the source of all light, so that it is evidently a contradiction that He should deceive us, that is to say, that He should be properly and positively the cause of the errors to which we are conscious of being subject. For although the capacity for deceit would seem to be a mark of subtlety of mind amongst men, yet the will to deceive proceeds only from malice, or fear, or weakness, and it cannot consequently be attributed to God.

Principle XXX

And consequently all that we perceive clearly is true, and this delivers us from the doubts put forward above.

Whence it follows that the light of nature, or the faculty of knowledge which God has given us, can never disclose to us any object which is not true, inasmuch as it comprehends it, that is, inasmuch as it apprehends it clearly and distinctly. Because we should have had reason to think God a deceiver if He had given us this faculty perverted, or such that we should take the false for the true [when using the faculty aright]. And this should deliver us from the supreme doubt which encompassed us when we did not know whether our nature had been such that we had been deceived in things that seemed most clear. It should also protect us against all the other reasons already mentioned which we had for doubting. The truths of mathematics should now be above suspicion, for they are of the clearest. And if we perceive anything by our senses, either waking or sleeping, if it is clear and distinct, and if we separate it from what is obscure and confused, we shall easily assure ourselves of what is the truth. I do not require to say more on this particular subject here, since I have treated of it fully in the Meditations on Metaphysics, and what I intend to say later will serve to explain it more accurately.

Principle XLIV

That we shall always judge ill when we assent to what we do not clearly perceive, although our judgment may be true; and that it frequently is our memory that deceives us by leading us to believe that certain things had been satisfactorily established by us.

It is also quite certain that whenever we give our assent to some reason which we do not exactly understand, we either deceive ourselves, or, if we arrive at the truth, it is only by chance, and thus we cannot be certain that we are not in error. It is true that it happens but rarely that we judge of a matter at the same time as we observe that we do not apprehend it, because the light of nature teaches us that we must not judge of anything that we do not understand. But we frequently err when we presume we have known certain things as being stored up in our memory, to which on recollection we give our assent, and of which we have never possessed any knowledge at all.

Principle XLV

What a clear and distinct perception is.

There are even a number of people who throughout all their lives perceive nothing so correctly as to be capable of judging of it properly. For the knowledge upon which a certain and incontrovertible judgment can be

formed, should not alone be clear but also distinct. I
term that clear which is present and apparent to an
attentive mind, in the same way as we assert that we
see objects clearly when, being present to the regarding
eye, they operate upon it with sufficient strength. But
the distinct is that which is so precise and different
from all other objects that it contains within itself
nothing but what is clear.

PRINCIPLE XLVI

*It is shown from the example of pain that a percep-
tion may be clear without being distinct, but it cannot
be distinct unless it is clear.*

When, for instance, a severe pain is felt, the perception of this pain may be very clear, and yet for all that
not distinct, because it is usually confused by the suffer-
ers with the obscure judgment that they form upon its
nature, assuming as they do that something exists in
the part affected, similar to the sensation of pain of
which they are alone clearly conscious. In this way
perception may be clear without being distinct, and
cannot be distinct without being also clear.

PRINCIPLE XLVII

*That in order to remove the prejudices of our youth,
it must be considered what there is that is clear in each
of our simple notions.*

Indeed in our early years, our mind was so immersed
in the body, that it knew nothing distinctly, although it
perceived much sufficiently clearly; and because it even
then formed many judgments, numerous prejudices were
contracted from which the majority of us can hardly
ever hope to become free. But in order that we may

now free ourselves from them I shall here enumerate
all these simple notions which constitute our reflections,
and distinguish whatever is clear in each of them from
what is obscure, or likely to cause us to err.

Principle XLVIII

*That all the objects of our perceptions are to be
considered either as things or the affections of things,
or else as eternal truths; and the enumeration of things.*

I distinguish all the objects of our knowledge either
into things or the affections of things, or as eternal
truths having no existence outside our thought. Of the
things we consider as real, the most general are *substance, duration, order, number,* and possibly such other
similar matters as range through all the classes of real
things. I do not however observe more than two ultimate classes of real things—the one is intellectual things,
or those of the intelligence, that is, pertaining to the
mind or to thinking substance, the other is material
things, or that pertaining to extended substance, i.e. to
body. Perception, volition, and every mode of knowing
and willing, pertain to thinking substance; while to
extension pertain magnitude or extension in length,
breadth and depth, figure, movement, situation, divisibility of things into parts of themselves, and such like.
Besides these, there are, however, certain things which
we experience in ourselves and which should be attributed neither to mind nor body alone, but to the close
and intimate union that exists between the body and
mind as I shall later on explain in the proper place.
Such are the appetites of hunger, thirst, etc., and also
the emotions or passions of the mind which do not subsist in mind or thought alone, as the emotions of anger,
joy, sadness, love, etc.; and, finally all the sensations

such as pain, pleasure, light and colour, sounds, odours
tastes, heat, hardness, and all other tactile qualities.

Principle XLIX

*That eternal truths cannot be enumerated thus, and
that this is not requisite.*

What I have hitherto enumerated are regarded either
as the qualities of things or their modes.

[We must now talk of what we know as eternal
truths.]

When we apprehend that it is impossible that any
thing can be formed of nothing, the proposition *e
nihilo nihil fit* is not to be considered as an existing
thing, or the mode of a thing, but as a certain eternal
truth which has its seat in our mind, and is a common
notion or axiom. Of the same nature are the follow
ing: 'It is impossible that the same thing can be and
not be at the same time,' and that 'what has been done
cannot be undone,' 'that he who thinks must exist while
he thinks,' and very many other propositions the whole
of which it would not be easy to enumerate. But [this
is not necessary since] we cannot fail to recognise them
when the occasion presents itself for us to do so, and
if we have no prejudices to blind us.

Principle L

*That these eternal truths are clearly perceived, but
not by all, by reason of prejudice.*

As regards the common notions, indeed, there is no
doubt that they may be clearly and distinctly perceived
for otherwise they would not deserve to bear this name
but it is also true that there are some that do not in
regard to all men deserve the name equally with others

because they are not equally perceived by all. Not, however, that I believe the faculty of knowledge to extend further with some men than with others; it is rather that these common opinions are opposed to the prejudices of some who are thereby prevented from easily perceiving them, although they are perfectly manifest to those who are free from these prejudices.

PRINCIPLE LI

What substance is, and that it is a name which we cannot attribute in the same sense to God and to His creatures.

As regards these matters which we consider as being things or modes of things, it is necessary that we should examine them here one by one. And when we conceive of substance, we merely conceive an existent thing which requires nothing but itself in order to exist. To speak truth, nothing but God answers to this description as being that which is absolutely self-sustaining, for we perceive that there is no other created thing which can exist without being sustained by his power. That is why the word substance does not pertain *univoce* to God and to other things, as they say in the Schools, that is, no common signification for this appellation which will apply equally to God and to them can be distinctly understood.

PRINCIPLE LII

That it may be attributed univocally to the soul and to body, and how we know substance.

Created substances, however, whether corporeal or thinking, may be conceived under this common concept; for they are things which need only the concurrence of God in order to exist. But yet substance cannot be first discovered merely from the fact that it is a thing that exists, for that fact alone is not observed by us. We may, however, easily discover it by means of any one of its attributes because it is a common notion that nothing is possessed of no attributes, properties, or qualities. For this reason, when we perceive any attribute, we therefore conclude that some existing thing or substance to which it may be attributed, is necessarily present.

Principle LIII

That each substance has a principal attribute, and that the attribute of the mind is thought, while that of body is extension.

But although any one attribute is sufficient to give us a knowledge of substance, there is always one principal property of substance which constitutes its nature and essence, and on which all the others depend. Thus extension in length, breadth and depth, constitutes the nature of corporeal substance; and thought constitutes the nature of thinking substance. For all else that may be attributed to body presupposes extension, and is but a mode of this extended thing; as everything that we find in mind is but so many diverse forms of thinking. Thus, for example, we cannot conceive figure but as an extended thing, nor movement but as in an extended space; so imagination, feeling, and will, only exist in a thinking thing. But, on the other hand, we can conceive extension without figure or action, and thinking without imagination or sensation, and so on with the rest; as is quite clear to anyone who attends to the matter.

Principle LIV

How we may have clear and distinct notions of thinking substance, of corporeal substance, and of God.

We may thus easily have two clear and distinct notions or ideas, the one of created substance which thinks, the other of corporeal substance, provided we carefully separate all the attributes of thought from those of extension. We can also have a clear and distinct idea of an uncreated and independent thinking substance, that is to say, of God, provided that we do not suppose that this idea represents to us all that is exhibited in God, and that we do not mingle anything fictitious with it, but simply attend to what is evidently contained in the notion, and which we are aware pertains to the nature of an absolutely perfect Being. For no one can deny that such an idea of God exists in us, unless he groundlessly asserts that the mind of man cannot attain to a knowledge of God.

Principle LV

How we can also have a clear understanding of duration, order, and number.

We shall likewise have a very different understanding of *duration, order* and *number,* if, in place of mingling with the idea that we have of them what properly speaking pertains to the conception of substance, we merely consider that the duration of each thing is a mode under which we shall consider this thing in so far as it continues to exist; and if in the same way we think that order and number are not really different from the things that are ordered and numbered, but that they are only the modes under which we consider these things.

Principle LVI

What are modes, qualities, and attributes.

And, indeed, when we here speak of modes we mean nothing more than what elsewhere is termed *attribute* or *quality*. But when we consider substance as modified or diversified by them, I avail myself of the word *mode*; and when from the disposition or variation it can be named as of such and such a kind, we shall use the word *qualities* [to designate the different modes which cause it to be so termed] ; and finally when we more generally consider that these modes or qualities are in substance we term them *attributes*. And because in God any variableness is incomprehensible, we cannot ascribe to Him modes or qualities; but simply attributes. And even in created things that which never exists in them in any diverse way, like existence and duration in the existing and enduring thing, should be called not qualities or modes, but attributes.

Principle LVII

That there are attributes which pertain to things and others to thought; and what duration and time are.

Some of the attributes are in things themselves and others are only in our thought. Thus time, for example, which we distinguish from duration taken in its general sense and which we describe as the measure of movement, is only a mode of thinking; for we do not indeed apprehend that the duration of things which are moved is different from that of the things which are not moved, as is evident from the fact that if two bodies are moved for the space of an hour, the one quickly, the other slowly, we do not count the time longer in one case than in the other, although there is much more movement

in one of the two bodies than in the other. But in
order to comprehend the duration of all things under the
same measure, we usually compare their duration with
the duration of the greatest and most regular motions,
which are those that create years and days, and these
we term time. Hence this adds nothing to the notion
of duration, generally taken, but a mode of thinking.

Principle LVIII

*That number and all universals are simply modes of
thought.*

Similarly number when we consider it abstractly or
generally and not in created things, is but a mode of
thinking; and the same is true of all that which [in the
schools] is named *universals*.

Principle LIX

*How Universals are formed and what are the five
common ones:—genus, species, difference, property and
accident.*

Universals arise solely from the fact that we avail
ourselves of one and the same idea in order to think
of all individual things which have a certain similitude;
and when we comprehend under the same name all the
objects represented by this idea, that name is universal.
For example, when we see two stones, and without
thinking further of their nature than to remark that
there are two, we form in ourselves an idea of a certain
number which we term the number of two; and when
afterwards we see two birds or two trees, and we observe
without further thinking about their nature, that there
are two of them, we again take up the same idea which
we had before, which idea is universal; and we give to

this number the universal name 'two.' And in the same way when we consider a three-sided figure we form a certain idea which we call the idea of a triangle; and we afterwards make use of it as a universal in representing to ourselves all the figures having three sides. But when we notice more particularly that of three-sided figures some have a right angle and others have not, we form the universal idea of a rectangular triangle, which being related to the preceding as to a more general, may be termed *species*; and the right angle is the universal *difference* by which right-angled triangles are distinguished from all others. If we further observe that the square of the side which subtends the right angle is equal to the squares of the two other sides, and that this property belongs only to this species of triangle, we may term it a [universal] property of the species. Finally if we suppose that certain of the triangles are moved, and others are not moved we should take that to be a universal *accident* of the same; and it is thus that we commonly enumerate the five universals, viz.: genus, species, difference, property, accident.

PRINCIPLE LX

Of distinctions, and firstly of real distinction.

But as to the number in things themselves, this proceeds from the distinction which exists between them; and *distinction* is of three sorts, viz. *real, modal,* and *of reason.* The *real* is properly speaking found between two or more substances; and we can conclude that two substances are really distinct one from the other from the sole fact that we can conceive the one clearly and distinctly without the other. For in accordance with the knowledge which we have of God, we are certain that He can carry into effect all that of which we have

a distinct idea. That is why from the fact that we now
have e.g. the idea of an extended or corporeal substance,
although we do not yet know certainly whether such
really exists at all, we may yet conclude that it may
exist; and if it does exist, any one portion of it which
we can demarcate in our thought must be distinct from
every other part of the same substance. Similarly because each one of us is conscious that he thinks, and that
in thinking he can shut off from himself all other substance, either thinking or extended, we may conclude
that each of us, similarly regarded, is really distinct
from every other thinking substance and from every
corporeal substance. And even if we suppose that God
had united a body to a soul so closely that it was impossible to bring them together more closely, and made
a single thing out of the two, they would yet remain
really distinct one from the other notwithstanding the
union; because however closely God connected them
He could not set aside the power which He possessed
of separating them, or conserving them one apart from
the other, and those things which God can separate,
or conceive in separation, are really distinct.

PRINCIPLE LXI

Of the modal distinction.

There are two sorts of *modal distinctions,* i.e. the one
between the mode properly speaking, and the substance
of which it is the mode, and the other between two
modes of the same substance. The former we recognise
by the fact that we can clearly conceive substance
without the mode which we say differs from it, while
we cannot reciprocally have a perception of this mode
without perceiving the substance. There is, for example,
a modal distinction between figure or movement and the

corporeal substance in which both exist: there is also
a distinction between affirming or recollecting and the
mind. As to the other kind of distinction, its characteristic is that we are able to recognise the one mode without the other and *vice versâ,* but we can conceive neither
the one nor the other without recognising that both
subsist in one common substance. If, for example, a
stone is moved and along with that is square, we are
able to conceive the square figure without knowing that
it is moved, and reciprocally, we may be aware that it
is moved without knowing that it is square; but we cannot have a conception of this movement and figure
unless we have a conception of the substance of the
stone. As for the distinction whereby the mode of one
substance is different from another substance, or from
the mode of another substance, as the movement of one
body is different from another body or from mind, or
else as movement is different from duration; it appears
to me that we shall call it real rather than modal; because we cannot clearly conceive these modes apart
from the substances of which they are the modes and
which are really distinct.

PRINCIPLE LXII

Of the distinction created by thought.

Finally the *distinction of reason* is between substance
and some one of its attributes without which it is not
possible that we should have a distinct knowledge of it,
or between two such attributes of the same substance.
This distinction is made manifest from the fact that
we cannot have a clear and distinct idea of such a substance if we exclude from it such an attribute; or we
cannot have a clear idea of the one of the two attributes
if we separate from it the other. For example, because

there is no substance which does not cease to exist when it ceases to endure, duration is only distinct from substance by thought, and all the modes of thinking which we consider as though they existed in the objects, differ only in thought both from the objects of which they are the thought and from each other in a common object. I recollect having elsewhere conjoined this sort of distinction with modal distinction (near the end of the Reply made to the First Objection to the Meditations on the First Philosophy), but then it was not necessary to treat accurately of these distinctions, and it was sufficient for my purpose at the time simply to distinguish them both from the real.

Principle LXIII

How we may have distinct conceptions of thought and extension, inasmuch as the one constitutes the nature of mind, and the other that of body.

We may likewise consider thought and extension as constituting the natures of intelligence and corporeal substance; and then they must not be considered otherwise than as the very substances that think and are extended, i.e. as mind and body; for we know them in this way very clearly and distinctly. It is moreover more easy to know a substance that thinks, or an extended substance, than substance alone, without regarding whether it thinks or is extended. For we experience some difficulty in abstracting the notions that we have of substance from those of thought or extension, for they in truth do not differ but in thought, and our conception is not more distinct because it comprehends fewer properties, but because we distinguish accurately that which it does comprehend from all other notions.

Principle LXIV

How we may also conceive them as modes of substance.

We may likewise consider thought and extension as the modes which are found in substance; that is, in as far as we consider that one and the same mind may have many different thoughts, and that one body, retaining the same size, may be extended in many different ways, sometimes being greater in length and less in breadth or depth, and sometimes on the contrary greater in breadth and less in length. We then distinguish them modally from substance, and they may be conceived not less clearly and distinctly, provided that we do not think of them as substance or things separate from others, but simply as modes of things. Because when we regard them as in the substances of which they are the modes, we distinguish them from these substances, and take them for what they actually are; while, on the contrary, if we wish to consider them apart from the substances in which they are, that will have the effect of our taking them as self-subsisting things and thus confounding the ideas of mode and substance.

Principle LXV

How we may likewise know their diverse modes.

We shall similarly best apprehend the diverse modes of thought such as understanding, imagining, recollecting, willing, etc., and the diverse modes of extension, or which pertain to extension, such as all figures, the situation of parts, and their movements, provided that we consider them simply as modes of the things in which they are; and as for motion we shall best understand it, if we inquire only about locomotion, without taking

into account the force that produces it, which I shall nevertheless endeavour to set forth in its own place.

Principle LXVI

That we also have a clear knowledge of our sensations, affections, and appetites, although we frequently err in the judgments we form of them.

There remain our sensations, affections and appetites, as to which we may likewise have a clear knowledge, if we take care to include in the judgments we form of them that only which we know to be precisely contained in our perception of them, and of which we are intimately conscious. It is, however, most difficult to observe this condition, in regard to our senses at least, because we, everyone of us, have judged from our youth up that all things of which we have been accustomed to have sensation have had an existence outside our thoughts, and that they have been entirely similar to the sensation, that is the idea which we have formed of them. Thus, when, for example, we perceived a certain colour, we thought that we saw something which existed outside of us and which clearly resembled the idea of colour which we then experienced in ourselves, and from the habit of judging in this way we seemed to see this so clearly and distinctly as to be convinced that it is certain and indubitable.

Principle LXVII

That we frequently deceive ourselves in judging of pain itself.

The same is true in regard to all our other sensations, even those which have to do with agreeable sensation and pain. For although we do not believe that

these feelings exist outside of us, we are not wont to
regard them as existing merely in our mind or our perception, but as being in our hands, feet, or some other
part of our body. But there is no reason that we should
be obliged to believe that pain, for example, which we
feel in our foot, is anything beyond our mind which
exists in our foot, nor that the light which we imagine
ourselves to see in the sun really is in the sun [as it
is in us] ; for both these are prejudices of our youth,
as will clearly appear in what follows.

Principle LXVIII

*How we may distinguish in such matters that which
we know clearly from that in which we may err.*

But in order that we may here distinguish that which
is clear from that which is obscure we ought to observe
that we have a clear or distinct knowledge of pain,
colour, and other things of the sort when we consider
them simply as sensations or thoughts. But when we
desire to judge of such matters as existing outside of
our mind, we can in no wise conceive what sort of things
they are. And when anyone says that he sees colour
in a body or feels pain in one of his limbs, it is the
same as if he told us that he there saw or felt something but was absolutely ignorant of its nature, or else
that he did not know what he saw or felt. For although
when he examines his thoughts with less attention he
perhaps easily persuades himself that he has some
knowledge of it, because he supposes that there is
something resembling the sensation of colour or pain
which he experiences, yet if he investigates what is represented to him by this sensation of colour or pain appearing as they do to exist in a coloured body or suffering
part, he will find that he is really ignorant of it.

Principle LXIX

That we know magnitude, figure, etc., quite differently from colour and pain, etc.

This will be more especially evident if we consider that size in the body which is perceived, or figure or movement (local movement at least, for philosophers by imagining other sorts of motion than this, have rendered its nature less intelligible to themselves), or situation, or duration, or number, and those properties which we clearly perceive in all bodies, as has been already described, are known by us in a quite different way from that in which colour is known in the same body, or pain, odour, taste, or any of the properties which, as hitherto mentioned, should be attributed to the senses. For although in observing a body we are not less assured of its existence from the colour which we perceive in its regard than from the figure which bounds it, we yet know this property in it which causes us to call it figured, with much greater clearness than what causes us to say that it is coloured.

Principle LXX

That we may judge in two ways of sensible things, by one of which we shall avoid error, while by the other we shall fall into error.

It is thus evident when we say that we perceive colours in objects, that it is the same as though we said that we perceive something in the objects of whose nature we were ignorant, but which yet caused a very clear and vivid sensation in us, and which is termed the sensation of colours. But there is a great deal of difference in our manner of judging, for, so long as we believe that there is something in objects of which

we have no knowledge (that is in things, such as they are, from which sensation comes to us), so far are we from falling into error that, on the contrary, we rather provide against it, for we are less likely to judge rashly of a thing which we have been forewarned we do not know. But when we think we perceive a certain colour in objects although we have no real knowledge of what the name of the colour signifies, and we can find no intelligible resemblance between the colour which we suppose to exist in objects and what we are conscious of in our senses, yet, because we do not observe this, or remark in these objects certain other qualities like magnitude, figure, number, etc., which we clearly know are or may be in objects, as our senses or understanding show us, it is easy to allow ourselves to fall into the error of holding that what we call colour in objects is something entirely resembling the colour we perceive, and then supposing that we have a clear perception of what we do not perceive at all.

Principle LXXVI

That we ought to prefer the Divine authority to our perceptions, but, excluding this, we should not assent to anything which we do not clearly perceive.

Above all we should impress on our memory as an infallible rule that what God has revealed to us is incomparably more certain than anything else; and that we ought to submit to the Divine authority rather than to our own judgment even though the light of reason may seem to us to suggest, with the utmost clearness and evidence, something opposite. But in things in regard to which Divine authority reveals nothing to us, it would be unworthy of a philosopher to accept anything as true which he has not ascertained to be such, and to

trust more to the senses, that is to judgments formed without consideration in childhood, than to the reasoning of maturity.

SECOND PART

OF THE PRINCIPLES OF MATERIAL THINGS

PRINCIPLE I

What are the reasons for our having a certain knowledge of material things?

Although we are all persuaded that material things exist, yet because we have doubted this before and have placed it in the rank of the prejudices of our childhood, it is now requisite that we should inquire into the reasons through which we may accept this truth with certainty. To begin with we feel that without doubt all our perceptions proceed from some thing which is different from our mind. For it is not in our power to have one perception rather than another, since each one is clearly dependent on the object which affects our senses. It is true that we may inquire whether that object is God, or some other different from God. But inasmuch as we perceive, or rather are stimulated by sense to apprehend clearly and distinctly a matter which is extended in length, breadth, and depth, the various parts of which have various figures and motions, and give rise to the sensations we have of colours, smells, pains, etc., if God immediately and of Himself presented to our mind the idea of this extended matter, or merely permitted it to be caused in us by some other object which possessed no extension, figure, or motion, there would be nothing to prevent Him from being regarded as a deceiver. For we clearly apprehend this matter as different from God, or ourselves, or our mind, and appear to discern very plainly that the idea of it is due to objects outside of ourselves to which it is absolutely similar. But God cannot deceive us, because deception is repugnant to His nature, as has been explained. And hence we must conclude that there is an object in length, breadth, and depth, and possessing all those properties which we clearly perceive to pertain to extended objects. And this extended object is called by us either body or matter.

PRINCIPLE II

How we likewise know that the body of man is closely united to the mind.

It may be concluded also that a certain body is more closely united to our mind than any other, from the fact that pain and other of our sensations occur without our foreseeing them; and that mind is conscious that these do not arise from itself alone, nor pertain to it in so far as it is a thinking thing, but only in so far as it is united to another thing, extended and mobile, which is called the human body. But this is not the place to explain the matter further.

PRINCIPLE III

That the perceptions of the senses do not teach us what is really in things, but merely that whereby they are useful or hurtful to man's composite nature.

It will be sufficient for us to observe that the perceptions of the senses are related simply to the intimate union which exists between body and mind, and that while by their means we are made aware of what in external bodies can profit or hurt this union, they do not present them to us as they are in themselves unless occasionally and accidentally. For [after this observation] we shall without difficulty set aside all the prejudices of the senses and in this regard rely upon our understanding alone, by reflecting carefully on the ideas implanted therein by nature.

PRINCIPLE IV

That the nature of body consists not in weight, nor in hardness, nor colour and so on, but in extension alone.

In this way we shall ascertain that the nature of matter or of body in its universal aspect, does not consist in its being hard, or heavy, or coloured, or one that affects our senses in some other way, but solely in the fact that it is a substance extended in length, breadth and depth. For as regards hardness we do not know anything of it by sense, excepting that the portions of the hard bodies resist the motion of our hands when they come in contact with them; but if, whenever we moved our hands in some direction, all the bodies in that part retreated as soon as our hands approached them, we should never feel hardness; and yet we have no reason to believe that the bodies which recede in this way would on this account lose what makes them bodies. It follows from this that the nature of body does not consist in hardness. The same reason shows us that weight, colour, and all the other qualities of the kind that is perceived in corporeal matter, may be taken from it, it remaining meanwhile entire: it thus follows that the nature of body depends on none of these.

PRINCIPLE VIII

That quantity and number differ only in thought from what has quantity and is numbered.

For quantity differs from extended substance, or number from what is numbered, not in reality but only in our conception. Thus, to take an example, we may consider the whole nature of corporeal substance which is comprised within a space of ten feet, although we do not attend to this measure of ten feet; because it is clear that the thing conceived is the same in any one part of that space as in the whole. And *vice versâ*, we can comprehend the number ten, as also a continuous quantity of ten feet, without attending to any particular determinate substance, because the conception of the number of ten is plainly the same, whether considered in reference to the measure of ten feet, or to any other ten; and we cannot conceive a continuous quantity of ten feet without thinking of some extended substance of which it is the quantity, but yet we can conceive it without thinking of that determinate substance. In reality it is however impossible that even the least part of such quantity or extension can be taken away without taking away likewise an equal amount of substance; on the other hand, not the least part of the substance can be removed without our diminishing its quantity and extension by the same amount.

PRINCIPLE IX

That corporeal substance, when distinguished from its quantity, is confusedly conceived as something incorporeal.

Although however, some express themselves otherwise on this subject, I cannot think that they regard it otherwise than as I have just said; for when they distinguish substance from extension or quantity, they either mean nothing by the word substance, or they merely form in their minds a confused idea of incorporeal substance which they falsely attribute to corporeal, and leave to extension, which they nevertheless call an accident, that the true idea of this corporeal substance, but [so improperly that] it is easy to see that their words are not in harmony with their thoughts.

PRINCIPLE X

What space or internal place is.

Space or internal place and the corporeal substance which is contained in it, are not different otherwise than in the mode in which they are conceived of by us. For, in truth, the same extension in length, breadth, and depth, which constitutes space, constitutes body; and the difference between them consists only in the fact that in body we consider extension as particular and conceive it to change just as body changes; in space, on the contrary, we attribute to extension a generic unity, so that after having removed from a certain space the body which occupied it, we do not suppose that we have also removed the extension of that space, because it appears to us that the same extension remains so long as it is of the same magnitude and figure, and preserves the same position in relation to certain other bodies, whereby we determine this space.

PRINCIPLE XI

In what sense it may be said that space is not different from corporeal substance.

And it will be easy for us to recognise that the same extension which constitutes the nature of body likewise constitutes the nature of space, nor do the two mutually differ, excepting as the nature of the genus or species differs from the nature of the individual, provided that, in order to discern the idea that we have of any body,

such as stone, we reject from it all that is not essential
to the nature of body. In the first place, then, we may
reject hardness, because if the stone were liquefied or
reduced to powder, it would no longer possess hardness,
and yet would not cease to be a body; let us in the next
place reject colour, because we have often seen stones
so transparent that they had no colour; again we reject
weight, because we see that fire although very light is
yet body; and finally we may reject cold, heat, and all
the other qualities of the kind either because they are
not considered as in the stone, or else because with the
change of their qualities the stone is not for that reason
considered to have lost its nature as body. After examination we shall find that there is nothing remaining
in the idea of body excepting that it is extended in
length, breadth, and depth; and this is comprised in
our idea of space, not only of that which is full of body,
but also of that which is called a vacuum.

Principle XII

*How space is different from body in our mode of
conceiving it.*

There is, however, some difference in our mode of
conceiving them; for if we remove a stone from the
space or place where it was, we conceive that the extension of this stone has also been removed from it,
because we consider this to be singular, and inseparable
from the stone itself. But meantime we suppose that
the same extension of place occupied by the stone remains, though the place which it formerly occupied has
been taken up with wood, water, air, and any other
bodies, or even has been supposed to be empty, because
we now consider extension in general, and it appears

to us that the same is common to stones, wood, water, air, and all other bodies, and even to a vacuum, if there be such a thing, provided that it is of the same magnitude and figure as before, and preserves the same situation in regard to the external bodies which determine this space.

Principle XIII

What external place is.

The reason of this is that the words place and space signify nothing different from the body which is said to be in a place, and merely designate its magnitude, figure, and situation as regards other bodies. For it is necessary in order to determine this situation to observe certain others which we consider to be immovable; and according as we regard different bodies we may find that the same thing at the same time changes its place, and does not change it. For example, if we consider a man seated at the stern of a vessel when it is carried out to sea, he may be said to be in one place if we regard the parts of the vessel with which he preserves the same situation: and yet he will be found continually to change his position, if regard be paid to the neighbouring shores in relation to which he is constantly receding from one, and approaching another. And further, if we suppose that the earth moves, and that it makes precisely the same way from west to east as the vessel does from east to west, it will again appear to us that he who is seated at the stern does not change his position, because that place is determined by certain immovable points which we imagine to be in the heavens. But if at length we are persuaded that there are no points in the universe that are really immovable, as will presently be shown to be probable, we shall conclude that there is nothing that has a permanent place except in so far as it is fixed by our thought.

Principle XIV

Wherein place and space differ.

The terms place and space are however different, because place indicates situation more expressly than magnitude or figure; while, on the contrary, we more often think of the latter when we speak of space. For we frequently say that a thing has succeeded to the place of another, although it does not possess exactly either its magnitude or its figure; but we do not for all that mean that it occupies the same space as the other; and when the situation is changed, we say that the place also is changed, although the same magnitude and figure exist as before. And hence if we say that a thing is in a particular place, we simply mean that it is situated in a certain manner in reference to certain other things; and when we add that it occupies a certain space or place, we likewise mean that it is of a definite magnitude or figure [so as exactly to fill the space].

Principle XV

How external place is rightly taken to be the superficies of the surrounding body.

And thus we never distinguish space from extension in length, breadth and depth; but we sometimes consider place as in the thing placed, and sometimes as outside of it. Internal place is indeed in no way distinguished from space; but we sometimes regard external place as the superficies which immediately surrounds the thing placed in it. And it is to be observed that by

superficies we do not here mean any portion of the
surrounding body, but merely the extremity which is
between the surrounding body and that surrounded,
which is but a mode; or that we mean the common surface which is a surface that is not a part of one body
rather than of the other, and that it is always considered
the same, so long as it retains the same magnitude and
figure. For although all the surrounding body with its
superficies is changed, we should not imagine that the
body which was surrounded by it had for all that
changed its place, if it meanwhile preserved the same
situation in regard to other bodies that are regarded
as immovable. Thus if we suppose that a ship is carried along in one direction by the current of a stream,
and is impelled by a contrary wind in another direction
in an equal degree, so that its situation is not changed
with regard to the banks, we are ready to admit that
it remains in the same place although we see the whole
surrounding superficies is in a state of change.

Principle XVI

*That it is contrary to reason to say that there is a
vacuum or space in which there is absolutely nothing.*

As regards a vacuum in the philosophic sense of the
word, i.e. a space in which there is no substance, it is
evident that such cannot exist, because the extension of
space or internal place, is not different from that of
body. For, from the mere fact that a body is extended
in length, breadth, or depth, we have reason to conclude
that it is a substance, because it is absolutely inconceivable that nothing should possess extension, we ought
to conclude also that the same is true of the space which
is supposed to be void, i.e. that since there is in it extension, there is necessarily also substance.

Principle XVII

That a vacuum, in the ordinary sense, does not exclude all body.

And when we take this word vacuum in its ordinary sense, we do not mean a place or space in which there is absolutely nothing, but only a place in which there are none of those things which we expected to find there. Thus because a pitcher is made to hold water, we say that it is empty when it contains nothing but air; or if there are no fish in a fish-pond, we say there is nothing in it, even though it be full of water; similarly we say a vessel is empty, when, in place of the merchandise which it was designed to carry, it is loaded only with sand, so that it may resist the impetuous violence of the wind; and finally we say in the same way that a space is empty when it contains nothing sensible, even though it contain created matter and self-existent substance; for we are not wont to consider things excepting those with which our senses succeed in presenting us. And if, in place of keeping in mind what we should comprehend by these words—vacuum and nothing— we afterwards suppose that in the space which is termed vacuum there is not only nothing sensible, but nothing at all, we shall fall into the same error as if, because a pitcher is usually termed empty since it contains nothing but air, we were therefore to judge that the air contained in it is not a substantive thing.

Principle XVIII

How the prejudice concerning the absolute vacuum is to be corrected.

We have almost all lapsed into this error from the beginning of our lives, for, seeing that there is no necessary connection between the vessel and the body it contains, we thought that God at least could remove all the body contained in the vessel without its being necessary that any other body should take its place. But in order that we may be able to correct this error, it is necessary to remark that while there is no connection between the vessel and that particular body which it contains, there is an absolutely necessary one between the concave figure of the vessel and the extension considered generally which must be comprised in this cavity ; so that there is not more contradiction in conceiving a mountain without a valley, than such a cavity without the extension which it contains, or this extension without the substance which is extended, because nothing, as has already been frequently remarked, cannot have extension. And therefore, if it is asked what would happen if God removed all the body contained in a vessel without permitting its place being occupied by another body, we shall answer that the sides of the vessel will thereby come into immediate contiguity with one another. For two bodies must touch when there is nothing between them, because it is manifestly contradictory for these two bodies to be apart from one another, or that there should be a distance between them, and yet that this distance should be nothing; for distance is a mode of extension, and without extended substance it cannot therefore exist.

PRINCIPLE XXIII

That all the variety in matter, or all the diversity of its forms, depends on motion.

There is therefore but one matter in the whole universe, and we know this by the simple fact of its being extended. All the properties which we clearly perceive in it may be reduced to the one, viz. that it can be divided, or moved according to its parts, and consequently is capable of all these affections which we perceive can arise from the motion of its parts. For its partition by thought alone makes no difference to it; but all the variation in matter, or diversity in its forms, depends on motion. This the philosophers have doubtless observed, inasmuch as they have said that nature was the principle of motion and rest, and by nature they understood that by which all corporeal things become such as they are experienced to be.

PRINCIPLE XXIV

What motion is in common parlance.

But motion (i.e. local motion, for I can conceive no other kind, and do not consider that we ought to conceive any other in nature), in the vulgar sense, is nothing more than the *action by which any body passes from one place to another.* And just as we have remarked above that the same thing may be said to change and not to change its place at the same time, we can say that it moves and does not move at the same time. For he who is seated in a ship setting sail, thinks he is moving when he looks at the shore he has left, and considers it as fixed, but not if he regards the vessel he is on, because he does not change his position in reference to its parts. Likewise, because we are accustomed to think that there is no motion without action and that in rest there is cessation of action, the person thus seated may more properly be said to be in repose than in motion, since he is not conscious of any action in himself.

PRINCIPLE XXV

What movement properly speaking is.

But if, looking not to popular usage, but to the truth of the matter, let us consider what ought to be understood by motion according to the truth of the thing; we may say, in order to attribute a determinate nature to it, that it is the *transference of one part of matter or one body from the vicinity of those bodies that are in immediate contact with it, and which we regard as in repose, into the vicinity of others.* By *one body* or by a *part of matter* I understand all that which is transported together, although it may be composed of many parts which in themselves have other motions. And I say that it is the *transportation* and not either the force or the action which transports, in order to show that the motion is always in the mobile thing, not in that which moves; for these two do not seem to me to be accurately enough distinguished. Further, I understand that it is a mode of the mobile thing and not a substance, just as figure is a mode of the figured thing, and repose of that which is at rest.

THIRD PART

OF THE VISIBLE WORLD

PRINCIPLE I

That we cannot think too highly of the works of God.

Having now ascertained certain principles of material things which were derived, not from the prejudices of the senses, but from the light of reason, so that we cannot doubt of their truth, it is for us to examine whether from these alone we can explain all the phenomena of nature. And we shall commence with those which are the most general, and on which the others depend, such as the general structure of the visible world. But in order that we may philosophise correctly in this matter, two things are to be observed. The first is that we must ever keep before our minds the infinitude of the power and goodness of God, and not fear to fall into error by imagining His works to be too great, too beautiful, and too perfect, but that, on the contrary, we must take care lest, if we suppose any limits to exist in them of which we have no certain knowledge, we may seem to be insufficiently sensible of the greatness and power of the Creator.

PRINCIPLE II

That we ought to beware lest we presume too much in supposing ourselves to understand the ends which God set before Himself in creating the world.

The second is that we ought to beware lest we think too highly of ourselves. This we should appear to do if we supposed the universe to have certain limits not presented to our knowledge without at the same time being assured of the fact by divine revelation, which would be making our knowledge extend beyond that which God has made; but this would be even more so if we persuaded ourselves that it was only for us that all things were created by God, or even were we to suppose that by the powers of our mind we could comprehend the ends which He set before Himself in creating the universe.

PRINCIPLE III

In what sense it can be said that all things were created for man.

For although it may be a pious thought, as far as Morals are concerned, to believe that God has created all things for us in as far as that incites us to a greater gratitude and affection toward Him, and although it is in some respect true, because there is nothing created from which we cannot derive some use, if it be but the exercise of our minds in considering it and the being incited to worship God by its means, it is yet not at all probable that all things have been created for us in such a manner that God has had no other end in creating them. And it seems to me that such a supposition would be certainly ridiculous and inept in reference to questions of Physics, for we cannot doubt that an infinitude of things exist, or did exist, though now they have ceased to exist, which have never been beheld or comprehended by man and which have never been of any use to him.

FOURTH PART

OF THE EARTH

Principle CLXXXVIII

Of what is to be borrowed from disquisitions on animals and man in order to advance the knowledge of material things.

I should add no more to this Fourth Part of the Principles of Philosophy, did I (as I had formerly in my mind) purpose writing other sections, viz. a Fifth and a Sixth Part, the fifth treating of living things, that is of animals and plants, and the sixth of man. But because I am not yet quite clear about all of the matters of which I should like to treat in these two last parts, and do not know whether I am likely to have sufficient leisure [or be able to make the experiments necessary] to complete them, I shall here add a little

about the objects of the senses in order not to delay
the earlier part too long to prevent [their lacking completeness or] anything being amissing which I should
have reserved for the latter. For up to this point I
have described the earth, and all the visible world, as
if it were simply a machine in which there was nothing
to consider but [the] figure and movements [of its
parts], and yet our senses cause other things to be
presented to us, such as colours, smells, sounds, and
other such things, of which, if I did not speak, it might
be thought that I had omitted the main part of the explanation of the objects of nature.

Principle CLXXXIX

What sensation is, and how it operates.

We must know, therefore, that although the mind
of man informs the whole body, it yet has its principal
seat in the brain, and it is there that it not only understands and imagines, but also perceives; and this by
means of the nerves which are extended like filaments
from the brain to all the other members, with which
they are so connected that we can hardly touch any
part of the human body without causing the extremities
of some of the nerves spread over it to be moved; and
this motion passes to the other extremities of those
nerves which are collected in the brain round the seat
of the soul, as I have just explained quite fully enough
in the fourth chapter of the Dioptrics. But the movements which are thus excited in the brain by the nerves,
affect in diverse ways the soul or mind, which is intimately connected with the brain, according to the diversity of the motions themselves. And the diverse

affections of our mind, or thoughts that immediately arise from these motions, are called perceptions of the senses, or, in common language, sensations.

PRINCIPLE CXCVI

That the soul does not perceive excepting in as far as it is in the brain.

It is however easily proved that the soul feels those things that affect the body not in so far as it is in each member of the body, but only in so far as it is in the brain, where the nerves by their movements convey to it the diverse actions of the external objects which touch the parts of the body [in which they are inserted]. For, in the first place, there are many maladies, which, though they affect the brain alone, yet either disorder or altogether take away from us the use of our senses; just like sleep itself which affects the brain alone, and yet every day takes from us during a great part of our time the faculty of perception, which is afterwards restored to us on awakening. Secondly, from the fact that though the brain be healthy [as well as the members in which the organs of the external senses are to be found], if the paths by which the nerves pass from the external parts to the brain are obstructed, that sensation is lost in these external parts of the body. And finally we sometimes feel pain as though it were in certain of our members, and yet its cause is not in these members where it is felt, but in others through which the nerves pass that extend to the brain from the parts where the pain is felt. And this I could prove by innumerable experiments; here, however, one will suffice. When a girl suffering from a serious affection of the hand was visited by the surgeon, her eyes were usually bandaged lest seeing the dressing should have a bad effect upon her. After some days, as gangrene set in, her arm had to be cut off from the elbow and several linen cloths tied together were substituted in place of the amputated limb, in such a way that she was quite ignorant of what had been done; meanwhile, however, she had various pains, sometimes in one of the fingers of the hand which was cut off, and sometimes in another. This could clearly only happen because the nerves which previously had been carried all the way from the brain to the hand, and afterwards terminated in the arm near the elbow, were there affected in the same way as it was their function to be stimulated for the purpose of impressing on the mind residing in the brain the sensation of pain in this and that finger. [And this shows clearly that pain in the hand is not felt by the mind inasmuch as it is in the hand, but as it is in the brain.]

Principle CXCVII

That mind is of such a nature that from the motion of the body alone the various sensations can be excited in it.

It may, in the next place, be [easily] proved that our mind is of such a nature that the motions which are in the body are alone sufficient to cause it to have all sorts of thoughts, which do not give us any image of any of the motions which give rise to them; and specially that there may be excited in it those confused thoughts called feelings or sensations. For [first of all] we observe that words, whether uttered by the voice or merely written, excite in our minds all sorts of thoughts and emotions. On the same paper, with the same pen and ink, by moving the point of the pen ever so little over the paper in a certain way, we can trace letters which bring to the minds of our readers thoughts of battles, tempests or furies, and the emotions of indignation and sadness; while if the pen be moved in another way, hardly different, thoughts may be given of quite a different kind, viz. those of quietude, peace, pleasantness, and the quite opposite passions of love and joy. Someone will perhaps reply that writing and speech do not immediately excite any passions in the mind, or imaginations of things different from the letters and sounds, but simply so to speak various acts of the understanding; and from these the mind, making them the occasion, then forms for itself the imaginations of a variety of things. But what shall we say of the sensations of what is painful and pleasurable? If a sword moved towards our body cuts it, from this alone pain results which is certainly not less different from the local movement of the sword or of the part of the body which is cut, than are colour or sound or smell or taste. And therefore, as we see clearly that the sensation of pain is easily excited in us from the fact alone that certain parts of our body are locally disturbed by the contact with certain other bodies, we may conclude that our mind is of such a nature that certain local motions can excite in it all the affections belonging to all the other senses.

Principle CXCVIII

That there is nothing known of external objects by the senses but their figure, magnitude or motion.

Besides this, we observe in the nerves no difference which may cause us to judge that some convey to the brain from the organs of the external sense any one thing rather than another, nor again that anything is conveyed there excepting the local motion of the nerves themselves. And we see that this local motion excites in us not alone the sensations of pleasure or pain, but also the sensations of sound and light. For if we receive a blow in the eye hard enough to cause the vibration to reach the retina, we see myriads of sparks which are yet not outside our eye; and when we place our finger on our ear to stop it, we hear a murmuring sound whose cause cannot be attributed to anything but the agitation of the air which is shut up within it. Finally we can likewise frequently observe that heat and the other sensible qualities, inasmuch as they are in objects, and also the forms of these bodies which are purely material, such as e.g., the forms of fire, are produced in them by the motions of certain other bodies, and that these again also produce other motions in other bodies. And we can very well conceive how the movement of one body can be caused by that of another, and diversified by the size, figure, and situation of its parts, but we can in nowise understand how these same things (viz. size, figure and motion) can produce something entirely different in nature from themselves, such as are those substantial forms and real qualities which many suppose to exist in bodies; nor likewise can we understand how these forms of qualities possess the force adequate to cause motion in other bodies. But since we know that our mind is of such a nature that the diverse motions of body suffice to produce in it all the diverse sensations that it has, and as we see by experience that some of the sensations are really caused by such motions, though we do not find anything but these movements to pass through the organs of the external senses to the brain, we may conclude that we in no way likewise apprehend that in external objects like light, colour, smell, taste, sound, heat, cold, and the other tactile qualities, or what we call their substantial forms, there is anything but the various dispositions of these objects which have the power of moving our nerves in various ways.

Principle CXCIX

That there is no phenomenon in nature which has not been dealt with in this treatise.

And thus by a simple enumeration it may be deduced that there is no phenomenon in nature whose treatment has been omitted in this treatise. For there is nothing that can be counted as a phenomenon of nature, excepting what we are able to perceive by the senses. And with the exception of motion, magnitude, and figure [or the situation of the parts of each body], which things I have explained as they exist in every body, we perceive nothing outside us by means of our senses, but light, colours, smells, tastes, sounds, and the tactile qualities; and of all these I have just proved that they are nothing more, as far as is known to us, than certain dispositions of objects consisting of magnitude, figure, and motion [so well have I demonstrated that there is nothing in all the visible world, in as far as it is merely visible or sensible, but the things I have there explained].

Principle CCI

That certain sensible bodies are composed of insensible particles.

I consider that there are many particles in each body which cannot be perceived by our senses, and this will perhaps not be approved by those who take their

senses as a measure of the things they can know. [But
it seems to me to be doing great wrong to human reason
if we do not consider that knowledge goes beyond the
seen]; for no one can doubt that there are bodies so
small that they cannot be perceived by any of our senses,
if only we consider what is being added each moment
to those bodies which increase little by little, and what
is removed from those which diminish in the same
fashion. We day by day see a tree grow, and it is impossible to comprehend how it becomes larger than it
was before, unless by conceiving that some body is
added to it. But who has ever observed by means of
the senses what are the small bodies which are each
day added to the plant that grows? Those at least
who hold quantity to be finitely divisible should acknowledge that the particles may become so small as to be
absolutely imperceptible. And indeed it should not be
wondered at that we are unable to perceive very minute
bodies, for the nerves, which must be moved by objects
in order to cause us to perceive, are not very minute,
but are like small cords which consist of a quantity
of yet smaller fibres, and thus they cannot be moved
by the minutest of bodies. Nor do I think that anyone
who uses his reason will deny that we do much better
to judge of what takes place in small bodies which their
minuteness alone prevents us from perceiving, by what
we see occurring in those that we do perceive [and thus
explain all that is in nature, as I have tried to do in
this treatise], than, in order to explain certain given
things, to invent all sorts of novelties, that have no
relation to those that we perceive [such as are first
matter, substantial forms, and all the great array of
qualities which many are in the habit of assuming,
any of which it is more difficult to understand than all
the things which we profess to explain by their means].

Principle CCVII

Nevertheless all my opinions are submitted to the authority of the church.

At the same time, recalling my insignificance, I affirm nothing, but submit all these opinions to the authority of the Catholic Church, and to the judgment of the more sage; and I wish no one to believe anything I have written, unless he is personally persuaded by the force and evidence of reason.

SELECTIONS FROM THE WORLD; OR ESSAY ON LIGHT

CHAPTER I

Of the difference between our sensations and the things which produce them

Proposing, as I do, to treat of the nature of light, the first thing of which I wish you to take note is, that there may be a difference between the sensation which we have in ourselves, that is to say, the idea which is formed within our imagination by the help of our eyes, and that which exists in the objects that produce within us the sensation, namely, that which exists in the flame, or in the sun, and is called by the name of light; because, although everyone is commonly persuaded that the ideas that we have in our thought are altogether similar to the objects whence they proceed, I see no reason, nevertheless, to assure us that this is true; but, on the contrary, I observe many facts which should incline us to question it.

You know that words, while having no resemblance to the things which they signify, do not fail to make them intelligible to us, and often, even without our paying attention to the sound of the words, or to their syllables; so that it may happen that after having listened to a discourse, the meaning of which we have completely understood, we are not able to say in what language it was spoken. But if words, which signify nothing except by human institution, are capable of making conceivable for us things to which they have no

resemblance, why may not nature also have established
a certain sign which should make us feel the sensation
of light, although this sign should have nothing in itself
resembling sensation? Has she not thus appointed
laughter and tears to make us read joy and sadness in
the human countenance?

But you will say, perhaps, that our ears make us
perceive in reality merely the sound of the words, and
our eyes only the face of him who laughs or who weeps,
and that it is our mind, which, having retained what
these words and this countenance signify, represents
it to us at the same time. To that I may reply that,
just in the same way, it is our mind which represents
to us the idea of light whenever the action which signifies it touches our eye; but, without wasting time in dispute, I will at once bring forward another illustration.

Do you think that when we pay no attention to the
meaning of words, and only hear the sound of them,
that the idea of this sound, which is formed within our
thought, is anything like the object which is the cause of
it? A man opens his mouth, moves his tongue, expels
his breath; I see nothing in all these motions which is
not quite different from the idea of the sound which
they cause us to imagine. And most philosophers assure
us that the sound is nothing but a certain trembling
of the air which has just struck our ears; so that, if
the sense of hearing brought to our thought the true
image of its object, it would be necessary, in place of
making us conceive the sound, that it should make us
conceive the motion of the portions of the air which is
trembling at the time against our ears. But because,
perhaps, everybody will not believe what the philosophers say, I will adduce still another example. Touch
is the one of all the senses which we consider the least
deceptive and the most trustworthy; so that, if I prove

to you that even touch makes us conceive many ideas which do not at all resemble the objects which produce them, I do not think you ought to consider it strange if I say that sight may do the same.

But there is no one who does not know that the ideas of pleasure and of pain which are formed within our thought on occasion of bodies touching us externally have no resemblance to them. A person gently passes a feather over the lips of a child asleep, and he perceives the tickling; do you suppose that the idea of the tickling which he conceives has any resemblance to anything there is in the feather? A soldier returns from a fight; during the heat of the combat he might have been wounded without perceiving it, but now that he begins to cool off he feels pain, he thinks he has been wounded; a surgeon is called, his uniform is stripped off, he is examined, and at last it is found that what he felt was nothing but a buckle or a strap, which, being twisted underneath his uniform, pressed upon him and hurt him. If his sense of touch, while making him feel the strap, had impressed the image of it on his thought, he would not have needed a surgeon to tell him what he felt.

But I see no reason which obliges us to think that what is in the objects from which the sensation of light comes to us is any more like that sensation than the action of a feather and a buckle is like the tickling and the pain; and yet I have not adduced these examples in order to make you believe absolutely that this light is something different in the objects from what it is in our eyes, but simply that you may question it, and that, being on your guard against a prejudice to the contrary, you may now the better inquire with me into the true state of the case.

CHAPTER II

In what the heat and light of a fire consist

I know only two kinds of bodies in the universe in which light is found, namely, the stars, and flame or fire; and because the stars are without question further removed from the knowledge of men than fire or flame is, I will attempt to explain in the first place what I observe in respect to flame. When it burns wood or any similar material, we can see at a glance that it removes small particles of this wood, and separates them one from another transforming thus the finer parts into fire, into vapor and smoke, and leaving the grosser parts as ashes. Anyone else, if he pleases, may imagine in this wood the form of fire, the quality of heat, and the energy which burns it, as all different things; as for me, who am afraid of deceiving myself if I suppose anything more to be there than what I see must necessarily be present, for my part, I am content with conceiving there the movement of its parts: because, put the fire there, put the heat there, and make it burn as much as you please, if you do not suppose, along with that, that there are some of its parts in motion, and that they detach themselves from their neighbours, I cannot imagine that it receives any alteration or change; and, on the contrary, remove the fire, remove the heat, prevent it from burning, provided only that you grant me that there is some power which sets in violent motion its minutest parts, and which separates them from the grosser parts, I find that that by itself could effect in it all the changes which take place when it burns.

But, inasmuch as it does not seem to me possible to conceive that one body can move another, unless it is also in motion itself, I conclude from this that the body of flame, which acts upon the wood, is composed of small parts which are in motion separately one from another, with a motion very rapid and very violent, and which, thus moving themselves, push and move with themselves the parts of the bodies which they touch, and which do not offer them too great resistance. I say that the parts move separately one from another, because, although they often accord and conspire, many together, to produce a single effect, we see nevertheless that each of them acts in its own particular way upon the bodies which they touch. I say, also, that their motion is very rapid and very violent; because, being too small for sight to distinguish, they would not have the force they do for acting on other bodies, if the rapidity of their motion did not make up for the want of its extent.

I add nothing in respect to the direction which each part takes; for if you consider that the power of moving itself, and that which determines the direction which the movement shall take, are two entirely different things, one of which might exist without the other (as I have explained in the second discourse of the Dioptrics), you will readily decide that each moves in the way that is made the least difficult to it by the disposition of the bodies which surround it, and that in the same flame there may be parts which would move up and others down, in a straight line and in a curve, and in all directions, without thereby changing its nature at all; so that, if you see almost all of them tending upward, it need not be supposed that this happens so for any other reason than that the other bodies which touch them are almost in every case disposed to offer them more resistance on every other side.

But having taken note that the parts of the flame move in this manner, and that it is sufficient to conceive its motions in order to comprehend how it has the power to consume wood and to burn, let us inquire, pray, whether the same (conception) will not enable us to comprehend how it warms us and how it illuminates us: for, if this should prove to be the case, it will not be necessary that there should exist in it any other quality, and we can say that it is this motion alone, which, according to the different effects which it produces, is called now heat and now light.

But as concerns the nature of heat, the sensation which we have of it may, as it seems to me, be regarded as a kind of pain when it is violent, and sometimes as a kind of pleasure when it is moderate; and as we have said before that there is nothing external to our thought which is like the ideas that we conceive of pleasure and pain, we can easily believe also that there is nothing like that which we conceive of as heat, but that whatever can put in motion in divers ways the minute particles of our hands, or any other portion of our body, may excite in us this sensation.

Many things which we experience also favor this view; for, in simply rubbing the hands, they become warm, and every other body also may be made warm without putting it before the fire, provided only it be moved and shaken so that many of its minute particles are set in motion, and along with them those of our hands.

As for what light is, it can easily be conceived that the same motion which exists in the flame may be sufficient to enable us to perceive it; but inasmuch as it is in this that the principal part of my design consists, I wish to attempt to explain it at length, and to carry on my discourse further.

*   *   *   *   *   *

CHAPTER VI

Description of a new world and of the qualities of the matter of which it is composed

Let, then, your thought pass for a little while beyond this world, that you may behold another wholly new one, which I shall cause to rise to view in imaginary spaces. Philosophers tell us that these spaces are infinite; and they surely ought to be believed, since it is themselves who have made them; but that this infinity may not hinder us or prove an embarrassment, let us not try to get to the end of it: let us proceed so far only as to lose sight of all the creatures God has made in five or six thousand years; and when we have come to a stand there at some fixed point, let us imagine that God creates anew all around us so much matter as that, whatever direction our imagination may take, it shall discover no empty place. Grant that the ocean is not infinite, those who are on a ship in the middle of it can extend their view apparently to infinity, and nevertheless there is water beyond what they can see. Thus, although our imagination seems to be able to stretch to infinity, and this new matter may not be supposed to be infinite, we may nevertheless well suppose that it fills spaces far greater than all those we shall have imagined; and yet, in order that there may be no ground for objection in all this, let us not allow our imagination to stretch itself as far as it can, but let us purposely confine it within a certain space, which need not be very great—for example, the distance between the earth and the principal stars of the firmament; and let us suppose that the matter which God shall have created stretches far beyond, to an indefinite distance in all directions; for this is, indeed, more likely, and we can more easily prescribe

limits to the activity of our thought than to the works
of God.

Now, since we take the liberty to fashion this matter
according to our fancy, we will attribute to it, if you
please, a nature in which there is nothing at all that
anyone cannot know as perfectly as possible; and, in
order to do this, let us suppose expressly that it has not
the form of earth, or fire, or air, or of any other thing
in particular, as wood, stone, or metal; nor the qualities
of being hot or cold, dry or moist, light or heavy; or
that it has any taste, or odour, or sound, or colour, or
light, or other similar quality, in the nature of which it
could be said there was something which is not clearly
known by everybody.

And, on the other hand, let us not think of it as being
that primary matter of philosophers, which has been
so stripped of all its forms and qualities that there is
nothing remaining which can be clearly conceived; but
let us conceive of it as a true substance perfectly solid,
which uniformly fills all the length, breadth, and depth
of that great space, in the midst of which we have stayed
our thought, so that each one of its particles always
occupies a portion of that space so related to its magnitude that it could not fill a greater, nor contract itself
into a less, nor allow, while it remains there, any other
to enter it.

Add to this, that this matter can be divided into all
the parts and according to all the figures we can imagine,
and that each one of its parts is capable of taking on
also all the motions which we can conceive of; and suppose, further, that God has actually divided it into many
such parts, some greater, some smaller; some of one
figure, others of another, whatever we may be pleased
to fancy; not that, in doing so, he has separated them

one from another, so that there should be any empty
space between two of them; but let us suppose that the
only distinction to be met with consists in the variety
of the motions he gives to them, in causing that, at the
very instant that they are created, some of them begin
to move in one direction, others in another; some more
swiftly, others more slowly (or, if you please, not at all),
and that they continue thereafter their motions according to the ordinary laws of nature; for God has so mar-
vellously ordained these laws that, although we should
suppose that he had created nothing more than what I
have said, and even that he had established therein no
order or proportion, but that he had made a chaos the
most confused and the most perplexed that poets could
describe, they would be sufficient to cause the parts
of this chaos to disentangle themselves, and to arrange
themselves in such good order that they would take the
form of a very perfect world, and one in which not only
light would be seen, but also all other things, in general
and particular, which appear in this real world.

But, before I go on to explain this more at length,
pause to consider yet a little further this chaos, and observe that it contains nothing which is not so perfectly
known to you that you cannot even pretend to be ignorant of it; for as to the qualities I have assigned to it,
if you have attended, you have noticed that I have supposed such only as you could conceive. And as for the
matter of which I have composed it, there is nothing
more simple or more easy to understand in the inanimate
world; and the idea of it is so comprehended in all those
objects which our imagination can frame that it must
necessarily be that you conceive it, or that you could
never conceive anything. Nevertheless, since philosophers are so acute that they know how to find difficulties

in things which seem extremely clear to other men, and the recollection of their primary matter—which they know to be very hard to conceive of—might prevent them from understanding that of which I am speaking, I must tell them just here that, if I am not mistaken, the whole difficulty which they experience in regard to it arises from their desire to distinguish it from its quantity and extension, that is to say, from its property of occupying space; wherein, indeed, I am quite willing that they should think themselves to be right, for I do not mean to stop to refute them; but on their part they ought not to find it strange if I suppose that the quantity of the matter which I have described does not differ from its substance any more than number does from things numbered, and if I conceive its extension—or its property of occupying space—not at all as an accident, but as its true form and its essence; for they cannot deny that it is very easy to conceive it in this way.

And my purpose is not to explain, like them, things which really exist in the actual world; but simply to fancy one at pleasure, in which there should be nothing which the dullest minds are not capable of conceiving, and which might not, nevertheless, be created just as I have imagined it. If I should introduce therein the least thing which should prove obscure, it would be owing to the fact that included in that obscurity there was some concealed contradiction of which I had not been aware, and thus, without knowing it, I had supposed something impossible; whereas, on the other hand, if I am able distinctly to conceive all I include in it, it is certain that, although there may be nothing like it in the old (real) world, God might nevertheless create it in a new one, for it is certain that he can create everything we can conceive.

CHAPTER VII

Of all the natural laws of this new world

But I will no longer delay to tell you by what reasons nature alone will be able to disentangle the confusion of the chaos of which I have spoken, and what are the laws which God has imposed upon it.

Know, then, in the first place, that by nature I do not here understand any goddess or any other sort of imaginary power, but I make use of this word to signify matter itself, in so far as I consider it with all the qualities I have attributed to it, taken as a whole, and under this condition, that God continues to preserve it in the same way that he has created it; for, from the simple fact that he continues thus to preserve it, it necessarily follows that there must be many changes in its parts, which not being, as it seems to me, properly attributed to the Divine activity—because that does not change—I attribute them to nature; and the rules in accordance with which these changes occur I call the laws of nature.

In order the better to understand this, remember that among the qualities of matter we have supposed that its particles have had various motions from the instant of their creation, and, besides that, they are all in contact on every side, so that there is no empty space between any two of them; whence it follows of necessity that at the time they began to move they began to change also and to vary their movements as they encountered one another; and thus, even if God preserved them thereafter in the same manner as he created them, he does not preserve them in the same condition—that is to say, while God always acts in the same way, and consequently always produces the same effect in substance, there result, as it were by accident, many diversities in this effect.

And it is easy to believe that God, who, as everybody ought to know, is immutable, acts always in the same way. But without involving myself further in these metaphysical considerations, I will lay down two or three principal rules in accordance with which it must be thought that God causes the nature of this new world to act, and which are sufficient, I believe, to enable you to comprehend all the rest.

The first is, that each individual particle of matter remains always in one and the same state, so long as contact with others does not compel it to change it; that is to say, if it have a certain magnitude it will never become smaller, unless others divide it; if it be round or square, it will never change this figure, unless the rest compel it to do so; if it be at rest in any place, it will never leave it, unless others drive it therefrom; and if it have once begun to move with uniform energy until others stop or retard it.

There is no one who does not believe that this same rule is of force in the old (real) world, in respect to magnitude, figure, rest, and a thousand other matters of a like kind; but philosophers have made an exception in the case of motion, which is, nevertheless, the thing which I desire most expressly to include in it. Do not think, however, that I intend to oppose them: the motion of which they speak is so very different from that which I have in mind, it may easily happen that what is true of the one should not be so of the other.

They admit themselves that the nature of theirs is very little understood, and to render it intelligible in any way they have been unable to explain it more clearly than in these terms: *motus est actus entis in potentia prout in potentia est,* which are so obscure to me that I am constrained to leave them here in their own language, because I cannot interpret them (and indeed

these words, *le mouvement est l'acte d'un être en puissance, en tant qu'il est en puissance,* are no clearer
in French). But, on the other hand, the nature of the
motion I intend here to speak of is so easy to comprehend, that the geometers themselves, who, of all men,
have made the greatest efforts to conceive very distinctly
the things they have treated of, have judged the nature
of motion more simple and more intelligible than that
of their surfaces and their lines, as appears in the fact
that they have explained the line by the motion of a
point, and the surface by that of a line.

The philosophers suppose, also, many motions which
they think could occur without a body changing its place,
as those which they call *motus ad formam, motus ad
calorem, motus ad quantitatem* (motion as to form, motion as to heat, motion as to quantity), and a thousand
others; for my part, I know of none more easy to conceive than the lines of the geometers, which bodies make
in passing from one place to another and successively
occupying all the spaces between the two.

Besides, they attribute to the least of these motions
an existence much more substantial and real than they
do to the rest, which they say is merely privation; for
my part, I conceive that rest is as much a quality to be
attributed to matter, as long as it remains in one place,
as motion is, so long as it changes its place.

Finally, the motion of which they speak is of a nature
so strange that, whereas all other things have for their
end their perfection, and aim only to preserve themselves, this has no other end or aim but rest, and, contrary to all the laws of nature, it aims at its own destruction; but, on the contrary, that which I have in
mind follows the same laws of nature which bring about
in general all the arrangements and all the qualities
which are found in matter, as well as those which the

learned call *modos et entia rationis cum fundamento in re* (modes and entities of reason with foundation in things), together with *qualitates reales* (real qualities), in which I candidly confess that I find no more reality than in the rest.

I suppose, for the second rule, that when one body impels another, it cannot impart to it any motion without at the same time losing so much of its own, nor take from it but so much as its own is thereby increased. This rule, together with the preceding, agrees very well with all the facts which we observe when a body begins or ceases to move, on account of being pushed or stopped by another. For, having assumed the preceding rule, we are free from the difficulty in which the learned find themselves when they wish to give a reason why a stone continues to move for some time after it has left the hand of one who has thrown it; for we ought rather to ask ourselves why it should not continue to move on forever. But the reason is easy to give; for who can deny that the air in which it is moving offers it some resistance? We can hear the air whistle when it is parted, and if set in motion by a fan, or any other very light and very broad body, it can be sensibly felt by the hand that it hinders the movement rather than helps it, as some would have us say. But if the effect of its resistance is not explained according to our second rule, and it is thought that the more a body can resist the more capable it becomes of stopping the movement of others, as perhaps one might at first be inclined to think, there would be considerable difficulty in giving a reason why the movement of this stone is sooner overcome when it meets a soft body, the resistance of which is moderate, than when it meets a harder one which resists it more; as, also, why, as soon as it has made a slight effort against this last, it instantly returns upon its path rather than arrest or interrupt its motion on account of it. Whereas, admitting this rule, there is no difficulty at all; for it instructs us that the motion of the body is not retarded on meeting another in proportion to the degree with which this resists it, but only in proportion to the degree in which its own resistance of it is overcome, and that, in submitting to it, it receives into itself the energy of motion which the other loses.

Now, although in most of the movements which we observe in the real world, we might not perceive that the bodies which begin or cease to move are impelled or arrested by any others, we have no ground on that account to conclude that these two rules are not exactly observed; for it is certain that these bodies may frequently be set in motion by the two elements of air and fire, which are always intermixed with them, though they cannot be perceived there, as was said a while ago; or even by this grosser atmosphere, which also cannot be perceived; and that they may be able to transmit it presently to this grosser air, and again to the whole mass of the earth, in which, being dispersed, it may also not be perceived. But although all that our senses have ever experienced in the real world might appear contrary to these two rules, the reason which has indicated them to me seems so strong that I cannot help thinking myself obliged to admit them in the new one which I am describing to you; for what firmer or more solid foundation could be found to establish a truth, although one were at liberty to choose what he would, than the constancy and immutability of God?

Now these two rules follow manifestly from the simple fact that God is immutable, and that, acting always in the same way, he produces always the same effect: for granting that he has put a certain quantity of motion into all matter universally at the first instant that he created it, it must be admitted that he also preserves as much of it there, or else it cannot be thought that he acts always in the same way; and granting with this that from that first instant the various parts of matter, in which those motions are found unequally distributed, have begun to retain them or to transfer them one to another, according as they had power to do, it must necessarily be thought that he makes them always continue to do the same thing; and this is what these two rules contain.

I will add, for the third, that when a body moves, although its movement is most frequently in a curved line, and can never be otherwise than circular in some degree, as has been said above, nevertheless each one of its particles in particular tends always to continue its own motion in a straight line. And so their action— that is to say, their inclination to move—is different from their movement.

For example, if a wheel be turned on its axle, although all its parts move in a circle, because being joined together they could not move otherwise, nevertheless their tendency is to move in a right line, as plainly appears if by chance any one is detached from the rest; for, as soon as it is set free, its movement ceases to be circular, and it continues on in a straight line. Likewise, when a stone is whirled in a sling, not only does it go in a straight line as soon as it leaves it, but further, all the time it is in it, it presses upon the center of the sling, and stretches the cord, thus showing plainly that it always has a tendency to go in a straight line, and that it moves in a circle only by constraint.

This rule rests on the same foundation as the other

two, and depends only on the fact that God preserves each thing by one continuous activity, and that, consequently, he does not preserve it such as it may have been some time before, but precisely such as it is at the very instant that he preserves it. Now the case is that, among all movements, that which is in a straight line is the only one which is entirely simple, and one the whole nature of which may be embraced in a single instant; for, in order to conceive it, it is enough to think of a body actually moving in one fixed direction, which is the case in every one of the instants which can be determined during the time it is in motion; whereas, to conceive circular movement, or any other that can exist, it is necessary to consider at least two of these instants, or rather two of its parts, and the relation between them; but in order that philosophers or sophists rather, may not take occasion here to practise their superfluous subtleties, notice that I do not say that movement in a straight line can take place in an instant, but simply all that is required to produce it exists in the body in every instant which can be determined during its movement, and not all that is required to produce the circular . . . . It must then be said, according to this rule, that God alone is the author of all the movements in the universe, in so far as they exist, and in so far as they are in straight lines; but that there are various arrangements of matter which render them irregular and curved, just as the theologians teach us that God is the author of all our actions, in so far as they exist, and in so far as they have any goodness in them, but that it is the various dispositions of our wills which make them bad.

I might add here many rules to determine in particular when, and how, and how much the movement of any body can be deflected, and increased or diminished, by meeting others, in which are summarily comprehended all natural phenomena; but I shall content myself with informing you that, besides the three laws which I have explained, I do not intend to assume any others except those which follow infallibly from the eternal verities, I say, in accordance with which God himself has taught us that he has disposed all things by number, weight, and measure, and the knowledge of which is so natural to our minds that we cannot help knowing them infallibly when we conceive them distinctly, nor doubting that, had God created many worlds, they would be no less true in all than in this.

So that those who shall have sufficiently examined the consequences of these verities, and of our rules, will be able to know effects by their causes, and, to express myself in the language of the school, may have *a priori* demonstrations of all that can come to pass in this new world. And, in order that there may be no exception whatever to embarrass us, we will add to our assumptions, if you please, that God will never work any miracle there, and that the intelligences, or reasonable minds, which we shall hereafter assume to be there, will never interfere in any way with the ordinary course of nature. In what follows, nevertheless, I do not promise to place before you exact demonstrations of all that I have to say; it will be enough that I open the way by which you shall be able to find them out for yourselves, when you will take pains to seek them. Most minds are displeased when things are made too easy for them. And to paint a picture here which shall please you, I must make use of shadows as well as colours. Accordingly I shall content myself with following out the description which I have begun, having no other design than to tell you a story.

CHAPTER VIII

Of the formation of the sun and the stars of this new world

Whatever inequality and confusion we might suppose God had introduced at the beginning among the particles of matter, it is necessary, according to the laws which he has imposed upon nature, that nearly all of them should afterward be reduced to one size and one moderate motion, and thus that they should take the form of the second element, such as I have explained it above. For, considering this matter in the state in which it might have been before God had set it in motion, it should be conceived of as being like the hardest and most solid body in the world. And as one could not push a single particle of such a body without also, by the same means, pushing or drawing all the rest, so it must be thought that the action or force of motion, or division, which at the first had been placed in any of its particles, would have expanded and distributed itself at the same instant to all the rest as uniformly as possible.

It is true that this uniformity could not have been absolutely perfect, for, in the first place, because there is no void at all in this world, it would have been impossible that all the particles of matter should move in a straight line; but being very nearly equal, and one being almost as easily deflected as another, they should all agree together in a circular motion of some sort. And nevertheless, inasmuch as we suppose that God has moved them variously at the first, we must not think that they would all agree in revolving about a single center, but about many different ones, which we may conceive of as being differently situated with respect to one another.

Accordingly we must conclude that they would naturally be in less rapid motion or smaller, or both at once,
in the places nearer these centers than in those more
remote; for all having a disposition to continue their
movement in a straight line, it is certain that those are
the strongest—that is, the largest, among those which
may be equally swift in their motion, and the swiftest
among those which may equal in size—which have to
describe the greater circles, as being the nearest to the
straight line. And as for the matter contained between
three or more of these circles, it might well be at first
much less divided and less swift in its motion than all
the rest; and what is more, inasmuch as we suppose that
God at the beginning has put all sorts of inequality into
the different parts of this matter, we ought to think
that from that time it has had all sorts of sizes and
shapes, and has been disposed to move, or not to move,
in every way and manner.

But this does not prevent them afterward becoming
nearly all uniform, especially those which remain at an
equal distance from the centers around which they revolve; for, being unable to move independently, it was
necessary that the swifter communicate of their motion
to those which had less, and that the greater break up
and divide, in order to be able to pass over the same
spaces as those which preceded them, or, at least, that
they mount higher; and thus they would arrange themselves, in a short time, all in order, so that each one
would find itself more or less distant from the center
around which it had taken its course, according as it
had more or less of size or swiftness than the rest; and
also, inasmuch as size always conflicts with speed, it
must be that the most distant from each center were
those which, being a little smaller than those nearer,
have been also much swifter.

The same would be true of their figures. Although we may suppose that these at the beginning were of every sort, and that they had, for the most part, many angles and many sides, like the pieces which split off from a stone when it is broken, it is certain that afterward, in moving and striking against one another, they would have rubbed off, little by little, the small points of their angles, and blunted the edges of their sides, until they became by degrees almost all round, as grains of sand and flint do when rolled about in running water; so that there might not now be any noticeable difference between those which are near enough together, nor even between those which are very distant, except in the fact that they can move a little faster, and be a little smaller or larger, one than the other; and this does not prevent our attributing to all of them the same form. Only an exception must be made of some which, having been from the first much larger than the rest, have not easily become divided, or which, having had very irregular and resistant shapes, have tended to unite in a mass rather than to break up and become round, and thus they have retained the form of the third element, and have served to compose the planets and the comets, as I shall hereafter explain to you.

Further, it is to be noted that the matter which has come off from the surface of the parts of the second element, in proportion as they have broken up and blunted the sharp corners of their angles in becoming round, has necessarily acquired a motion much swifter than theirs, and at the same time a facility of dividing and changing its shape at every moment to accommodate itself to that of the places where it happens to be, and so it has taken the form of the first element.

It is also to be noted that what there is of this first element, more than is needed to fill the small interspaces that the particles of the second, which are spherical, necessarily leave around them, must move toward the centers about which they (the particles of the second element) revolve, because, these occupy all the other places more distant, and that it must there form round bodies perfectly liquid and rare, which, turning incessantly much more rapidly and in the same direction as the particles of the second element which environ them, have power to increase the motion of those to which they are nearest, and also to push them all in every direction, drawing them from the center to the circumference, so that they also push one another, and this by a mode of action which it is necessary that I presently describe as exactly as I am able to do; for I apprise you here in advance that it is this action which we take to be light, just as we take those round bodies composed of matter of the first element quite pure, the one to be the sun, the others to be the fixed stars, of the new world I am describing to you, and the matter of the second element, which revolves around them, to be the heavens. . . . . . .

CHAPTER IX

Of the origin and course of the planets and comets in general, and in particular of the comets

Now—to begin to speak to you of the planets and comets—consider that as respects the diversity of the parts of the matter which I have assumed, although the larger part of them, through clashing and breaking up on encountering one another, would take the form of the first or second element, there would still be found two sorts which have necessarily retained the form of the third, namely, those whose figure was so extended and so resistant that, on meeting one another, it was easier for several of them to join together and by this means to become larger, than to break up and become smaller, and those which were from the beginning the largest and most massive of all were well able to break and shatter the others on striking them, but not, reciprocally, to be broken and shattered. If now, you should conceive that these two sorts of parts were at first in very rapid motion, or even that they moved very slowly, or not at all, it is certain that afterward they would have to move at the same rate as the matter of the heavens which contained them; for, if at first they moved more swiftly than this matter, as they would unavoidably push it forward as they encountered it in their path, they must in a short time have transferred to it a part of their own momentum; and if, on the contrary, they had not in themselves any disposition to move, nevertheless, being surrounded on all sides by this matter of the heavens, they would necessarily have followed its course; just as we see every day that boats and various other bodies which float upon the water, the largest and most massive, as well as the smallest, follow the current of the water in which they are, whenever there is nothing else to prevent them.

And observe that, among the various bodies which thus float upon the water, those which are solid and massive enough, as boats commonly are, especially the larger and more heavily laden, have always much more force than it (the water) to continue their movement, even though it may be received from it above; and that, on the contrary, those which are very light, such as the masses of white foam which are seen floating along on rivers during a storm, have less force. So that if you imagine two rivers which unite at a certain point and separate soon after, before their waters, which must be conceived as very calm and uniform in force, but also

very rapid, have had time to mingle, boats or other
bodies massive and heavy enough, which are carried
along by the current of one, might easily pass into the
other, whereas the lighter ones would keep separate
from it, and be borne by the force of this stream toward
parts where it is less rapid. . . . . . .

From this illustration it is easy to understand that,
in whatever place there may be found, at the beginning,
parts of matter which could not take the form of the
second element, nor of the first, all the largest and most
massive among them would have been compelled in a
short time to take their course toward the outer circle
of the heavens which contain them, and to pass continually thereafter from one of these heavens into another, without ever stopping for any long time together
in the same heavens; and that, on the contrary, all the
less massive must have been pushed in turn toward the
center of the heavens which contained them, by the current of the matter of those heavens; and that, considering the forms I have attributed to them, they must, on
meeting, have united themselves many of them together,
and formed those great globes which, revolving in the
heavens, have there a motion the resultant of all those
which their parts would have when moving separately,
so that some of them would tend toward the circumfer-
ences of these heavens, and others toward their centers.
And understand that it is those which tend thus to move
toward the center of any heavens that we must here call
the planets, and those which pass across the different
heavens we must call comets.

Now, in the first place, in regard to the comets, it must
be observed that there would be but few of them in this
new world, in comparison to the number of the heavens;
for although, indeed, there might have been many of
them at the beginning, they must, in course of time, in

their passage across the different heavens, nearly all of them have struck against one another and gone to pieces, as I have said two vessels might do by running into one another, so that only the biggest might now remain. It is necessary, also, to observe that, when they pass thus from one heaven into another, they always push before themselves a little of the matter of that which they leave, and remain for some time enveloped in it, until they have entered pretty well within the borders of the next heavens; on being there, they finally free themselves of it all at once, as it were, and without taking any more time perhaps than the sun does to rise in the morning above our horizon; so that they move much more slowly when they tend to pass out of any heaven than they do a little after entering it. . . . . . .

CHAPTER X

Of the planets in general, and in particular of the earth and the moon

There are, likewise, in regard to the planets, many things to be noted: the first of which is that, although they all tend toward the centers of the heavens which contain them, they never can reach those centers; for, as I have already said above, it is the sun and the fixed stars which occupy them. . . . . . .

If I have not yet made you sufficiently understand the cause which makes the parts of the heaven which are outside (the orbits of the planets), being incomparably smaller than the planets, have greater power than these to continue their movement in a straight line, consider that this force does not depend solely on the quantity of the matter in each body, but also on the extent of its surface. For although when two bodies are moving with equal velocity, it may be correct to say that if one con-

tain twice as much matter as the other, it has, also, twice
as much momentum; it cannot on that account be said
that it has twice as much power to continue to move in
a straight line; but it will have twice as much if along
with that, its surface be exactly twice as great, because
it will always meet twice as many bodies which will
resist it; and it will have much less if its surface is
much more than twice as great.

Now you know that the particles which compose the
heavens are almost quite spherical, and so they have
that figure which of all others contains the most matter
within the least surface; and that on the contrary, the
planets, being composed of small parts which are of
very irregular and extended figure, have great surface
in proportion to the quantity of their matter, so that
they may have much more than most of the parts of the
heaven, and yet also have less than some of the smaller
parts and those nearer the centers; for it must be understood that, as between two globes quite solid—as are
those parts of the heaven—the smaller has always more
surface, in proportion to its quantity, than the larger
has.

And all this may easily be confirmed by experience.
For if a great globe, made of the boughs of trees all
matted together, as the parts of the matter composing
the planets may be conceived as being, should be set in
motion, it is certain that it would not continue its movement so far, although impelled by a force entirely pro-
portionate to its size, as would another globe much
smaller and made of the same wood, but quite solid: it
is certain, also, quite to the contrary, that another
globe might be made of the same wood and quite solid,
but which should be so extremely small that it would
have much less power to continue its movement than
the first; finally it is certain that this first would have

more or less power to continue its movement, according
as the boughs which composed it were more or less
large and compacted together. From this you see how
different planets may be suspended within the outer-
most circle at different distances from the sun, and how
it is not those simply which appear the largest outside,
but those which are in their interior most solid and
massive, which must be the more distant.

It is to be observed, further, that as we find that
boats which follow the currents of a river never move
so swiftly as the waters which bear them, nor the largest
among them so fast as the smallest; so, although the
planets follow the course of the matter of the heavens
without resistance, and move by the same impetus as
that, it cannot be said, on that account, that they ever
move so swiftly; and, also, the inequality of their movement must have some relation to that which exists
between the greatness of their mass and the smallness
of the parts of the heavens which environ them. The
reason of which is this, that, generally speaking, the
larger a body is, the easier it is for it to communicate
a part of its motion to other bodies, and the more difficult for other bodies to communicate to it any of theirs;
for although many small bodies when combining together to act upon a greater, might have as much force
as it, nevertheless they never could make it move so
fast in every way as they move themselves; because,
if they agree in certain of their movements which they
communicate to it at the same time, they inevitably
differ in others which they do not communicate to it.

Now, there follow from this two things, which seem
to me to be of considerable importance: the first is that
the matter of the heavens must not only cause the
planets to revolve about the sun, but also about their
own center (except when there is any particular cause

to hinder them), and, accordingly, that it must be composed of small heavens around them which move in the same way as the greater. And the second is that, if there meet together two planets unequal in size, but so situated as to take their course in the heavens at the same distance from the sun, so that one were exactly so much more solid than the other was large, the smaller of these two, having a motion more rapid than the larger, will unite itself with the small heaven which is around this larger one and revolve continually with it. . . . . . .

CHAPTER XI

Of gravity

But I desire now that you consider what the gravity of this earth is, that is to say, the force which unites all its parts, and which makes them all tend toward its center, everyone more or less according as they are more or less large and solid; which is nothing else and consists only in this, that the parts of the small heaven which surrounds it, turning much more swiftly than its own do around its center, tend also with much more force to withdraw themselves from it, and consequently push them back there.

In which if you find any difficulty from the fact that I have said so many times that the more massive and solid bodies, such as I have assumed the comets to be, would tend toward the circumference of these heavens, and it would be only the less so which would be pushed back toward their centers, as if it should follow from that it would be only the less solid parts of the earth which could be pushed towards its center, and the others would necessarily withdraw from it; observe that, when I said that the most solid and massive bodies tend to

withdraw from the center of a heaven, I assumed that
they were moving already with the same impetus as the
matter of that heaven: because it is certain that if they
had not yet begun to move, or if they were in motion,
provided that this motion were less rapid than was
necessary to follow the current of this matter, they
must be forced by it toward the center around which it
turned; and, also, it is certain that, in proportion as
they were greater and more solid, they would be pushed
with more force and swiftness.

And nevertheless, this would not prevent that, if
they were solid enough to compose comets, they would
tend but little toward the exterior circles of the heavens,
inasmuch as the energy which they should have acquired
in descending toward any one of their centers would
inevitably impart to them force to pass beyond it and
reascend toward its circumference. . . . . . .

Now it is evident that a stone, containing in itself
more of the matter of the earth, and in return containing much less of that of the heaven, then a quantity
of air of equal extent, and also its parts being less impelled by the matter of this heaven than that of this
air, it would not have power to mount above it, but
rather, on the contrary, it would have the power to
make this descend below it, so that the air would be
light when compared with the stone; but heavy when
compared with the heaven itself. . . . . . .

And you can understand from this that the arguments
which many philosophers employ, to refute the motion
of the real earth, have no force against that of the earth
which I am describing to you; as when they say that
if the earth were in motion heavy bodies would not fall
plumb toward its center, but rather would stray this
way and that toward the sky, and that cannon pointed
toward the west would carry much further than when

pointed toward the east, and that great winds would be
felt and great noises in the air, and such like things,
which could happen only on the supposition that the
earth is not carried forward by the current of the
heaven which surrounds it, but is moved by some other
force and in some other way than this heaven moves.

CHAPTER XII

Of light

I have repeatedly said that bodies which revolve in
a circle tend always to withdraw from the centers of
the circles which they describe; but I must here determine more precisely in what directions the parts of the
matter of which the heavens and the stars are composed
have a tendency to move. Accordingly, it must be
understood that when I speak of a body tending to
move in any direction, I do not wish it to be supposed
on that account that it has in it any thought or design
which carries it hither, but simply that it is disposed
to move that way, whether it actually does move thither,
or some other body prevents it from doing so; and it
is principally in this latter signification that I employ
the word "tend," because it seems to signify some effort,
and all effort presupposes resistance. Now, inasmuch
as there are often various causes which, acting together
upon the same body, counteract one another, it may be
said, for various reasons, that the same body tends to
move in different directions at the same time, as has
just been said that the particles of the earth tend to
withdraw from its center, so long as they are considered
independently, and that they tend on the contrary to
approach it when the force of the particles of the
heavens which push them thither is considered; and
again that they tend to withdraw from it when con-

trasted with other terrestrial particles which compose
bodies more massive than they are. As, for example, a
stone whirled in a sling. . . . . . .

Still further I reply that their other motions which
continue in them (the particles of the second element),
while thus advancing toward the circumference, not
allowing them to remain a single instant arranged in
the same way, prevent them from coming in contact,
or at least cause that as soon as they touch they instantly separate again, and thus they do not cease to
advance without interruption toward the circumference
until the whole space is filled. Accordingly we can
draw from this no other conclusion than that the force
by which they tend toward (the circumference) is
probably, as it were, a tremulous one, and increases
and diminishes in varying minute vibrations, according
as they change their situation, which seems to me a
property very well agreeing with light. . . . Finally,
the particles of the first element which . . . compose
the body of the sun, revolving in a circular manner
very swiftly about (its center), tend to scatter themselves in every direction in straight lines. . . . As for
the rest, although they must thus advance toward (the
circumference) if this space be occupied only by the
first element, it is certain that they tend to move thither
just the same if it be filled with any other body, and
that, consequently, they push and strive against this
body, as it were, to drive it from its place. So that if
the eye of a man should be at (a point in this circumference) it would be really pushed upon by the sun as
much as by any of the matter (in the intervening
space). Now it is to be understood that the inhabitants
of this new world are of such a nature that, when their
eyes are thus pushed upon, they have a sensation in
every respect resembling that which we have of light.

CHAPTER XIII

Of the properties of light

But I wish to delay a little longer at this point to explain the properties of the energy (*de l'action*) by which their eyes can be excited. For they agree so perfectly with those which we observe in light, that when you shall have considered them, I am sure that you will declare, as I do, that there is no need of conceiving in the stars, nor in the heavens, any other quality than this energy, which is called by the name of light.

The principal properties of light are: 1, That it spreads itself around on all sides about bodies which we call luminous; 2, and to every degree of distance; 3, and instantaneously; 4, and usually in straight lines, which must be understood as rays of light; 5, and that many of these rays, coming from different points, may gather at one point; 6, or, coming from the same point, may proceed to different points; 7, or, coming from different points, and going toward different points, may pass by the same point without interference with one another; 8, and that they may also sometimes hinder one another, to wit, when their force is very unequal, and that of some is very much greater than that of others; 9, and finally, that they can be turned aside by reflection; 10, or by refraction; 11, and that their force may be increased; 12, or diminished by the different dispositions or qualities of the matter which receives them.

These are the principal properties observed in light, all of which agree with this energy, as you shall see:

1. That this energy must spread itself in all directions around luminous bodies, the reason whereof is evident, because it is from the circular movement of their particles that it proceeds.

2. It is also evident that it can extend itself to every degree of distance; because, for example, supposing that the particles of the heavens which are contained in the space between (the sun and some point in the circumference of those heavens) are already of themselves disposed to move toward (the circumference), as we have said they are, it cannot be doubted that the force with which the sun impels those which are (about it) must make them reach as far as the (circumference), even although it were a distance greater than that between the most distant stars of the firmament and ourselves.

3. And considering that the particles of the second element which are between [the sun and some point on the circumference] touch upon and press each other as much as possible, it cannot be doubted also that the energy by which the first are impelled must pass in an instant as far as the last, just as that by which one end of a stick is pushed in the same instant to the other end. . . . . . .

4. In regard to the lines along which this energy is communicated, and which are properly rays of light, it must be observed that they differ from the particles of the second element, by the medium of which this same energy is propagated, and that they are nothing material in the medium through which they pass, but that they signify simply in what way and in what direction the luminous body acts upon that which it illuminates; and thus they are not to be conceived otherwise than as exactly straight, although the particles of the second element, which serves to transmit this energy or light, might almost never be so directly situated one after another as to compose perfectly straight lines.

9, 10. As for reflection and refraction, I have already sufficiently explained them elsewhere. Nevertheless,

because for the illustration of the movement, I then
made use of a ball instead of speaking of rays of light,
in order by this means to make my discourse more intelligible; it remains to me here to bring to your attention the fact that the energy, or inclination to move,
which is transmitted from one place to another by
means of many bodies which are in contact and which
exist without break throughout all the space between
both, follows precisely the same path wherein this same
energy might cause the first of these bodies to move,
if the others were not in its way, with no other difference except that time would be required for this body
to move, whereas the energy which is in it may, through
the intervention of those which are in contact with it,
extend itself to all distances in an instant; whence it
follows that, in like manner as a ball is reflected when
it hits against the wall of a tennis-court, and that it
suffers refraction when it enters obliquely into water,
or passes out of it, so also when the rays of light meet
a body which does not allow them to pass through, they
must be reflected; and when they enter obliquely into
any place through they can extend themselves more or
less easily than through that whence they proceed, they
must also, at the point of this change, be deflected and
suffer refraction.

11, 12. Finally, the energy of light is not only more
or less great in each place, according to the quantity
of rays which meet there, but it can also be increased
and diminished by the different dispositions of the bodies
which happen to be in the places through which it
passes, just as the velocity of a ball or stone thrown
into the air may be increased by the winds which blow
in the same direction in which it is moving, and diminished by those which oppose it.

CHAPTER XIV

*That the heavens of this new world must appear to its
inhabitants the same as ours*

Having thus explained the nature and properties of
that energy which I understand light to be, it is necessary also that I explain how by means of it the inhabitants of the planet, which I have assumed for the earth,
may see the face of their heavens as one quite like ours.
In the first place, there is no doubt that they must see
the [central body] all full of light like our sun, seeing
that that body sends its rays from every point of its
surface toward their eyes; and because it is much nearer
them than the stars, it must appear much larger. . . . . .
It must be understood that the great heavens, that
is to say, those which have a fixed star or sun for their
center, although, perhaps, quite unequal in extent, must
always be of exactly equal energy; for, if this equilibrium did not exist, they would inevitably perish in a
short time, or at least they would change until they
acquired this equilibrium. . . . But it is necessary that
you further observe, in regard to their situation, that
the stars can never appear in the places where they
really are. . . . The reason of this is that the [different]
heavens being unequal in extent, the surfaces which
separate them never happen to be so disposed that the
rays, which cross them in going from these stars toward
the earth, meet them at right angles; and, meeting them
obliquely, it is certain, according to what has been
shown in the "Dioptrics," that they must be bent and
suffer considerable refraction, inasmuch as they pass
much more easily through one of the sides of this surface than through the other. . . . . . .
Consider, also, as regards the number of these stars,
that frequently the same one might appear in several

places, because of the different surfaces which deflect
its rays toward the earth . . . just as objects are multi-
plied when seen through glasses or other transparent
bodies cut with many faces.

Further consider, in regard to their size, that although
they must appear much smaller than they are, because
of their extreme distance, and also that, for the same
reason, the larger part of them cannot appear at all,
and others can appear only as the rays of many uniting
together make the parts of the firmament through which
they pass a little whiter, and like certain stars which
astronomers call nebulous, or that great belt of the
heavens which the poets feign was washed in the milk
of Juno; nevertheless, as for those which are less distant, it is enough to assume them to be about equal to
our sun, in order to conclude that they would appear
as large as the largest in our world.

. . . Beside that, it is very probable that the [limit-
ing] surfaces of the heavens being of an extremely fluid
matter, which is incessantly in motion, would constantly
shake and undulate somewhat; and, consequently, that
the stars which are seen through it would appear scintillating and trembling, as it were, as do our own, and
also, because of their trembling, a little larger, as does
the image of the moon upon a lake, the surface of which
is not greatly disturbed nor tossed, but only slightly
ruffled by a breeze.

And finally, it may come about in the course of time,
these limiting surfaces change a little, or even again
that some [of them] bend as much in a short time—on
occasion, it may be, of a comet approaching them—
and, by this means, many stars appear, after a long
time, to be a little changed in position without being
so in magnitude, or slightly changed in magnitude
without being so in position; or even that some begin

suddenly to appear or to disappear, as is seen to happen
in the real world.

As for the planets and comets which are in the same
heavens as the sun, remembering that the particles of
the third element of which they are composed are so
large, or so many of them compacted together, that they
can resist the action of light, it is easy to understand
that they must shine by means of the rays that the sun
sends toward them, and which they reflect thence toward the earth; just as opaque or dark objects in a
chamber can be seen by means of the rays which a
torch lighted there sends toward them, and which return thence toward the eyes of the observers.   And
besides, the rays of the sun have a very considerable
advantage over those of a torch, which consists in this,
that their energy is preserved or even increased more
and more in proportion to their distance from the sun,
until they reach the exterior surface of its heavens,
because all the matter of those heavens tends thither;
whereas the rays of a torch grow feebler as they recede,
in proportion to the extent of the spherical surfaces
which they illuminate, and also, in some small degree,
on account of the resistance of the air through which
they come.   Whence it arises that objects which are in
the vicinity of the torch are noticeably brighter than
those which are at a distance from it; and that the inferior planets are not in the same proportions more
illuminated by the sun than the superior, nor even than
the comets, which are, beyond comparison, more distant.

Now, experience shows that the same thing happens,
also, in the real world; and, nevertheless, I do not
believe it possible to give a reason for it, if it be assumed that light be anything else in objects than an
energy [*une action*] or disposition, such as I have ex-

plained it to be. I say an energy or disposition; for if you have paid good attention to what I have recently proved, that, if the space where the sun is were quite empty, the particles of its heavens would not cease to tend toward the eyes of the observers in the same way as when they are impelled by its matter, and even with almost as much force, you may easily conclude that there would be hardly any need of its having in it any activity, or even, as it were, any being, other than pure space, in order to appear such as we see it. As to the rest, the movement of these planets about their center is the cause of their scintillating, yet much less strongly and in a different way from the fixed stars; and, because the moon is devoid of this movement, it does not scintillate at all. . . . . . .

SELECTIONS FROM THE TREATISE ON MAN

These men[1] shall be composed, as we are, of a soul and a body; and I must describe to you first the body by itself, afterward the soul, also by itself, and finally I must show you how both these natures are to be joined and united to compose men which resemble us.

I assume that the body is nothing else than a statue or machine of clay which God forms expressly to make it as nearly like as possible to ourselves, so that not only does he give it externally the colour and the form of all our members, but also he puts within it all the parts necessary to make it walk, eat, breathe and, in fine, imitate all those of our functions which may be supposed to proceed from matter and to depend merely on the arrangement of organs.

We see clocks, artificial fountains, mills, and other similar machines, which, although made by men, are not without the power of moving of themselves in many different ways; and it seems to me that I should not be able to imagine so many kinds of movements in this one, which I am supposing to be made by the hand of God, nor attribute to it so much of artifice that you would not have reason to think there might still be more.

Now, I will not stop to describe to you the bones, nerves, muscles, veins, arteries, stomach, liver, spleen, heart, brain, nor all the other different parts of which

[1] The men of the world described in the treatise "The World, an Essay on Light."

it is to be composed; for I assume them to be in every respect similar to the parts of our own body which have the same names, and which you can have shown to you by any learned anatomist, at least those which are large enough to be seen, if you do not already know them well enough yourselves; and as for those which, because of their minuteness, are invisible, I shall be able to make you more easily and clearly understand them, by speaking of the movements which depend upon them; so that it is only necessary here for me to explain in order these movements, and to tell you by the same means what functions of our own they represent. . . .

But what is here to be chiefly noted is that all the most active, vigorous, and finest particles of the blood tend to run into the cavities of the brain, inasmuch as the arteries which carry them are those which come in the straightest line of all from the heart, and, as you know, all bodies in motion tend, as far as possible, to continue their motion in a straight line. . . . . . .

In regard to the particles of blood which penetrate to the brain, they serve not only to nourish and support its substance, but chiefly, also, to produce there a certain very subtle breath, or rather flame, very active and very pure, which is called the *animal spirits*. For it must be understood that the arteries which carry them from the heart, after being divided into an infinitude of small branches, and having formed those small tissues which are spread like tapestries at the base of the cavities of the brain, collect about a certain small *gland* situated nearly at the middle of the substance of the brain, just at the entrance of its cavities, and have at this place a great number of small openings through which the finest particles of the blood they contain can run into this gland, but which are too narrow to admit the larger.

It must also be understood that these arteries do not end there, but that—many of them there joined together in one—they mount directly upward and empty into that great artery which is like a Euripus [aqueduct] by which the whole exterior surface of the brain is irrigated. And, moreover, it is to be noted that the larger particles of the blood may lose much of their onward motion in the winding passages of the small tissues through which they pass, inasmuch as they have the power to push on the smaller ones among them, and so transfer it to them; but that these smaller ones cannot in the same way lose their own, inasmuch as it is even increased by that which the larger transfer to them, and there are no other bodies around them to which they can so easily transfer it.

Whence it is easy to conceive that, when the larger ones mount straight toward the exterior surface of the brain, where they serve for the nourishment of its substance, they cause the smaller and more rapidly moving particles all to turn aside and enter into this gland, which is to be conceived of as a very copious fountain, whence they flow on all sides at once into the cavities of the brain; and thus, with no other preparation or change, except that they are separated from the larger, and that they still retain the extreme swiftness which the heat of the heart has imparted to them, they cease to have the form of blood and are called animal spirits.

Now, in proportion as these spirits enter thus the cavities of the brain, they pass thence into the pores of its substance, and from these pores into the nerves; where, according as they enter, or even only as they tend to enter, more or less into some rather than into others, they have the power to change the form of the muscles into which their nerves are inserted and by this means to cause all the limbs to move; just as you may have seen in grottoes and fountains in the royal gardens that the force alone with which the water moves, in passing from the spring, is enough to move various machines, and even to make them play on instruments, or utter words, according to the different arrangement of the pipes which conduct it.

And, indeed, the nerves of the machine that I am describing to you may very well be compared to the pipes of the machinery of these fountains, its muscles and its tendons to various other engines and devices which serve to move them, its animal spirits to the water which sets them in motion, of which the heart is the spring, and the cavities of the brain the outlets. Moreover, respiration and other such functions as are natural and usual to it, and which depend on the course of the spirits, are like the movements of a clock or a mill, which the regular flow of the water can keep up. External objects which, by their presence alone, act upon the organs of its senses, and which by this means determine to move in many different ways, according as the particles of its brain are arranged, are like visitors, who, entering some of the grottoes of these fountains, bring about of themselves, without intending it, the movements which occur in their presence; for they cannot enter without stepping on certain tiles of the pavement so arranged that, for example, if they approach a Diana taking a bath, they make her hide in the reeds; and, if they pass on in pursuit of her, they cause a Neptune to appear before them who menaces them with his trident; or if they turn in some other direction they will make a marine monster come out, who will squirt water into their faces, or something similar will happen, according to the fancy of the engineers who construct them. And finally, when the *reasonable soul* shall be in this machine, it will have its principal seat in the brain, and it will be there like the fountain-maker, who must be at the openings where all the pipes of these machines discharge themselves, if he wishes to start, to stop, or to change in any way their movements.

I desire you to consider next that all the functions which I have attributed to this machine, such as the digestion of food, the beating of the heart and arteries, the nourishment and growth of the members, respiration, waking, and sleeping; the impressions of light, sounds, odours, tastes, heat and other such qualities on the organs of the external senses; the impression of their ideas on the common sense and the imagination; the retention of imprinting of these ideas upon the memory; the interior motions of the appetites and passions; and, finally, the external movements of all the members, which follow so suitably as well as the actions of objects which present themselves to sense, as the passions and impressions which are found in the memory, that they imitate in the most perfect manner possible those of a real man; I desire, I say, that you consider that all these functions follow naturally in this machine simply from the arrangement of its parts, no more nor less than do the movements of a clock, or other *automata,* from that of its weights and its wheels; so that it is not at all necessary for their explanation to conceive it in any other soul, vegetative or sensitive, nor any other principle of motion and life, than its blood and its spirits, set in a motion by the heat of the fire which burns continually in its heart, and which is of a nature no different from all fires in inanimate bodies.

AUTOMATISM OF BRUTES

Letter to the Marquis of Newcastle

. . . As for the understanding or thought attributed by Montaigne and others to brutes, I cannot hold their opinion; not, however, because I am doubtful of the truth of what is commonly said, that men have absolute dominion over all the other animals; for while I allow that there are some which are stronger than we are, and I believe there may be some, also, which have natural cunning capable of deceiving the most sagacious men; yet I consider that they imitate or surpass us only in those of our actions which are not directed by thought; for it often happens that we walk and that we eat without thinking at all upon what we are doing; and it is so much without the use of our reason that we repel things which harm us, and ward off blows struck at us, that, although we might fully determine not to put our hands before our heads when falling, we could not help doing so. I believe, also, that we should eat as the brutes do, without having learned how, if we had no power of thought at all; and it is said that those who walk in their sleep sometimes swim across rivers, where, had they been awake, they would have been drowned.

As for the movements of our passions, although in ourselves they are accompanied with thought, because we possess that faculty, it is, nevertheless, very evident that they do not depend upon it, because they often arise in spite of us, and, consequently, they may exist in brutes, and even be more violent than they are in the men, without warranting the conclusion that brutes can think; in fine there is no one of our external actions which can assure those who examine them that our body

is any thing more than a machine which moves of itself,
but which also has in it a mind which thinks—excepting
words, or other signs made in regard to whatever subjects present themselves, without reference to any passion. I say words, or other signs, because mutes make
use of signs in the same way as we do of the voice, and
these signs are pertinent; but I exclude the talking of
parrots, but not that of the insane, which may be
apropos to the case in hand, although it is irrational;
and I add that these words or signs are not to relate
to any passion, in order to exclude, not only cries of
joy or pain and the like, but, also, all that can be
taught to any animal by art; for if a magpie be taught
to say "good-morning" to its mistress when it sees her
coming, it may be that the utterance of these words is
associated with the excitement of some one of its passions; for instance, there will be a stir of expectation
of something to eat, if it has been the custom of the
mistress to give it some dainty bit when it spoke those
words; and in like manner all those things which dogs,
horses, and monkeys are made to do are merely motions
of their fear, their hope, or their joy, so that they might
do them without any thought at all.

Now, it seems to me very remarkable that language,
as thus defined, belongs to man alone; for although
Montaigne and Charron have said that there is more
difference between one man and another than between
a man and a brute, nevertheless there has never yet
been found a brute so perfect that it has made use of a
sign to inform other animals of something which had
no relation to their passions; while there is no man so
imperfect as not to use such signs; so that the deaf and
dumb invent particular signs by which they express
their thoughts, which seems to me a very strong argu-

ment to prove that the reason why brutes do not talk as we do is that they have no faculty of thought, and not at all that the organs for it are wanting. And it cannot be said that they talk among themselves, but we do not understand them; for, as dogs and other animals express to us their passions, they would express to us as well their thoughts, if they had them. I know, indeed, that brutes do many things better than we do, but I am not surprised at it; for that, also, goes to prove that they act by force of nature and by springs, like a clock, which tells better what the hour is than our judgment can inform us. And, doubtless, when swallows come in the spring, they act in that like clocks. All that honey-bees do is of the same nature; and the order that cranes keep in flying, or monkeys drawn up for battle, if it be true that they do observe any order, and, finally, the instinct of burying their dead is no more surprising than that of dogs and cats, which scratch the ground to bury their excrements, although they almost never do bury them, which shows that they do it by instinct only, and not by thought. It can only be said that, although the brutes do nothing which can convince us that they think, nevertheless, because their bodily organs are not very different from ours, we might conjecture that there was some faculty of thought joined to these organs, as we experience in ourselves, although theirs be much less perfect, to which I have nothing to reply, except that, if they could think as we do, they would have an immortal soul as well as we, which is not likely, because there is no reason for believing it of some animals without believing it of all, and there are many of them too imperfect to make it possible to believe it of them, such as oysters, sponges, etc.

Letter to Henry More, 1649

. . . But the greatest of all the prejudices we have retained from infancy is that of believing that brutes think. The source of our error comes from having observed that many of the bodily members of brutes are not very different from our own in shape and movements, and from the belief that our mind is the principle of the motions which occur in us; that it imparts motion to the body and is the cause of our thoughts. Assuming this, we find no difficulty in believing that there is in brutes a mind similar to our own; but having made the discovery, after thinking well upon it, that two different principles of our movements are to be distinguished—the one entirely mechanical and corporeal, which depends solely on the force of the animal spirits and the configuration of the bodily parts, and which may be called corporeal soul, and the other incorporeal, that is to say, mind or soul, which you may define a substance which thinks—I have inquired with great care whether the motions of animals proceed from these two principles or from one alone. Now, having clearly perceived that they can proceed from one only, I have held it demonstrated that we are not able in any manner to prove that there is in the animals a soul which thinks. I am not at all disturbed in my opinion by those doublings and cunning tricks of dogs and foxes, nor by all those things which animals do, either from fear, or to get something to eat, or just for sport. I engage to explain all that very easily, merely by the conformation of the parts of the animals. Nevertheless, although I regard it as a thing demonstrated that it cannot be proved that the brutes have thought, I do not think that it can be demonstrated that the contrary is not true, because the human mind cannot penetrate into the heart to know what goes on there; but, on examining into the probabilities of the case, I see no reason whatever to prove that brutes think, if it be not that having eyes, ears, a tongue, and other organs of sense like ours, it is likely that they have sensations as we do, and, as thought is involved in the sensations which we have, a similar faculty of thought must be attributed to them. Now, since this argument is within the reach of everyone's capacity, it has held possession of all minds from infancy. But there are other stronger and more numerous arguments for the opposite opinion, which do not so readily present themselves to everybody's mind; as, for example, that it is more reasonable to make earthworms, flies, caterpillars, and the rest of the animals, move as machines do, than to endow them with immortal souls.

Because it is certain that in the body of animals, as in ours, there are bones, nerves, muscles, blood, animal spirits, and other organs, disposed in such a manner that they can produce themselves, without the aid of any thought, all the movements which we observe in the animals, as appears in convulsive movements, when, in spite of the mind itself, the machine of the body moves often with greater violence, and in more various ways than it is wont to do with the aid of the will; moreover, inasmuch as it is agreeable to reason that art should imitate nature, and that men should be able to construct divers *automata* in which there is movement without any thought, nature, on her part, might produce these *automata,* and far more excellent ones, as the brutes are, than those which come from the hand of man, seeing no reason anywhere why thought is to be found wherever we perceive a conformation of bodily members like that of the animals, and that it is more surprising that there should be a soul in every human body than that there should be none at all in the brutes.

But the principal argument, to my mind, which may convince us that the brutes are devoid of reason, is that, although among those of the same species, some are more perfect than others, as among men, which is particularly noticeable in horses and dogs, some of which have more capacity than others to retain what is taught them, and although all of them make us clearly understand their natural movements of anger, of fear, of hunger, and others of like kind, either by the voice or by other bodily motions, it has never yet been observed that any animal has arrived at such a degree of perfection as to make use of a true language; that is to say, as to be able to indicate to us by the voice, or by other signs, anything which could be referred to thought alone, rather than to a movement of mere nature; for the word is the sole sign and the only certain mark of the presence of thought hidden and wrapped up in the body; now all men, the most stupid and the most foolish, those even who are deprived of the organs of speech, make use of signs, whereas the brutes never do anything of the kind; which may be taken for the true distinction between man and brute. . . . I omit, for the sake of brevity, the other arguments which deny thought to the brutes. It must, however, be observed that I speak of thought, not of life, nor of sensation; for I do not deny the life of any animal, making it to consist solely in the warmth of the heart. I do not refuse to them feeling even, in so far as it depends only on the bodily organs. Thus, my opinion is not so cruel to animals as it is favourable to men; I speak to those who are not committed to the extravagances of Pythagoras, which attached to those who ate or killed them the suspicion even of a crime. . . . . . .

THE PASSIONS[1] OF THE SOUL

PART FIRST

OF THE PASSIONS IN GENERAL, AND INCIDENT-ALLY OF THE WHOLE NATURE OF MAN

ARTICLE I

That what in respect of a subject is passion, is in some other regard always action.

There is nothing in which the defective nature of the sciences which we have received from the ancients appears more clearly than in what they have written on the passions; for, although this is a matter which has at all times been the object of much investigation, and though it would not appear to be one of the most difficult, inasmuch as since every one has experience of the passions within himself, there is no necessity to borrow one's observations from elsewhere in order to discover their nature; yet that which the ancients have taught regarding them is both so slight, and for the most part so far from credible, that I am unable to entertain any hope of approximating to the truth excepting by shunning the paths which they have followed. This is why I shall be here obliged to write just as though I were treating of a matter which no one had ever touched on before me; and, to begin with, I consider that all that which occurs or that happens anew, is by the philosophers, generally speaking, termed a passion, in as far

---

[1] The expression 'Passions' is, in this Treatise, of course used in its etymological significance.

as the subject to which it occurs is concerned, and an action in respect of him who causes it to occur. Thus although the agent and the recipient [patient] are frequently very different, the action and the passion are always one and the same thing, although having different names, because of the two diverse subjects to which it may be related.

ARTICLE II

That in order to understand the passions of the soul its functions must be distinguished from those of body.

Next I note also that we do not observe the existence of any subject which more immediately acts upon our soul than the body to which it is joined, and that we must consequently consider that what in the soul is a passion is in the body commonly speaking an action; so that there is no better means of arriving at a knowledge of our passions than to examine the difference which exists between soul and body in order to know to which of the two we must attribute each one of the functions which are within us.

ARTICLE III

What rule we must follow to bring about this result.

As to this we shall not find much difficulty if we realise that all that we experience as being in us, and that to observation may exist in wholly inanimate bodies, must be attributed to our body alone; and, on the other hand, that all that which is in us and which we cannot in any way conceive as possibly pertaining to a body, must be attributed to our soul.

ARTICLE IV

That the heat and movement of the members proceed from the body, the thoughts from the soul.

Thus because we have no conception of the body as thinking in any way, we have reason to believe that every kind of thought which exists in us belongs to the soul; and because we do not doubt there being inanimate bodies which can move in as many as or in more diverse modes than can ours, and which have as much heat or more (experience demonstrates this to us in flame, which of itself has much more heat and movement than any of our members), we must believe that all the heat and all the movements which are in us pertain only to body, inasmuch as they do not depend on thought at all.

ARTICLE V

That it is an error to believe that the soul supplies the movement and heat to body.

By this means we shall avoid a very considerable error into which many have fallen; so much so that I am of opinion that this is the primary cause which has prevented our being able hitherto satisfactorily to explain the passions and the other properties of the soul. It arises from the fact that from observing that all dead bodies are devoid of heat and consequently of movement, it has been thought that it was the absence of soul which caused these movements and this heat to cease; and thus, without any reason, it was thought that our natural heat and all the movements of our body depend on the soul: while in fact we ought on the contrary to believe that the soul quits us on death only because this heat ceases, and the organs which serve to move the body disintegrate.

Article VI

The difference that exists between a living body and a dead body.

In order, then, that we may avoid this error, let us consider that death never comes to pass by reason of the soul, but only because some one of the principal parts of the body decays; and we may judge that the body of a living man differs from that of a dead man just as does a watch or other automaton (i.e., a machine that moves of itself), when it is wound up and contains in itself the corporeal principle of those movements for which it is designed along with all that is requisite for its action, from the same watch or other machine when it is broken and when the principle of its movement ceases to act.

Article VII

A brief explanation of the parts of the body and some of its functions.

In order to render this more intelligible, I shall here explain in a few words the whole method in which the bodily machine is composed. There is no one who does not already know that there are in us a heart, a brain, a stomach, muscles, nerves, arteries, veins, and such things. We also know that the food that we eat descends into the stomach and bowels where its juice, passing into the liver and into all the veins, mingles with, and thereby increases the quantity of the blood which they contain. Those who have acquired even the minimum of medical knowledge further know how the heart is composed, and how all the blood in the veins can easily flow from the vena cava into its right side and from thence pass into the lung by the vessel which we term the arterial vein, and then return from the lung into the left side of the heart, by the vessel called the venous artery, and finally pass from there into the great artery, whose branches spread throughout all the body. Likewise all those whom the authority of the ancients has not entirely blinded, and who have chosen to open their eyes for the purpose of investigating the opinion of Harvey regarding the circulation of the blood, do not doubt that all the veins and arteries of the body are like streams by which the blood ceaselessly flows with great swiftness, taking its course from the right cavity of the heart by the arterial vein whose branches are spread over the whole of the lung, and joined to that of the venous artery by which it passes from the lung into the left side of the heart; from these, again, it goes into the great artery whose branches, spread throughout all the rest of the body, are united to the branches of the vein, which branches once more carry the same blood into the right cavity of the heart. Thus these two cavities are like sluices through each of which all the blood passes in the course of each circuit which it makes in the body. We further know that all the movements of the members depend on the muscles, and that these muscles are so mutually related one to another that when the one is contracted it draws toward itself the part of the body to which it is attached, which causes the opposite muscle at the same time to become elongated; then if at another time it happens that this last contracts, it causes the former to become elongated and it draws back to itself the part to which they are attached. We know finally that all these movements of the muscles, as also all the senses, depend on the nerves, which resemble small filaments, or little tubes, which all proceed from the brain, and thus contain like it a certain very subtle air or wind which is called the animal spirits.

Article VIII

What is the principle of all these functions?

But it is not usually known in what way these animal spirits and these nerves contribute to the movements and to the senses, nor what is the corporeal principle which causes them to act. That is why, although I have already made some mention of them in my other writings, I shall not here omit to say shortly that so long as we live there is a continual heat in our heart, which is a species of fire which the blood of the veins there maintains, and that this fire is the corporeal principle of all the movements of our members.

Article IX

How the movement of the heart is carried on.

Its first effect is to dilate the blood with which the cavities of the heart are filled; that causes this blood, which requires a greater space for its occupation, to pass impetuously from the right cavity into the arterial vein, and from the left into the great artery; then when this dilation ceases, new blood immediately enters from the vena cava into the right cavity of the heart, and from the venous artery into the left; for there are little membranes at the entrances of these four vessels, disposed in such a manner that they do not allow the blood to enter the heart but by the two last, nor to issue from it but by the two others. The new blood which has entered into the heart is then immediately afterwards rarefied, in the same manner as that which preceded it; and it is just this which causes the pulse, or beating of the heart and arteries; so that this beating repeats itself as often as the new blood enters the heart. It is also just this which gives its motion to the blood, and causes it to flow ceaselessly and very quickly in all the arteries and veins, whereby it carries the heat which it acquires in the heart to every part of the body, and supplies them with nourishment.

ARTICLE X

How the animal spirits are produced in the brain.

But what is here most worthy of remark is that all the most animated and subtle portions of the blood which the heat has rarefied in the heart, enter ceaselessly in large quantities into the cavities of the brain. And the reason which causes them to go there rather than elsewhere, is that all the blood which issues from the heart by the great artery takes its course in a straight line towards that place, and not being able to enter it in its entirety, because there are only very narrow passages there, those of its parts which are the most agitated and the most subtle alone pass through, while the rest spreads abroad in all the other portions of the body. But these very subtle parts of the blood form the animal spirits; and for this end they have no need to experience any other change in the brain, unless it be that they are separated from the other less subtle portions of the blood; for what I here name spirits are nothing but material bodies and their one peculiarity is that they are bodies of extreme minuteness and that they move very quickly like the particles of the flame which issues from a torch. Thus it is that they never remain at rest in any spot, and just as some of them enter into the cavities of the brain, others issue forth by the pores which are in its substance, which pores conduct them into the nerves, and from there into the

muscles, by means of which they move the body in all
the different ways in which it can be moved.

ARTICLE XI

How the movements of the muscles take place.

For the sole cause of all the movements of the members is that certain muscles contract, and that those
opposite to them elongate, as has already been said;
and the sole cause of one muscle contracting rather than
that set against it, is that there comes from the brain
some additional amount of animal spirits, however
little it may be, to it rather than to the other. Not
that the spirits which proceed immediately from the
brain suffice in themselves to move the muscles, but
they determine the other spirits which are already in
these two muscles, all to issue very quickly from the
one of them and to pass into the other. By this means
that from which they issue becomes longer and more
flaccid, and that into which they enter, being rapidly
distended by them, contracts, and pulls the member
to which it is attached. This is easy to understand
provided that we know that there are but very few
animal spirits which continually proceed from the brain
to each muscle, but that there are always a quantity of
others enclosed in the same muscle, which move there
very quickly, sometimes by only turning about in the
place where they are—that is, when they do not find
any passage open from which to issue forth from it—
and sometimes by flowing into the opposite muscle; and
inasmuch as there are little openings in each of these
muscles by which the spirits can flow from one to the
other, and which are so arranged that when the spirits
that come from the brain to one of them have ever so
little more strength than those that proceed to the

other, they open all the entrances by which the spirits of the other muscle can pass into this one, and at the same time close all those by which the spirits of this last can pass into the other. By this means all the spirits formerly contained in these two muscles very quickly collect in one of them and then distend and shorten it, while the other becomes elongated and flaccid.

Article XVI

How all the members may be moved by the objects of the senses and by the animal spirits without the aid of the soul.

We must finally remark that the machine of our body is so formed that all the changes undergone by the movement of the spirits may cause them to open certain pores in the brain more than others, and reciprocally that when some one of the pores is opened more or less than usual (to however small a degree it may be) by the action of the nerves which are employed by the senses, that changes something in the movement of the spirits and causes them to be conducted into the muscles which serve to move the body in the way in which it is usually moved when such an action takes place. In this way all the movements which we make without our will contributing thereto (as frequently happens when we breathe, walk, eat, and in fact perform all those actions which are common to us and to the brutes), only depend on the conformation of our members, and on the course which the spirits, excited by the heat of the heart, follow naturally in the brain, nerves, and muscles, just as the movements of a watch are produced simply by the strength of the springs and the form of the wheels.

Article XVII

What the functions of the soul are.

After having thus considered all the functions which
pertain to the body alone, it is easy to recognise that
there is nothing in us which we ought to attribute to our
soul excepting our thoughts, which are mainly of two
sorts, the one being the actions of the soul, and the
other its passions. Those which I call its actions are
all our desires, because we find by experience that they
proceed directly from our soul, and appear to depend
on it alone: while, on the other hand, we may usually
term one's passions all those kinds of perception or
forms of knowledge which are found in us, because it is
often not our soul which makes them what they are,
and because it always receives them from the things
which are represented by them.

Article XVIII

Of the Will.

Our desires, again, are of two sorts, of which the
one consists of the actions of the soul which terminate
in the soul itself, as when we desire to love God, or
generally speaking, apply our thoughts to some object
which is not material; and the other of the actions
which terminate in our body, as when from the simple
fact that we have the desire to take a walk, it follows
that our legs move and that we walk.

Article XIX

Of the Perceptions.

Our perceptions are also of two sorts, and the one
have the soul as a cause and the other the body. Those

which have the soul as a cause are the perceptions of
our desires, and of all the imaginations or other thoughts
which depend on them. For it is certain that we
cannot desire anything without perceiving by the same
means that we desire it; and, although in regard to our
soul it is an action to desire something, we may say that
it is also one of its passions to perceive that it desires.
Yet because this perception and this will are really one
and the same thing, the more noble always supplies the
denomination, and thus we are not in the habit of calling
it a passion, but only an action.

Article XXX

*That the soul is united to all the portions of the body
conjointly.*

But in order to understand all these things more
perfectly, we must know that the soul is really joined
to the whole body, and that we cannot, properly speaking, say that it exists in any one of its parts to the
exclusion of the others, because it is one and in some
manner indivisible, owing to the disposition of its
organs, which are so related to one another that when
any one of them is removed, that renders the whole
body defective; and because it is of a nature which has
no relation to extension, nor dimensions, nor other
properties of the matter of which the body is composed,
but only to the whole conglomerate of its organs, as
appears from the fact that we could not in any way
conceive of the half or the third of a soul, nor of the
space it occupies, and because it does not become smaller
owing to the cutting off of some portion of the body,
but separates itself from it entirely when the union of
its assembled organs is dissolved.

Article XXXI

That there is a small gland in the brain in which the soul exercises its functions more particularly than in the other parts.

It is likewise necessary to know that although the soul is joined to the whole body, there is yet in that a certain part in which it exercises its functions more particularly than in all the others; and it is usually believed that this part is the brain, or possibly the heart: the brain, because it is with it that the organs of sense are connected, and the heart because it is apparently in it that we experience the passions. But, in examining the matter with care, it seems as though I had clearly ascertained that the part of the body in which the soul exercises its functions immediately is in nowise the heart, nor the whole of the brain, but merely the most inward of all its parts, to wit, a certain very small gland which is situated in the middle of its substance and so suspended above the duct whereby the animal spirits in its anterior cavities have communication with those in the posterior, that the slightest movements which take place in it may alter very greatly the course of these spirits; and reciprocally that the smallest changes which occur in the course of the spirits may do much to change the movements of this gland.

Article XXXII

How we know that this gland is the main seat of the soul.

The reason which persuades me that the soul cannot have any other seat in all the body than this gland wherein to exercise its functions immediately, is that

I reflect that the other parts of our brain are all of them double, just as we have two eyes, two hands, two ears, and finally all the organs of our outside senses are double; and inasmuch as we have but one solitary and simple thought of one particular thing at one and the same moment, it must necessarily be the case that there must somewhere be a place where the two images which come to us by the two eyes, where the two other impressions which proceed from a single object by means of the double organs of the other senses, can unite before arriving at the soul, in order that they may not represent to it two objects instead of one. And it is easy to apprehend how these images or other impressions might unite in this gland by the intermission of the spirits which fill the cavities of the brain; but there is no other place in the body where they can be thus united unless they are so in this gland.

Article XXXIII

That the seat of the passions is not in the heart.

As to the opinion of those who think that the soul receives its passions in the heart, it is not of much consideration, for it is only founded on the fact that the passions cause us to feel some change taking place there; and it is easy to see that this change is not felt in the heart excepting through the medium of a small nerve which descends from the brain towards it, just as pain is felt in the foot by means of the nerves of the foot, and the stars are perceived as in the heavens by means of their light and of the optic nerves; so that it is not more necessary that our soul should exercise its functions immediately in the heart, in order to feel its passions there, than it is necessary for the soul to be in the heavens in order to see the stars there.

Article XXXIV

How the soul and the body act on one another.

Let us then conceive here that the soul has its principal seat in the little gland which exists in the middle of the brain, from whence it radiates forth through all the remainder of the body by means of the animal spirits, nerves, and even the blood, which, participating in the impressions of the spirits, can carry them by the arteries into all the members. And recollecting what has been said above about the machine of our body, i.e., that the little filaments of our nerves are so distributed in all its parts, that on the occasion of the diverse movements which are there excited by sensible objects, they open in diverse ways the pores of the brain, which causes the animal spirits contained in these cavities to enter in diverse ways into the muscles, by which means they can move the members in all the different ways in which they are capable of being moved; and also that all the other causes which are capable of moving the spirits in diverse ways suffice to conduct them into diverse muscles; let us here add that the small gland which is the main seat of the soul is so suspended between the cavities which contain the spirits that it can be moved by them in as many different ways as may also be moved in diverse ways by the soul, whose nature is such that it receives in itself as many diverse impressions, that is to say, that it possesses as many diverse perceptions as there are diverse movements in this gland. Reciprocally, likewise, the machine of the body is so formed that from the simple fact that this gland is diversely moved by the soul, or by such other cause, whatever it is, it thrusts the spirits which surround it towards the pores of the brain, which conduct them by the nerves into the muscles, by which means it causes them to move the limbs.

Article XXXV

Example of the mode in which the impressions of the objects unite in the gland which is in the middle of the brain.

Thus, for example, if we see some animal approach us, the light reflected from its body depicts two images of it, one in each of our eyes, and these two images form two others, by means of the optic nerves, in the interior surface of the brain which faces its cavities; then from there, by means of the animal spirits with which its cavities are filled, these images so radiate towards the little gland which is surrounded by these spirits, that the movement which forms each point of one of the images tends towards the same point of the gland towards which tends the movement which forms the point of the other image, which represents the same part of this animal. By this means the two images which are in the brain form but one upon the gland, which, acting immediately upon the soul, causes it to see the form of this animal.

Article XXXVI

Example of the way in which the passions are excited in the soul.

And, besides that, if this figure is very strange and frightful—that is, if it has a close relationship with the things which have been formerly hurtful to the body, that excites the passion of apprehension in the soul and then that of courage, or else that of fear and consternation according to the particular temperament of the body or the strength of the soul, and according as we have to begin with been secured by defence or by flight against the hurtful things to which the present impression is related. For in certain persons that disposes the brain in such a way that the spirits reflected from the image thus formed on the gland, proceed thence to take their places partly in the nerves which serve to turn the back and dispose the legs for flight, and partly in those which so increase or diminish the orifices of the heart, or at least which so agitate the other parts from whence the blood is sent to it, that this blood being there rarefied in a different manner from usual, sends to the brain the spirits which are adapted for the maintenance and strengthening of the passion of fear, i.e., which are adapted to the holding open, or at least reopening, of the pores of the brain which conduct them into the same nerves. For from the fact alone that these spirits enter into these pores, they excite a particular movement in this gland which is instituted by nature in order to cause the soul to be sensible of this passion; and because these pores are principally in relation with the little nerves which serve to contract or enlarge the orifices of the heart, that causes the soul to be sensible of it for the most part as in the heart.

Article XL

The principal effect of the passions.

For it is requisite to notice that the principal effect of all the passions in men is that they incite and dispose their soul to desire those things for which they prepare their body, so that the feeling of fear incites it to desire to fly, that of courage to desire to fight, and so on.

Article XLI

The power of the soul in regard to the body.

But the will is so free in its nature, that it can never be constrained; and of the two sorts of thoughts which I have distinguished in the soul (of which the first are its action, i.e., its desires, the others its passions, taking this word in its most general significance, which comprises all kinds of perceptions), the former are absolutely in its power, and can only be indirectly changed by the body, while on the other hand the latter depend absolutely on the actions which govern and direct them, and they can only indirectly be altered by the soul, excepting when it is itself their cause. And the whole action of the soul consists in this, that solely because it desires something, it causes the little gland to which it is closely united to move in the way requisite to produce the effect which relates to this desire.

Article XLII

How we find in the memory the things which we desire to remember.

Thus when the soul desires to recollect something, this desire causes the gland, by inclining successively to different sides, to thrust the spirits towards different parts of the brain until they come across that part where the traces left there by the object which we wish to recollect are found; for these traces are none other than the fact that the pores of the brain, by which the spirits have formerly followed their course because of the presence of this object, have by that means acquired a greater facility than the others in being once more opened by the animal spirits which come towards them in the same way. Thus these spirits in coming in contact with these pores, enter into them more easily than into the others, by which means they excite a special movement in the gland which represents the same object to the soul, and causes it to know that it is this which it desired to remember.

Article XLIII

How the soul can imagine, be attentive, and move the body.

Thus when we desire to imagine something we have never seen, this desire has the power of causing the gland to move in the manner requisite to drive the spirits towards the pores of the brain by the opening of which pores this particular thing may be represented; thus when we wish to apply our attention for some time to the consideration of one particular object, this desire holds the gland for the time being inclined to the same side. Thus, finally, when we desire to walk or to move our body in some special way, this desire causes the gland to thrust the spirits towards the muscles which serve to bring about this result.

PART SECOND

OF THE NUMBER AND ORDER OF THE PASSIONS AND AN EXPOSITION OF THE SIX PRIMITIVE PASSIONS

Article LI

What are the first causes of the passions.

We know from what has been said above that the ultimate and most proximate cause of the passions of the soul is none other than the agitation with which the spirits move the little gland which is in the middle of the brain. But that does not suffice to distinguish one from another; it is necessary to investigate their sources, and to examine their first causes: and, although they may sometimes be caused by the action of the soul which determines itself to conceive of this or that object, and also simply by the temperament of the body or by the impressions which are fortuitously met with in the brain, as happens when we feel sad or joyous without being able to give a reason, it yet appears by what has been said, that in all cases the same passions can also be excited by the objects which move the senses, and that these objects are their most ordinary and principal causes; from which it follows that in order to find them all, it is sufficient to consider all the effects of these objects.

ARTICLE LII

What is their mode of operation and how they may be enumerated.

I notice besides, that the objects which move the senses do not excite diverse passions in us because of all the diversities which are in them, but only because of the diverse ways in which they may harm or help us, or in general be of some importance to us; and that the customary mode of action of all the passions is simply this, that they dispose the soul to desire those things which nature tells us are of use, and to persist in this desire, and also bring about that same agitation of spirits which customarily causes them to dispose the body to the movement which serves for the carrying into effect of these things; that is why, in order to enumerate them, we must merely examine in their order in how many diverse ways which are significant for us, our senses can be moved by their objects; and I shall here make an enumeration of all the principal passions according to the order in which they may thus be found.

Article LXIX

That there are only six primitive passions.

But the number of those which are simple and primitive is not very large. For, in making a review of all those which I have enumerated, we may easily notice that there are but six which are such, i.e., wonder, love, hatred, desire, joy and sadness; and that all the others are composed of some of these six, or are species of them. That is why, in order that their multitude may not embarrass my readers, I shall here treat the six primitive passions separately; and afterwards I shall show in what way all the others derive from them their origin.

Article LXX

Of Wonder; its definition and cause.

Wonder is a sudden surprise of the soul which causes it to apply itself to consider with attention the objects which seem to it rare and extraordinary. It is thus primarily caused by the impression we have in the brain which represents the object as rare, and as consequently worthy of much consideration; then afterwards by the movement of the spirits, which are disposed by this impression to tend with great force towards the part of the brain where it is, in order to fortify and conserve it there; as they are also disposed by it to pass thence into the muscles which serve to retain the organs of the senses in the same situation in which they are, so that it is still maintained by them, if it is by them that it has been formed.

Article LXXI

That in this passion no change occurs in the heart or in the blood.

And this passion has this particular characteristic, that in it we do not notice that it is accompanied by any change which occurs in the heart and blood like the other passions. The reason of this is that not having good or evil as its object, but only the knowledge of the thing that we wonder at, it has no relation with the heart and blood on which all the good of the body depends, but only with the brain where are the organs of the senses which are the instruments of this knowledge.

Article LXXIV

The end which the passions serve, and to what they are detrimental.

And it is easy to understand from what has been said above, that the utility of all the passions consists alone in their fortifying and perpetuating in the soul thoughts which it is good it should preserve, and which without that might easily be effaced from it. And again, all the harm which they can cause consists in the fact that they fortify and conserve these thoughts more than necessary, or that they fortify and conserve others on which it is not good to dwell.

Article LXXIX

The definition of Love and Hate.

Love is an emotion of the soul caused by the movement of the spirits which incites it to join itself willingly to objects which appear to it to be agreeable. And hatred is an emotion caused by the spirits which

incite the soul to desire to be separated from the objects
which present themselves to it as hurtful. I say that
these emotions are caused by the spirits in order to
distinguish love and hate, which are passions and depend on the body, both from the judgments which also
induce the soul by its free will to unite itself with the
things which it esteems to be good and to separate itself
from those it holds to be evil, and from the emotions
which these judgments excite of themselves in the soul.

Article LXXXII

*How very different passions agree, inasmuch as they
participate in love.*

There is also no need to distinguish as many kinds
of love as there are diverse objects which we may love;
for, to take an example, although the passions which
an ambitious man has for glory, a miser for money, a
drunkard for wine, a brutal man for a woman whom he
desires to violate, a man of honour for his friend or mistress, and a good father for his children, may be very
different, still, inasmuch as they participate in love,
they are similar. But the four first only have love for
the possession of the objects to which their passion
relates, and do not have any for the objects themselves,
for which they only have desire mingled with other
particular passions. But the love which a good father
has for his children is so pure that he desires to have
nothing from them, and does not wish to possess them
otherwise than he does, nor to be united with them more
closely than he already is. For, considering them as
replicas of himself, he seeks their good as his own, or
even with greater care, because, in setting before himself that he or they form a whole of which he is not
the best part, he often prefers their interests to his, and

does not fear losing himself in order to save them. The affection which honourable men have for their friends is of this nature even though it is rarely so perfect; and that which they have for their mistress participates largely in it, but it also participates a little in the others.

Article LXXXVI

The definition of Desire.

The passion of desire is an agitation of the soul caused by the spirits which dispose it to wish for the future the things which it represents to itself as agreeable. Thus we do not only desire the presence of the absent good, but also the conservation of the present, and further, the absence of evil, both of that which we already have, and of that which we believe we might experience in time to come.

Article XCI

The definition of Joy.

Joy is an agreeable emotion of the soul in which consists the enjoyment that the soul possesses in the good which the impressions of the brain represent to it as its own. I say that it is in this emotion that the enjoyment of the good consists; for as a matter of fact the soul receives no other fruits from all the good things that it possesses; and while it has no joy in these, it may be said that it does not enjoy them more than if it did not possess them at all. I add also that it is of the good which the impressions of the brain represent to it as its own, in order not to confound this joy, which is a passion, with the joy that is purely intellectual, and which comes into the soul by the action of the soul alone, and which we may call an agreeable emotion excited in it, in which the enjoyment consists which it has in the good which its understanding represents to it as its own. It is true that while the soul is united to the body this intellectual joy can hardly fail to be accompanied by that which is a passion; for as soon as our understanding perceives that we possess some good thing, even although this good may be so different from all that pertains to the body that it is not in the least capable of being imagined, imagination does not fail immediately to make some impression in the brain from which proceeds the movement of the spirits which excites the passion of joy.

Article XCII

The definition of Sadness.

Sadness is a disagreeable languor in which consists the discomfort and unrest which the soul receives from evil, or from the defect which the impressions of the brain set before it as pertaining to it. And there also is an intellectual sadness which is not passion, but which hardly ever fails to be accompanied by it.

Article XCVI

The movements of the blood and the spirits to which the five preceding passions are due.

The five passions which I have here commenced to explain are so united or opposed the one to the other, that it is easier to consider them all together than to treat each of them separately, as wonder has been treated; and their cause is not, as is that of the latter, in the brain alone, but also in the heart, the spleen, the liver, and in all the other portions of the body in as far as they serve for the production of the blood and consequently of the spirits. For, although all the veins conduct the blood which they contain towards the heart, yet it sometimes happens that the blood of certain of them is driven there with greater strength than that of others; it also happens that the openings by which it enters into the heart, or else those by which it issues out, are more enlarged or contracted on one occasion than on the other.

Article XCVII

The chief experiences that furnish us with the knowledge of these movements in Love.

Now in considering the various alterations which experience causes us to observe in our body while our soul is agitated by various passions, I notice in love that when it occurs alone, that is, when it is unaccompanied by any strong joy, desire, or sadness, the beating of the pulse is equal and much fuller and stronger than is usually the case, that we feel a gentle heat in the breast, and that the digestion of food is accomplished very quickly in the stomach. In this way this passion is useful to health.

Article XCVIII

In Hatred.

I notice, on the other hand, that in hatred the pulse is unequal, feebler, and often quicker; that we have fits of cold interspersed with a severe and biting heat in the breast difficult to describe; that the stomach ceases to fulfil its functions and is inclined to vomit and reject the food that has been eaten, or at least to corrupt them and convert them into evil humours.

Article XCIX

In Joy.

In joy, that the pulse is equal and quicker than usual, but that it is not so strong or full as in love, and that we feel an agreeable heat which is not only in the breast, but also spreads throughout all the other exterior parts of the body with the blood which we see present there in abundance; and yet that we sometimes lose our appetite because the digestion is not so active as usual.

Article C

In Sadness.

In sadness, that the pulse is feeble and slow, and that we feel as it were constrictions round the heart which press upon it, and icy chills which congeal it and communicate their cold to the rest of the body; and that nevertheless we continue in certain cases to have a good appetite and to feel that the stomach does not fail to do its duty, provided that there is no hatred mingled with the sadness.

Article CI

In Desire.

I finally notice this peculiarity about desire, that it agitates the heart more violently than any of the other passions, and furnishes more spirits to the brain, which, passing from thence into the muscles, render all the senses more acute, and all the parts of the body more mobile.

Article CXII

The external signs of these Passions.

That which I have set down here makes sufficiently clear the cause of the differences in the pulse and of all the other properties which I have above attributed to these passions, without there being any necessity for me to pause in order to explain them further. But because I have only remarked in each that which may be observed to accompany it when it is alone, and which serves for a knowledge of the movements of the blood and the spirits which produce them, it still remains for me to treat of the several exterior signs which usually accompany them, and which are much better observed when several are mingled with one another as they usually are, than when they are separated. The principal of these signs are the actions of the eyes and face, changes of colour, tremors, languor, swooning, laughter, tears, groans and sighs.

Article CXIII

Of the actions of the Eyes and Face.

There is no passion that is not evidenced by some particular action of the eyes. And that is so manifest in certain emotions that even the stupidest servants can remark by the eye of their master if he is or is not angry with them. But although these actions of the eyes are easily perceived, and that which they signify is known, it is not, for all that, easy to describe them, since each is composed of many changes which take place in the movement and shape of the eye and which are so unique and so slight that we cannot perceive each one separately, although the result of their conjunction is very easily observed. We may say almost the same of the actions of the face which also accompany the passions, for although they are of greater extent than those of the eyes, it is at the same time hard to distinguish them; and they are so little different that there are men who present almost the same mien when they

weep as when they laugh. It is true that there are
some which are remarkable enough, as are the seams
in the forehead which come in anger, and certain movements of nose and lips in indignation and scorn; but
they do not so much appear to be natural as voluntary.
And generally speaking all actions, whether of face or
eyes, may be changed by the soul when, desiring to
hide a passion, it vigorously calls up the image of a
contrary one: so that we may make use of these actions
as well in dissimulating our passions as in evidencing
them.

Article CXXIV

Of Laughter.

Laughter consists in the fact that the blood, which
proceeds from the right orifice in the heart by the
arterial vein, inflating the lungs suddenly and repeatedly,
causes the air which they contain to be constrained to
pass out from them with an impetus by the windpipe,
where it forms an inarticulate and explosive utterance;
and the lungs in expanding equally with the air as it
rushes out, set in motion all the muscles of the dia-
phragm from the chest to the neck, by which means
they cause motion in the facial muscles, which have a
certain connection with them. And it is just this action
of the face with this inarticulate and explosive voice
that we call laughter.

Article CXXV

Why it does not accompany the greatest joys.

But although it seems as though laughter were one
of the principal signs of joy, nevertheless joy cannot
cause it except when it is moderate and has some wonder or hate mingled with it. For we find by experience

that when we are extraordinarily joyous the subject of this joy never causes us to burst into laughter, and we cannot even be so easily induced to do so by some other cause as when we are sad. And the reason of this is that in great joys the lung is always so full of blood that it cannot be further inflated by repeated gushes.

ARTICLE CXXVI

What are its principal causes.

And I can only observe two causes which make the lung thus inflate suddenly. The first is the surprise of admiration or wonder, which, being united to joy, may open the orifices of the heart so quickly that a great abundance of blood suddenly entering on its right side by the *vena cava,* rarefies there, and, passing from thence by the arterial vein, inflates the lung. The other is the admixture of some liquor which increases the rarefaction of the blood, and I can find nothing which could do that but the most liquid part of that which proceeds from the spleen, which part of the blood being driven to the heart by some slight emotion of hatred, assisted by the surprise of wonder, and mingling itself there with the blood which proceeds from the other parts of the body which joy causes to enter there in abundance, may cause this blood to dilate there much more than usual. We observe the same thing in many other liquids which, when on the fire, suddenly dilate when we throw a little vinegar into the vessel where they are; for the most liquid portion of the blood which comes from the spleen is in nature similar to vinegar. Experience also causes us to see that in all the possible occurrences which can produce this explosive laughter which proceeds from the lung, there is always some little element of hatred, or at least of wonder. And those whose spleen is not in a very healthy condition are subject to being not alone more sad, but also at intervals more gay and more disposed to laughter than the others, inasmuch as the spleen sends two sorts of blood to the heart, the one thick and coarse, which causes sadness, the other very fluid and subtle, which causes joy. And often, after having laughed much, we feel ourselves naturally inclined to sadness because the more fluid portion of the blood of the spleen being exhausted, the other, more coarse, follows it towards the heart.

ARTICLE CXXVII

Its cause in indignation.

As to the laughter which sometimes accompanies indignation, it is usually artificial and feigned; but when it is natural, it appears to proceed from the joy that we have in observing the fact that we cannot be hurt by the evil at which we are indignant, and, along with that, from the fact that we find ourselves surprised by the novelty or by the unexpected encountering of this evil. In this way joy, hatred and wonder contribute to it. At the same time I would fain believe that it may also be produced without any joy, by the movement of aversion alone, which sends blood from the spleen to the heart, where it is rarefied and driven from thence to the lung; and this it easily inflates when it finds it almost empty. And speaking generally, all that can suddenly inflate the lung in this way causes the outward action of laughter, excepting when sadness changes it into that of groans, and the cries which accompany tears. In reference to which Vives[1] writes of himself regarding

---

[1] In the margin of the first edition: "I. L. Vives, 3, de Animâ. cap. de Risu."

a time when he had been long without eating, that the
first pieces of food which he placed in his mouth caused
him to laugh; and this might proceed from the fact
that his lung, emptied of blood by lack of nourishment,
was promptly inflated by the first juice which passed
from his stomach to his heart, and which the mere
imagination of eating could conduct there, even before
the arrival of the food he was eating.

Article CXXVIII

Of the origin of Tears.

As laughter is never caused by the greatest joys, so
tears do not proceed from an extreme sadness but only
from that which is moderate and accompanied or followed by some feeling of love or likewise of joy. And
in order to understand their origin properly, we must
remark that although a mass of vapours continually
escapes from all the portions of our body, there are at
the same time none from which so much issues as the
eyes, because of the size of the optic nerves and the
multitude of little arteries by which the vapours reach
them; and as the sweat is simply composed of vapours
which, issuing from the other parts of the body, are con-
verted into water on their surface, so tears are formed
from the vapours which issue from the eyes.

Article CXXXII

Of the groans which accompany tears.

And then the lungs are also sometimes inflated suddenly by the abundance of the blood which enters them,
and which drives out from them the air which they had
contained, which, issuing by the windpipe, begets the
groans and cries which usually accompany tears. And

these cries are as a rule shriller than those which accompany laughter, although they are produced almost in the same way. The reason of this is that the nerves which serve to enlarge or contract the organs of the voice in order to make it louder or sharper, being united to those which open the orifices of the heart in joy, and contract them in sadness, cause these organs to enlarge or contract at the same time.

Article CXLV

Of those Desires which depend only on other things, and what is the meaning of chance.

As to the things which in nowise depend on us, good as they may be, we should never desire them with passion, not only because they may not happen and thus may vex us so much the more in proportion to the strength of our desire for them, but principally because, in occupying our thought, they turn us away from applying our affection to other things, the acquisition of which depends on us. And there are two general remedies for these vain desires: the first is generosity, of which I shall speak later: the second is that we ought frequently to cause ourselves to reflect on divine Providence and represent to ourselves that it is impossible that anything should happen in any other way than as it has been determined by this Providence from all eternity. In this way it is, so to speak, a fatality or an immutable necessity, which must be opposed to chance, in order to destroy it by treating it as a chimera which only proceeds from the error of our understanding. For we can desire nothing but that which we hold to be in some manner possible, and we can only hold to be possible those things that do not depend on us, in so far as we reflect that they depend on chance, i.e. that we judge that they may happen, and that similar things have formerly happened. And this opinion is founded only on the fact that we do not know all the facts that contribute to each effect; for when a thing that we have judged to depend on chance does not come to pass, that shows that some one of the causes that were necessary in order to produce it has failed, and in consequence that it was absolutely impossible, and that no such thing has ever happened—that is, a thing in the production of which a similar cause was also lacking—so that if we had not been ignorant of that beforehand, we should not have ever judged it possible, nor consequently have desired it.

Article CXLVI

Of those that depend on us and on others.

We must, then, entirely set aside the vulgar opinion that there is outside of us a Fortune which causes things to happen or not to happen in accordance with its pleasure, and we must recognise that all is conducted by divine Providence, whose eternal decree is so infallible and immutable, that, excepting the things that this same decree has willed to leave dependent on our free will, we ought to reflect that in relation to us nothing happens which is not necessary, and so to speak decreed by fate, and that thus we cannot without error desire that it should happen otherwise. But because the greater part of our desires extends to things which do not depend entirely on us, nor entirely on others, we ought to distinguish exactly in them what depends only on us, in order to extend our desire to that alone; and as to what remains, although we ought in this to hold success to be absolutely decreed by fate and immutable, in order that our desire may

not occupy itself therewith, we should not omit to consider the reasons which make it more or less to be hoped
for, in order that they may serve to regulate our actions.
Thus, to take an example, if we have business in some
particular place to which we may go by two different
roads, the one of which is usually much safer than the
other, although the decree of Providence is perhaps
such that, if we go by the road which we judge to be
safest, we shall not escape being robbed by so doing,
while, on the other hand, we might pass by the other
without danger, we should not for all that be indifferent
as to which one we choose, nor rest on the immutable
fatality of the said decree. But reason desires us to
choose the road which is usually most safe, and our
desire should be accomplished in respect to that when
we have followed it, whatever evil may thus befall us,
because this evil, having been relatively to us inevitable,
we have had no reason to expect exemption from it, but
merely claim to have done the best that our understanding has been able to point out, as I suppose to have
been the case. And it is certain that when we exercise
ourselves in thus distinguishing fatality from fortune,
we easily accustom ourselves so to regulate our desires,
that, in as far as their accomplishment depends only
on us, they may always provide us with complete satisfaction.

Article CXLVIII

*That the exercise of virtue is a sovereign remedy
against the passions.*

And, inasmuch as these inward emotions touch us
most nearly, and in consequence have much more power
over us than the passions from which they differ, and
which are met with in conjunction with them, it is certain that, provided our soul is always possessed of

something to content itself with inwardly, none of the troubles that come from elsewhere have any power to harm it, but rather serve to increase its joy, inasmuch as, seeing that it cannot be harmed by them, it is made sensible of its perfection. And in order that our soul may thus have something with which to be content, it has no need but to follow exactly after virtue. For whoever has lived in such a way that his conscience cannot reproach him for ever having failed to perform those things which he has judged to be the best (which is what I here call following after virtue) receives from this a satisfaction which is so powerful in rendering him happy that the most violent efforts of the passions never have sufficient power to disturb the tranquillity of his soul.

PART THIRD

OF PARTICULAR PASSIONS

Article CXLIX

Of Esteem and Disdain.

After having explained the six primitive passions which are so to speak the genera of which all the others are species, I shall here observe succinctly what in particular there is in each of these others, and I shall keep to the same order in which I have before enumerated them. The two first are esteem and disdain; for although their names usually signify only passionless opinions on our part as to the value of a particular thing, still, at the same time, because there often arises from these opinions passions to which we have not given particular names, it seems to me that such may be attributed to them. And esteem, in so far as it is a passion, is an inclination which the soul possesses to represent to itself the value of the thing esteemed, which inclination is caused by a particular movement of the animal spirits conducted into the brain in such a way that they there fortify the impression which serves for this end. The passion of disdain, on the contrary, is an inclination possessed by the soul to consider the baseness or smallness of that which it disdains, caused by the movement of the spirits which fortify the idea of this smallness.

Article CLXVII

Of Jealousy.

Jealousy is a species of fear which is related to the desire we have to preserve to ourselves the possession of some thing; and it does not so much proceed from the strength of the reasons that suggest the possibility of our losing that good, as from the high estimation in which we hold it, and which is the cause of our examining even the minutest subjects of suspicion, and taking them to be very considerable reasons for anxiety.

Article CLXXI

Of Courage and Bravery.

Courage, when it is a passion and not a custom or natural inclination, is a certain heat or agitation which disposes the soul forcibly to bend itself powerfully to the execution of the things which it desires to do, of whatever nature they may be; and bravery is a species of courage which disposes the soul to the execution of the things that are the most dangerous.

Article CLXXIV

Of Cowardice and Fear.

Cowardice is directly opposed to courage, and it is a languor or coldness which prevents the soul from proceeding to the execution of things which it would do were it exempt from this passion; and fear or terror, which is contrary to bravery, is not only coldness, but also a perturbation and astonishment of the soul, which takes from it the power of resisting the evils which it thinks lie at hand.

Article CLXXVIII.

Of Scorn.

Derision or scorn is a sort of joy mingled with hatred, which proceeds from our perceiving some small evil in a person whom we consider to be deserving of it; we have hatred for this evil, we have joy in seeing it in him who is deserving of it; and when that comes upon us unexpectedly, the surprise of wonder is the cause of our bursting into laughter, in accordance with what has been said above of the nature of laughter. But this evil must be small, for if it is great we cannot believe that he who has it is deserving of it, unless when we are of a very evil nature or bear much hatred towards him.

Article CLXXIX

Why the least perfect are usually most given to mockery.

And we notice that people with very obvious defects such as those who are lame, blind of an eye, hunched-backed, or who have received some public insult, are specially given to mockery; for, desiring to see all others held in as low estimation as themselves, they are truly rejoiced at the evils which befall them, and they hold them deserving of these.

Article CLXXX.

Of the function of ridicule.

As regards the modest bantering which is useful in reproving vices by making them appear ridiculous, so long as we do not laugh at them ourselves or bear any hatred towards the individuals concerned, it is not a passion, but a quality pertaining to the well disposed man which gives evidence of the gaiety of his temper and the tranquillity of his soul, which are characteristic marks of virtue; it often also shows the ingenuity of his mind in knowing how to present an agreeable appearance to the things which he ridicules.

Article CLXXXI

Of the function of laughter in ridicule.

And it is not wrong to laugh when we hear the jests of another; these jests may even be such that it would be difficult not to laugh at them; but when we ourselves jest, it is more fitting to abstain from laughter, in order not to seem to be surprised by the things that are said, nor to wonder at the ingenuity we show in inventing them. And that makes those who hear them all the more surprised.

Article CLXXXIV

From whence it comes that the envious are subject to have a leaden complexion.

For the rest, there is no vice which so detracts from the happiness of men as that of envy; for, in addition

to the fact that those who are tainted with it distress
themselves, they also disturb to the utmost of their
power the pleasure of others; and usually they have
a leaden hue, that is to say, one of mingled yellow and
black like battered blood, whence envy is in Latin called
livor, which accords very well with what has been said
above regarding the movements of the blood in sadness
and hatred.   For the former causes the yellow bile
which proceeds from the lower portion of the liver, and
the black which proceeds from the spleen, to expand
from the heart by the arteries into all the veins, and
the latter causes the blood in the veins to have less
heat, and to flow more slowly than usual, which suffices
to render the colour livid.   But because the bile, yellow
as well as black, may also be sent into the veins by
many other causes, and because envy does not send
them there in sufficiently great quantity to change the
shade of the colour, except when it is great and of long
duration, we must not think that all those in whom we
observe this colour are inclined thereto.

ARTICLE CXCIX

Of Anger.

Anger is also a species of hatred or aversion which
we have towards those who have done some evil to or
have tried to injure not any chance person but more
particularly ourselves.   Thus it has the same content
as indignation, and all the more so in that it is founded
on an action which affects us, and for which we desire
to avenge ourselves, for this desire almost always accompanies it; and it is directly opposed to gratitude,
as indignation is to favour.   But it is incomparably
more violent than these three other passions, because
the desire to repel harmful things and to revenge one-

self, is the most persistent of all desires. It is desire, united to self-love, which furnishes to anger the agitation of the blood that courage and bravery can cause; and hatred brings it to pass that it is mainly the bilious blood coming from the spleen and the small veins of the liver that experiences this agitation and enters into the heart, where, because of its abundance and of the nature of the bile with which it is mingled, it excites a heat which is more severe and ardent than is that which may be excited by love or by joy.

ARTICLE CC

Why those whom it makes flush are less to be feared than those whom it makes blanch.

And the external signs of this passion are different according to the difference of personal temperaments and the diversity of the other passions which compose it or unite themselves with it. We thus see people who become pale or who tremble when they become angry, and we see others who become flushed or who even weep; and we usually judge that the anger of those who grow pale is more to be feared than the anger of those who become red. And the reason of this is that when we do not desire to, or are unable to revenge ourselves otherwise than by our expression and words, we employ all our heat and all our strength from the commencement of our emotion, and this is the reason that we become red; besides which sometimes the regret and self-pity that we have, since we cannot avenge ourselves otherwise, is the reason why we weep. And, on the other hand, those who hold themselves in and make up their minds to a greater vengeance, become sad from thinking themselves obliged to behave so by the action which angers them; and they are sometimes also afraid by reason of the evils which may follow on the resolution which they have taken, which renders them pale, cold and trembling to begin with. But when they afterwards come to execute their vengeance, they become warm again in proportion as they had been cold to begin with, just as we notice that fevers which commence with chill usually become the most severe.

Article CCXI

A general remedy against the Passions.

And now that we are acquainted with them all, we have much less reason to fear them than we formerly had. For we see that they are all good in their nature and that we have nothing to avoid but their evil uses or their excesses, against which the remedies which I explained might suffice, if each one of us took sufficient heed to practise them. But because I have placed amongst these remedies the forethought and diligence whereby we can correct our natural faults in exercising ourselves in separating within us the movements of the blood and spirits from the thoughts to which they are usually united. I confess that there are few people who are sufficiently prepared in this way to meet all the accidents of life, and that these movements excited in the blood by the objects of the passions follow so promptly from these single impressions that are made in the brain and from the disposition of the organs, although the soul contributes in no wise to them, that there is no human wisdom capable of resisting them when sufficient preparation is not made for doing so. Thus many people cannot prevent themselves from laughing on being tickled, even though they have no pleasure in it; for the impression of joy and surprise which caused them formerly to laugh for the same reason, being once more awakened in their imagination, causes their lung to be suddenly inflated in spite of themselves by the blood which the heart sends to it. In this way those who are naturally much carried away by their disposition towards emotions of joy or pity, or fear or anger, cannot prevent themselves from fainting, weeping, or trembling, or from having their blood agitated just as though they had a fever, when their imagination is violently affected by the object of some one of these passions. But what we can always do on such occasions, and what I think I can here put forward as the most general remedy and the most easy to practise against all excesses of the passions, is that, when we feel our blood to be thus agitated, we should be warned of the fact, and recollect that all that presents itself before the imagination tends to delude the soul and causes the reasons which serve to urge it to accomplish the object of its passion to appear much stronger than they are, and those which serve to dissuade it to be much weaker. And when the passions urge us only towards things the execution of which necessitates some delay, we ought to abstain from pronouncing any judgment on the spot, and to divert ourselves by other thoughts until time and rest shall have entirely calmed the emotion which is in the blood. And finally, when it incites us to actions regarding which it is requisite that an immediate resolution should be taken, the will must make it its main business to consider and follow up the reasons which are contrary to those set up by the passions, although they appear to be less strong; just as when we are suddenly attacked by some enemy, the occasion does not permit of our taking time to deliberate. But it seems to me that what those who are accustomed to reflect on their actions can always do when they feel themselves to be seized with fear, is to try to turn their thoughts away from the consideration of danger by representing to themselves the reasons which prove that there is much more certainty and honour in resistance than in flight. And on the other hand, when they feel that the desire of vengeance and anger incites them to run thoughtlessly towards those who attack them, they will recollect that it is imprudence to lose their lives when they can without dishonour save themselves, and that, if the match is very unequal, it is better to beat an honourable retreat or ask quarter, than to expose oneself doggedly to certain death.

Article CCXII

That it is on them alone that all the good and evil of this life depends.

For the rest, the soul may have pleasures of its own, but as to those which are common to it and the body, they depend entirely on the passions, so that the men whom they can most move are capable of partaking most of enjoyment in this life. It is true that such men may also find most bitterness when they do not know how to employ them well, or fortune is contrary to them. But the principal use of prudence or self-control is that it teaches us to be masters of our passions, and to so control and guide them that the evils which they cause are quite bearable, and that we even derive joy from them all.